Women in Japan
from Ancient Times to the Present

by
MARJORIE WALL BINGHAM & SUSAN HILL GROSS
edited by
Janet Donaldson

Women in World   Area Studies

The Ise Cultural Foundation of Tokyo provided
funding for the printing of *Women in Japan*.

Distributed by:

Glenhurst
Publications, Inc.

Publishers of Women's History Curriculum
Central Community Center, 6300 Walker St., St. Louis Park, MN 55416   (612) 925-3632

Picture Credits

Cover Photos (Clockwise from top):

Shoda Michiko in Bridal Costume at Her Marriage to Prince Akihito — Roby Eunson, *100 Years: The Amazing Development of Japan Since 1860* (Tokyo, Japan: Kodansha International Ltd., 1965).

Haruko in Summer Kimono — Courtesy Gail Lee Bernstein.

Yoshino Chiba — A "Designated Living National Treasure" for her Indigo Dyeing Techniques. By permission of Standard Advertising, Inc., Tokyo, Japan.

Peasant Woman in late 19th century photograph Anna C. Hartshorne, *Japan and Her People*, Vol. II (Philadelphia: Henry T. Coates & Co., 1902).

Ise Shrine from 19th century photograph (upper left). Shintō shrine to Amaterasu, the female sun deity.

Nijō Castle — Doranne Jacobson (upper right). Built by the first Tokugawa emperor. The Tokugawa period represented a time of steep decline in Japanese women's rights.

Text Photos:

John Batchelor, *Ainu Life and Lore* (Tokyo: Kyobunkwan, 1892) A Tattooed Ainu Woman / 185

Gail Lee Bernstein, *Haruko's World* (Stanford: Stanford University Press, 1983) By permission of Stanford University — Haruko in Face Mask / 286

Michael Cooper, S.J., ed., *The Southern Barbarians* (Tokyo, Japan: Kodansha International Ltd., in cooperation with Sophia University, Tokyo, 1971) — Kannon / 120

Baroness Albert d'Anethan, *Fourteen Years of Diplomatic Life in Japan* (London: Stanley Paul & Co., 1912) — Fisherwoman Collecting Driftwood / 133

Roby Eunson, *100 Years: The Amazing Development of Japan Since 1860.* Published by Kodansha International Ltd., Tokyo, Japan, 1965.
Ise Shrine / 6

Buddhist Nun / 28
Pickle Sellers / 129
Woman in Western Dress / 142
Women in School Uniforms / 143
Rokumeikan Pavilion / 144
Infamous Ball / 145
Five Japanese School Girls / 150
Prince Akihito and Shoda Michiko / 164
Japanese Spinning Mill Workers / 199
Modern Girls / 206
Soprano Muiri Tamaki / 207
Light Opera / 222
Woman in Traditional Dress / 223
Peasant Women Winnowing Rice / 226
Japanese Women Training as Militia / 232
Women Gathering 1000 Stitches / 233
Munitions Workers / 236
Survivors of the Atomic Holocaust / 241
Japanese Women Voting / 249
Child Nursemaids / 256

Anna C. Hartshorne, *Japan and Her People*, Vol.II (Philadelphia: Henry T. Coates & Co., 1902)
Peasant Family / 79
Woman Brush Painting / 102
Women Picking Tea Leaves / 130

Alfred M. Hitchcock, *Over Japan Way* (New York: Henry Holt and Company, 1917) — Tea Pickers / 227

International Society for Educational Information, Inc., Tokyo, Japan
Outer Shrine at Ise, Dedicated to Toyouke / 7
Tokeiji Temple / 27
Grave Site of Murasaki Shikibu / 47
Jakko-in Temple / 85
Fukuda Hideko / 199
Kishida Toshiko / 168
Hiratsuka Raichō / 171
Mori Arinori / 180

Baroness Shizue Ishimoto, *Facing Two Ways* (New York: Farrar & Rinehart, 1935)
Baroness Shizue Ishimoto with Her Family / 33
Princess Aya / 99

Library of Congress Catalog Card Number 86-080572
International Standard Book Number
0-914227-08-4 Paper Edition

Acknowledgments

Poem from *Sources of Japanese History*, By David John Lu., pages 39-40 (New York: McGraw Hill, 1974).

Excerpt from "Stories of My Life," in *The Japan Interpreter*, Vol. 12, No. 3-4 (Summer 1979) by Hani Motoka, pages 341-342. By permission of Center for Social Science Communication, Tokyo.

Excerpts from *Flowers in Salt*, by Sharon L. Sievers, pages 29, 163 (Stanford: Stanford University Press, 1983).

Excerpts from *Peasants, Rebels, and Outcastes*, by Mikiso Hane, pages 153, 157-158, 179, 233-235. © Copyright 1982 by Mikiso Hane. Reprinted by permission of Pantheon Books, a Division of Random House, Inc.

Chart from "Country Girls and Communication among Competitors in the Japanese Cotton-Spinning Industry," in Hugh Patrick, ed., *Japanese Industrialization and Its Social Consequences*, by Gary R. Saxonhouse, pages 99, 100 (Berkeley: University of California Press, 1976). By permission of the University of California Press.

Poem from "The Poetry of Yosano Akiko," by Atsumi Ikuko and Graeme Wilson, in the *Japan Quarterly*, Vol. 21, No. 2 (April-June 1974), page 184.

Excerpt from *My Japan 1930-1951*, by Hiroko Nakamoto, pages 52, 56-60 (New York: McGraw-Hill Book Co., 1970).

Excerpts from *Japanese Women: Constraint and Fulfillment*, by Takie Sugiyama Lebra, pages 142-144, 148, 254, 266 (Honolulu: University of Hawaii Press, 1984). By permission of University of Hawaii Press.

Excerpts from *A Half Step Behind — Japanese Women of the 80's*, by Jane Condon, pages 47, 228-229 (New York: Dodd, Mead and Company, 1985). By permission of Dodd, Mead and Company, publisher.

Excerpts from *The Tale of Genji*, by Murasaki Shikibu, translated by Edward G. Seidensticker, pages 158-165 (New York: Alfred A. Knopf, 1985).

Excerpts from *The Women of Suye Mura*, by Robert J. Smith and Ella Lury Wiswell, pages 3, 8, 45, 47-48, 75, 94, 95, 151, 188, 268 (Chicago: University of Chicago Press, 1982).

The project *Women in World Area Studies* began with the support of two Minneapolis suburban school districts — St. Louis Park and Robbinsdale. The project was funded by the Elementary and Secondary Education Act Title IV-C for three years.

The Northwest Area Foundation, the National Endowment for the Humanities, and the Japan Foundation funded the research and writing of *Women in Japan*.

The Ise Cultural Foundation of Tokyo provided funding for the printing of *Women in Japan*.

TABLE OF CONTENTS
Women in Japan

Women in Japan is an overview of the history of Japanese women from ancient times to the present. Two generally accepted ideas concerning Japanese women are investigated in this book. The first is a stereotype that views Japanese women as fitting the "Madam Butterfly" image — doll-like, long suffering, innocent victims who acquiesce to an undeserved fate. The second commonly held idea concerns the place of Japanese women in the history of Japan. According to this view the history of Japanese women has been shaped by Confucian philosophy imported from China in early Japanese times. Therefore, the major role for Japanese women in the history of Japan has been that of "good wife/wise mother" as dictated by the Confucian ethical system. These two assumptions reinforce each other. Both see Japanese women as passive, limited to support roles, with a history dictated by the constraints of Confucianism.

Women in Japan challenges both stereotypes. Powerful roles for women date from the distant, pre-historic past of Japan. A major deity in the Japanese Shintō religion is Amaterasu, the female sun god, looked to as the original ancestor of the Japanese imperial family, her place is central in the Japanese pantheon.

Female rulers were present in early Japanese history. There was Empress Jingu who reportedly conquered Korea in 420 A.D. Tradition says that she was pregnant when she led her troops into battle and so bound herself tightly to conceal her condition. Perhaps in honor of her, Japanese women still wear the obi or tight waistband over their traditional kimono to symbolize her waist binding. Empresses ruling Japan became so routine in early Japanese history that one scholar, Dorothy Robins-Mowry, has suggested that the period between 592 and 770 be called the "Epoch of the Queens."

By the Heian Period (794-1184 A.D.) upper-class women were writing some of the great works of world literature. In her diary Sei Shōnagon makes fun of the inadequacies she noticed in her society. During this time period Murasaki Shikibu wrote the first novel in world literature. Still considered great, her *Tale of Genji*, has had more commentaries written about it than any other work of secular literature except the plays of William Shakespeare.

1

In medieval Japan the samurai ideal of the warrior class developed out of feudalism. During this period (1185-1603 A.D.) women became less visible and influential. But for samurai-class women there was a complementary role to the warrior role of their husbands. At samurai weddings the bride was presented with a dagger which she was instructed to use to defend herself. When her husband was away from their castle fighting for the shōgun, the samurai wife was expected to know how to run the estate, organize the finances, and protect the property. During the medieval period, however, neo-Confucian ideals of a strict hierarchy of class and the subordination of women began to take hold in Japan. Peasant women lost some of their property rights. Samurai daughters of the nobility remained important assets in forming alliances through marriage, but women were seen as inferior to men in the Confucian hierarchy.

The Tokugawa Period (1603-1867 A.D.) marks the low point for women in the history of Japan. Many stereotypes of Japanese women as meek, suppressed people walking behind their husbands come from the generally low status of women in this time period. Reasons for this shift in the status of Japanese women will be explored.

With the end of Japan's isolation and the beginning of modernization during the Meiji period (1868-1913), changes in the status of women in Japan were influenced by Western views of women and the needs of industrialization. Indeed, Japan's early industrialization was built on the labor of teenage girls working long hours in the textile mills. Late 19th and early 20th century reform movements by Japanese women to obtain legal, social, and educational rights were organized. These movements, however, lost ground by the late 1920's and early 1930's, as Japan increasingly turned to imperialism, fascism, and war. The Allied occupation of Japan after World War II imposed constitutional changes giving women the vote and guaranteeing them equal rights.

For most of the history of Japan, the status of women might be viewed as a see-saw with various tilts, up and down depending upon a woman's class, time period, and individual talents. In the history of Japan, women have filled a variety of powerful and prominent roles. Meanwhile, ordinary women have contributed to the welfare of their families and society, and have created the social environment in which Japan's astonishing economic growth in the 20th century became possible. This book represents an attempt to present examples of the rich history of women in the long story of Japanese culture.

*   *   *   *   *

Note on style:

Japanese name order, family name first and given name last, has been used in *Women in Japan*. This stresses the importance of the family name in Japan. Reference books in footnotes and bibliographies have not, however, been changed if they were in the Western style with family name last. A macron has been placed over the long vowel sounds according to Japanese pronunciation. As Japanese nouns do not have *s* as plural signs they have not been used after nouns such as shōgun and geisha.

CHAPTER 1

ANCIENT JAPAN
FEMALE GODS AND
RULING EMPRESSES

A.   Amaterasu Ōmikami
Heaven-Shining-Great-August-Deity

The beaten path
Is covered with fallen leaves;
Brush them aside and see
The footprints of the Sun Goddess.
Ninomiya[1]

Looking back into the ancient history of Japan to find how women lived is rather like hunting for hidden footprints. The few written sources deal mainly with female religious figures and the lives of upper-class women. It is clear, even in these limited sources, that female roles in ancient Japan were often important ones.

One tradition concerns the female gods who, according to early Japanese mythology, helped create the islands of Japan and were ancestors of the imperial family. Unlike the Judeo-Christian belief in one god (primarily addressed in masculine terms), the creation of the human race as depicted in early Japanese mythology was seen as a joint effort between the gods Izanagi (male) and Izanami (female).[2]

These two gods (called Kami in Japanese, roughly meaning heavenly spirits) seem to have had affection for each other; yet they fell to quarreling and separated. Izanami retreated to the underworld. Izanagi tried to join her, but she rejected him and he fled. As Izanagi purified himself in the water of a river-mouth, from the pollution of the underworld, other

---

[1]Quoted in, Elizabeth Seeger, *Eastern Religions* (New York: Thomas Y. Crowell Co., 1973), p. 157.

[2]Floyd Hiatt Ross, *Shintō: The Way of Japan* (Boston: Beacon Press, 1965), p. 25.

5

The most honored Shintō shrines in Japan are at Ise, on the east coast of the island of Hōnshu. The inner shrine is dedicated to Amaterasu, the female sun god. The shrines at Ise were important in establishing the power of the emperors as they worshiped here and traced their ancestory to Amaterasu. This photograph was taken in 1871 during the Meiji era.

Kami sprung from his body. The most important of these Kami was Amaterasu.[3]

Amaterasu became the female sun god; her brothers, who were also created at the time of Izanagi's purification, became the moon god Tsuki and the storm god Susanō. Of the three, Amaterasu was given the most important role of ruling heaven while her brothers ruled the night and the earth. Accounts of this female god show her as the most responsible of the three. Amaterasu and her maidens are described in ancient myths as preparing feasts and festivals and making clothing for the gods in the weaving hall. The moon god Tsuki is seen as weak—in one source of these myths his activities are not described further.[4]

Susanō, the storm god, is seen as mischievous and destructive. Susanō broke the dikes in Amaterasu's rice fields. He even skinned a horse in an insulting and cruel way and then threw it through the roof of Amaterasu's weaving hall. Susanō's misbehavior was too much for his sister; in disgust she shut herself up in a cave. When Amaterasu retreated to the cave, the earth became dark and life on earth

---

[3]Some Japanese traditions say that Amaterasu was born of Izanami and was not just the child of her father. See, Ross, *Shintō: The Way of Japan*, p. 25.

[4]*Ibid.*, p. 25.

was threatened. To lure her out of the cave, the numerous gods—Kami—took council and did three things: they hung jewels on an evergreen tree which they placed near the cave, they hung a mirror near the entrance to the cave and then gathered for a comic dance which would make them laugh. Amaterasu became so curious as to why there should be laughter with her sunlight gone, that she peeked out of the cave door, saw the jewels, her own beautiful reflection, and the comic dance. As a result, she stayed outside the cave from that time on. Even her rambunctious brother Susanō tried to make up with her. He gave her a sword found in the dead body of a monster he had slain; and with that, the jewels, the mirror, and the sword became Amaterasu's special symbols.

To bring order to the earth, Amaterasu is said to have sent her grandson to rule the islands of Japan. According to legend, she told him:

"The Luxuriant Land of Reed Plains is a country which our descendants are to inherit. Go, therefore, Our Imperial Grandson, and rule over it! And may Our Imperial lineage continue unbroken and prosperous, co-eternal with Heaven and Earth!" [5]

The first Japanese emperor recorded in the early chronicles was Jinmu Tennō (711 B.C.-660 B.C.). It was written that he was a direct descendant of the female god Amaterasu. The Japanese emperors and empresses trace their origin in an unbroken line to Jinmu Tennō and, therefore, to Amaterasu. The sacred mirror of Amaterasu was kept at the

This is the outer shrine at Ise dedicated to the female god of food, Toyouke.

royal palace until 92 B.C., when the emperor entrusted it to his daughter who placed it in the Shrine of Ise, dedicated to the sun god Amaterasu. A female attendant is always in charge of the mirror, which is kept wrapped in silk in a special box. This woman, acting as protector of the mirror, is always a member of the imperial family and in charge of the shrine.[6]

The Japanese recognized many gods, both male and female; for example, the shrine of Toyouke, female god of food, is close to the famous one of Amaterasu's at Ise. Amaterasu has had a central place in Japanese history because of the importance of the sun to the success of agricultural endeavors, but particularly because she was thought to be the divine ancestor of the first emperor of Japan.

[5]Quoted in, *Ibid.*, p. 28.

[6]Seeger, *Eastern Religions*, p. 188-189.

Points to Consider

Out of ancient myths, like these of Amaterasu, developed the Japanese religion called Shintō. According to one modern scholar of Japan, J. Edward Kidder, the Shintō religion is still "a vital social force" in Japan, and "every Japanese hopes to visit the Shintō Shrine at Ise once in a 60-year period" to give homage to Amaterasu.[7] Another scholar, Tamie Kamiyama, feels this devotion to Amaterasu and Shintōism among Japanese peoples may be disappearing.

1. What roles and characteristics has Amaterasu that might still attract modern Japanese people to her worship?

2. In what way has the veneration of Amaterasu had political, as well as religious, implications in Japanese history?

3. Why might Shintōism as a "vital force" be fading in contemporary Japan?

---

[7]J. Edward Kidder, *Ancient Japan* (Oxford: Elsevier-Phaidon, 1977), p. 61, 68.

B. Ancient Japanese Empresses

During the period of the French Revolution in the late 18th century, a noted French philosopher, the Marquis de Condorcet, declared that a nation could be judged as civilized if it protected the civil rights and freedoms of women. But to the first Chinese travelers to Japan in the 3rd century A.D., and to Chinese commentators later, an opposite observation was made. Chinese visitors expressed dismay over the extent of freedom that Japanese women enjoyed and were startled by the presence of female rulers in Japanese history.[1] According to the philosophy of Confucius, the dominant one followed by the Chinese, women had a subordinate position to men. For a woman to rule would upset the natural order or be like "a hen crowing at dawn," as a Chinese saying put it. Therefore, the Japanese seemed an uncivilized people to these Chinese travelers because they allowed women freedom—and even accepted them as rulers.

A Chinese history written in 297 A.D. records the impressions of earlier Chinese travelers to the Land of Wa, as they called Japan. The history relates that "the men [of Wa] all tattoo their faces and adorn their bodies with designs . . . The women tie their hair in bows, and their clothing . . . is put on by slipping it over the head. They use pink and scarlet to smear their bodies . . . They take their food with their hands, but have bamboo and wooden

---

[1]Ivan Morris, *The World of the Shining Prince* (New York: Alfred A. Knopf, 1964), p. 11.

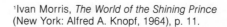

trays on which to put it."[2] The travelers also commented on the living arrangements of the Japanese. The men lived with men and the women with women, but they maintained a spirit of sexual equality. This same Chinese history described the queen who ruled the Land of Wa. She was called Himiko (or Pimiko), meaning "sun-daughter," and had come to power in about 183 A.D.[3] She was elderly and had never married. The Chinese history gave this description of how she came to rule:

"Formerly the country had men as rulers. However, for seventy or eighty years after that, the country had disturbances and warfare. Finally people agreed to take a woman as their ruler, and called her Himiko (Pimiko). She was adept in the ways of shamanism, [claiming to use supernatural powers], and could bewitch people. In her mature years, she was yet unmarried and had her younger brother help her rule the country. After she became the ruler, there were only a few who ever saw her. She had one thousand maidservants, but there was only one man servant attending her. His functions were to serve her food and drinks, to communicate messages, and to enter and leave her quarters. The queen resided in a palace surrounded by towers and barricades, with guards maintaining a constant watch . . . ."[4]

This early queen, Himiko, sent envoys to China to pay homage to the Chinese emperor and sent gifts of slaves and bolts of special cloth.[5] Her acts of friendship led to trade and diplomatic relations between China and Japan.

These very early ruling empresses like Himiko were probably also female shamans. Shamans were thought to have supernatural powers and to be able to act as intermediaries between humans and gods. The Japanese word for shaman is miko—literally divine woman. There is no Japanese word for a male shaman. This may suggest that one source of these early female rulers' power was their status as miko.

Other early women rulers followed Himiko.[6] When Himiko died, the Chinese account explained:

"A great mound was raised, more than a hundred paces in diameter. Over a hundred male and female attendants followed her to the grave. Then a king was placed on the throne, but the people would not obey him . . . [finally] a relative of Himiko named Iyo, a girl of thirteen, was made queen and order was restored."[7]

[2]Tsunoda Ryusaku, tr., *Japan in the Chinese Dynastic Histories* (South Pasadena: P. D. and Ione Perking, 1951), p. 1-2.

[3]J. Edward Kidder, *Ancient Japan* (Oxford: Elsevier-Phaidon, 1977), p. 4.

[4]Quoted in, David John Lu, *Sources of Japanese History*, Vol. 1 (New York: McGraw-Hill Book Co., 1974), p. 10.

[5]Dorothy Robins-Mowry, *The Hidden Sun: Women of Modern Japan* (Boulder, Colorado: Westview Press, 1983), p. 6.

[6]See: Yu Mizuno, "Shamanism In Early Japan," *The East*, Vol. 9, No. 6.

[7]Ryusaku, *Japan in the Chinese Dynastic Histories*, p. 16.

A later empress, Jingu (or Jingō), who ruled in the 3rd century A.D., became second only to the female god Amaterasu in the reverence shown her by the Japanese people.[8] Her story is a combination of legend and fact that makes historians unsure of her real history. A Japanese historian explained her importance this way: "The Empress Jingu (or Jingō) was our Joan of Arc. Fired by Divine inspiration, she displayed a military valor which was of incalculable service to her country in the crisis of its fortunes."[9]

Accounts of Empress Jingu's activities differ somewhat, but she seems to have become ruler of Japan upon the death of her husband. For awhile she managed to keep his death a secret and put down revolts within the kingdom, acting in his name. Although she was pregnant with the future emperor, she put on men's clothes and went into battle. Using her powers as a shaman she claimed to hear the will of a god tell her that the Japanese should invade Silla, now Korea. She said to her ministers:

"To listen to the will of God, to move the people to war, is a matter of great concern to the country. From above, I shall receive the support of the spirits of the Gods of Heaven and Earth, while, below, I shall avail myself of the assistance of you, my ministers. Brandishing our weapons, we shall cross the towering billows: preparing a fleet of ships, we shall take possession of the Land of Treasure. If this expedition is successful, it will be due to you, my ministers; and if not I alone am to blame." [10]

Empress Jingu's expedition to Korea succeeded, but she faced revolts at home upon her return. With these rebellions subdued, it is said she ruled for 70 years dying at the age of 100.

Several aspects of Empress Jingu's story have become part of Japanese culture and customs. The heroic deed of the pregnant empress binding herself to wear men's clothes into battle was commemorated in Japanese women's dress. In later times, Japanese women adopted a pregnancy "girdle," used partly in remembrance of Empress Jingu. Perhaps this girdle became the obi which is the sash worn over the kimono. The Empress has also been seen as a national hero. Western travelers to Japan in the 1870's found that the Japanese still referred to her military exploits with pride. This early empress had given them their first historical opportunity to display valor in making "the arms of Japan shine beyond the seas," as they put it.[11]

[8]Robins-Mowry, *The Hidden Sun*, p. 6-9.

[9]Tan Hamaguchi, "Some Striking Female Personalities in Japanese History," Annual Meeting of the Japan Society, London, May 13, 1903 (London: The Japan Society, 1904), p. 241.

[10]Mary R. Beard, *The Force of Women in Japanese History* (Washington, D.C.: Public Affairs Press, 1953), p. 25.

[11]Quoted in, William Elliot Griffis, *The Mikado's Empire*, (New York: Harper & Brothers, 1876), p. 79.

Tomb of Empress Suiko. She helped to establish Buddhism as a major religion in Japan.

Later empresses fulfilled the function of bringing together warring groups and adding to Japan's dignity by encouraging culture and religion. One scholar recently suggested that the period in Japanese history between 592 and 770 A.D. be called the "Epoch of the Queens" as one-half of the rulers during that time were women.[12] Historian E. Patricia Tsurumi calls these rulers "Female Emperors" to distinguish them as reigning sovereigns rather than wives of rulers. The six women who ruled as Female Emperors were:

Empress Suiko—592-628 A.D.

Empress Kōgyoku—642-645 A.D. (Empress Kōgyoku also reigned from 655-661 as Empress Saimei)

Empress Jitō—687-697 A.D.

Empress Genmyō—707-715 A.D.

Empress Genshō—715-724 A.D.

Empress Kōken—749-758 A.D. (Empress Kōken also reigned from 764-770 as Empress Shōtoku)

Generally, the reigns of these empresses-or female emperors—followed similar patterns.

* They were compromise candidates, chosen by warring factions, unable to agree upon a sovereign.

The empresses:

* favored Buddhism as a religion.

* worked to unify the state.

* were interested in cultural matters.

After the death or abdication of a male emperor, there frequently were conflicts between the nearest male relatives of the emperor, his sons or his brother, as to who should be the next ruler. In her role as emperor's wife, the empress, as in the case of Kōgyoku, was often the mother or sister of those desiring power. She might make an acceptable compromise candidate for emperor as someone both sides could trust. The Empress Suiko served as female emperor until her death in 628 A.D., but others abdicated in favor of a son (Kōgyoku as Empress Saimei), a grandson (Jitō), or a daughter (Genmyō). Sometimes the new ruler did not prove able, and in two cases the former ruling empress was recalled to rule. New "reign-names" were given to them, so eight names of reigning empresses appear in the

---

[12]Robins-Mowry, *The Hidden Sun*, p. 9. The Asuka (552-710 A.D.) and Nara (710-784 A.D.) periods of Japanese history span this "Epoch of the Queens."

The Tōdaiji Temple near Nara. Built during the reign of Empress Kōmyō in the 8th Century.

chronicles, but only six women reigned.[13]

As rulers, these empresses frequently supported the Buddhist religion. Both Confucianism and Buddhism were being introduced into Japan from China and Korea at this time. While the Buddhist religion did not always see women equal to men, it did not have the Confucian restrictions against women rulers, so Buddhism was more appealing to the empresses. Empress Suiko helped to establish Buddhism as a major religion in Japan by building a large monastery at Nara and bringing Buddhist scholars from Korea to encourage the spread of religious ideas. In her second reign, Empress Kōken made a Buddhist

priest her principal advisor and may have planned to make him her successor. The empress-consort Kōmyō (729-749), the wife Emperor Shomu chose to be empress, had Buddhist temples built, including the huge Buddha of Tōdaiji Temple in Nara. She was also known for charitable acts, including the cleansing of a leper. One scholar has suggested that she can be remembered as the "first volunteer

---

[13]E. Patricia Tsurumi, "Japan's Early Female Emperors," *Historical Reflections*, Vol. 8, No. 1 (Spring 1981), p. 41.

social worker in her country."[14] The Buddhist religion gave empresses outlets for their energies in the areas of scholarship, art and architecture, and helping the poor.

The empresses were attracted to the Buddhist faith introduced from Korea in the middle of the 6th century. They also accepted some of the ideas of an orderly and highly organized state introduced from China during the same time period. Most empresses became rulers as compromise candidates between warring factions. Once in power, they tended to work for a tightening of government organization and a centralizing of power. Empress Jitō supported efforts to write down a code of laws which later became the important Taihō Code of 701 A.D. Empress Genmyō established Nara as the first permanent capital of Japan which aided in strengthening and centralizing the government.[15] Empresses Jitō and Genmyō were interested in military affairs, and Jitō led troops in the field.

Another pattern common to the reigns of 7th and 8th century empresses was their promotion of culture and the arts. The Emperor Temmu and his wife, the Empress Jitō, ordered the oral histories of Japan written down. During her reign, the Empress Genmyō ordered the completion of the histories. The first written chronicle of Japan, called the Kojiki, is considered the most accurate of the early Japanese chronicles.[16] The writing of this history—chronicle—also involved a woman. The Shintō shrine maiden, Hieda no Are, was ordered to listen to the court storytellers and memorize the oral traditions, legends, and family chronologies. She then dictated these to the scholar Yasumaro, who wrote them down.

Empress Suiko supported the creation of art works, and Empress Shōtoku (Kōken) was responsible for printing one million religious charms in honor of a military victory. The printed charms that remain today are examples of the earliest printing in the world.[17] Jitō, Genmyō and Shōtoku encouraged the collection and writing down of Japanese poetry. The collection, called the *Manyōshū* or *Collection of Myriad Leaves*, became an important part of the cultural heritage of Japan. Empress Jitō is remembered for writing the first poem in a poetry game traditionally played at New Year:

Spring has passed away
And summer is come;
Look where white clothes are spread
* in the sun*
On the heavenly hill of Kagu![18]

[14]Robins-Mowry, *The Hidden Sun*, p. 10.

[15]*Ibid.*, p. 10.

[16]Yoshiko Wada, "Woman and Her Power in the Japanese Emperor System," *Feminist—Japan*, Vol. 1, No. 4 (February 1978), p. 15.

[17]Robins-Mowry, *The Hidden Sun*, p. 11.

[18]Quoted in, *Ibid.*, p. 10.

This line of female rulers—Suiko, Kōgyoku, Jitō, Genmyō, Genshō and Shōtoku—were effective governors who also encouraged the creation and preservation of the arts and culture of early Japan.

The line ended, however, with Shōtoku. She broke with the tradition of female rulers who balanced internal power groups and instead, associated herself with an outsider. The outsider was a Buddhist priest, Dōkyō, who was not a member of the imperial family. Because she was ill, the Empress Kōken, with the help of the medical-priest Dōkyō, abdicated in 758 A.D. She recovered from her illness. As Empress Shōtoku, Kōken took over the throne and elevated Dōkyō to chief advisor. She also indicated that he might be named her successor. His ambitions for the throne led to civil war. The year after Shōtoku's death, Dōkyō was banished and died in a temple in the mountains. With his banishment and death the tradition of having ruling empresses was discredited. After the "Epoch of the Queens," there were only two women who ruled as Japanese reigning female emperors. Both were children when they reigned and their reigns were brief ones.[26] Although the practice, then, of having female emperors was not officially made illegal until 1889 the custom virtually died out after the "Epoch of the Queens."

As the wives of emperors, empresses continued to affect Japanese history through their influence on their husband's decisions. Some empresses ruled as regents for minor sons and often continued to give them advice, once they became emperors. But the rule of Shōtoku marked the end of one powerful role for imperial Japanese women—that of leader of the empire. Women as female emperors were then only a memory recalled by reading the historical chronicles they had helped to produce.

Points to Consider

After reading over the following excerpts from speeches of two female monarchs answer the questions that follow.

1. One characteristic common to several early Japanese empresses was their military prowess and valor in battle. In the following account, Empress Jingu (200-269 A.D.) put on male clothing to lead her army in an invasion of Korea after her husband's death. She declared to her generals:

    "If I were to leave the whole conduct of the war in your hands, and you were unsuccessful, the responsibility would fall on your shoulders alone. But that I cannot bear. Although I am only a woman and unworthy of the post, yet it seems that I have the full approval of the god, and the hearty support of all you officers and of the soldiers. It is for these reasons I venture to marshal the army, and share both the successes and failures of the undertaking."

She then issued the following orders to her army on the eve of their departure:

"1. Unless the strictest discipline is preserved, success cannot be hoped for.

"2. Men who give themselves up to looting and to selfish considerations will in all probability fall into the enemies' hands.

"3. However weak your enemies may be, do not despise them.

"4. However strong they may be, do not be afraid of them.

"5. Do not spare those who are treacherous.

"6. Have mercy on those who surrender.

"7. When triumphant you will be rewarded amply.

"8. Severe punishment will fall upon cowards." [19]

In 1588, over 1300 years later, Queen Elizabeth I appeared before her troops at Tilsbury, England. The army of Elizabeth was assembled to meet the threatened invasion by the Spanish. At Tilsbury, Elizabeth gave a speech to her troops:

"... I have always so behaved myself that, under God, I have placed my chiefest strength and safeguard in the loyal hearts and goodwill of my subjects;

and therefore I am come amongst you, as you see, resolved, in the midst and heat of the battle, to live or die amongst you all, to lay down for my God, and for my kingdom, and for my people, my honor and my blood, even in the dust. I know I have the body of a weak and feeble woman, but I have the heart and stomach of a king, and of a king of England too, and think foul scorn that Parma or Spain or any prince of Europe should dare to invade the borders of my realm; to which, rather than any dishonor shall grow by me, I myself will take up arms, I myself will be your general, judge and rewarder of every one of your virtues in the field. I know already for your forwardness you have deserved rewards and crowns; and we do assure you, in the word of a prince, they shall be duly paid you." [20]

Compare and Contrast

In what specific ways are these two speeches alike?

In what specific ways are they different?

---

[19]Quoted in, Hamaguchi, "Some Striking Female Personalities in Japanese History," p. 239-240.

[20]Quoted in, Winston S., Churchill, *A History of the English-Speaking Peoples: The New World*, Vol. 2 (New York: Dodd, Mead & Company, 1956), p. 126.

In what ways were the occasions that inspired these speeches alike? In what ways different?

Why do you think both monarchs emphasize that they are "only a woman" or "I know I have the body of a weak and feeble woman . . .?" What advantages might they have had over a male leader in inspiring their troops?

2. A scholar of Japanese history, G. Cameron Hurst, wrote, "An empress came to the throne simply to avoid succession troubles and ensure transmission of the succession to the proper person [a male of the imperial family]. Once the troubles had been settled—one of the claimants had died, for example, or a younger crown prince had come of age—then there was no longer any need for the empress to remain on the throne."[21]

What specific things in the description of the six empresses would seem to agree with Hurst's theory?

What specific evidence would seem to refute (prove false) Hurst's theory?

Historian E. Patricia Tsurumi argues that Hurst's theory fits only the Empress Kogyoku/Saimei and "does not take into account [the empresses'] functions as rulers."[22] Why might historians judge these female emperors' roles differently than male emperors? How might the lack of information about Japan's ancient past lead to some of these differences in interpretation?

3. Although Empresses Jitō, (b. 646-d. 704 A.D.), who abdicated to her grandson Monmu but had reigned as ruling monarch, requested a modest, simple funeral without mourning ceremonies. After her death the following activities and rituals took place (read over the list and answer the questions that follow):

- "Five nobles, headed by an imperial prince, were appointed as a committee to oversee the erection of a temporary internment building to house [Jitō's] coffin. Another committee of four, also headed by an imperial prince, built a surrounding wall."

- "[Jitō's] coffin [was] moved to the Western Palace."

- "Funeral feasts [were held] in the Four Great Temples: Daian-ji, Yakushi-ji, Gankō-ji, and Kōfuku-ji."

- "Obarae, the national purification ceremony [was] not held."

- "Ogami (feast without meat, as a religious sacrifice) [were] celebrated in the Four Great Temples."

- "49th day ogami ceremonies [held] . . . in a total of 33 temples."

---

[21]Tsurumi, "Japan's Early Female Emperors," p. 41-42.

[22]*Ibid.*, p. 48.

17

- "100th day prayers [held] at the temporary internment building.

- "Two large funeral committees [were] appointed, one to deal with procedure and one to build a suitable crematorium."

- "Princes and officials read the funeral eulogy [before Empress Jitō was cremated]" The ex-empress was given an important posthumous [after death] title.

- Jitō was cremated and "buried in the Ōuchi tomb with the remains of Emperor Tenmu [her husband]." She was buried one year after her death.[23]

- Cremation was not a common form of funeral arrangement at the time of Jitō's death. After her death there was a "widespread adoption of cremation outside the priesthood."[24]

- One scholar has suggested that Jitō, who he feels made frequent pilgrimages for the purpose of communicating with the kami, can be considered to be a royal miko — mystics or shamans able to hear the kami or spirits.[25]

List specific things which indicate that the funeral was considered to be an important affair.

Speculate about possible reasons for planning such an elaborate funeral for an ex-empress who had not even been ruling upon her death.

How does Empress Jitō's funeral seem to refute the theory of Hurst about the six empresses? What other things suggest her importance?

Why might there be no single theory about the relative importance of these empresses?[26]

4. Recently historian Takamure Itsue examined archaeological and historical documents and concluded that until about 300 A.D. husbands and wives lived separately in matrilineal, matrilocal clans.

A. Define matrilineal, matrilocal, patrilineal, and patrilocal (virilocal.)

B. What evidence from ancient accounts is there in this selection that supports Takamure Itsue's theory?

C. Suggest ways that women might have more power in a matrilineal/matrilocal family system.

---

[23]J. Edward Kidder, "Problems of Cremation in early Japan: The Role of Empress Jitō," *Humanities Christianity and Culture*, Vol. 13 (Tokyo: International Christian University Publication IV-B), March 1979.

[24]*Ibid.*, p. 207

[25]*Ibid.*, p. p. 206-07.

[26]Myosho reigned from 1630-1643 and lived another 53 years after abdication; and Go-Sakuramachi reigned from 1763-1770 and lived for 44 years after her abdication.

CHAPTER 2

RELIGION AND JAPANESE WOMEN

A.   Shintō—Women as Gods and Shamans

Symbols from a variety of religions appear in the lives of modern Japanese people. Weddings may take place in several stages. A Japanese Shintō ceremony, with the bride dressed in traditional costume, is followed by a ceremony in which the bride dresses in a Western style white wedding dress. Although Japanese may be married at a Shintō shrine, they are often buried at a Buddhist temple.[1] In December, Christmas trees and decorations appear in public displays. The idea expressed recently by a community leader that ''Japan has been a country of men''[2] reflects the influence of Chinese Confucian ideals on later Japanese history and thought. There is not one dominant religion in Japan, but several—often blended—ones. For women, each religious tradition offers some unique benefits—as well as imposing specific

limitations on their lives.

The Shintō religion is based on a view of the world in which heavenly spirits (kami) interact with humans in both negative and positive ways. Amaterasu, the female sun god, represented a positive spirit, while her brother Susanō was an unruly one. Mountains, seas, rivers, and fields were thought to have a spiritual nature, and Mount Fuji was considered one of the most sacred of these natural creations. The aim of Shintō worship is to make the world better for human beings and to

---

[1] J. Edward Kidder, *Ancient Japan* (Oxford: Elsevier-Phaidon Press, 1977), p. 63.

[2] Dorothy Robins-Mowry, *The Hidden Sun: Women of Modern Japan* (Boulder, Colorado: Westview Press, 1983), p. 3.

achieve harmony with nature.[3] Many Shintō ceremonies were meant to achieve fertile harvests of crops.

Since kami were everywhere, both women and men were equally able to communicate with these heavenly spirits. From ancient times, some women have fulfilled the role of Shintō shaman. According to Shintō belief, a shaman is a person having supernatural powers, able to communicate with and interpret the will of the kami.[4] Many early empresses were shamans, such as the Empress Himiko (or Pimiko) mentioned in early Chinese accounts of Japan. At times these female shamans would go into a trance and, while in a state of possession, make predictions of future events or give advice to their followers.[5] In later Japanese history, during what is called medieval times, ruling Japanese lords would call in female shamans to decide difficult law cases where there were no witnesses to the crime. The female shaman would go into a trance and become possessed by kami. While in this trance, it was thought that her spoken words expressed the truth and so she decided the justice of the case.[6]

When separate Shintō shrines were first built in the 3rd century, female shamans were the ichiko, or those in charge. As time went on, the management of the shrines became professionalized, with male priests taking over their supervision.[7] Women have, however, continued to take an active part in ceremonies connected with some of the major Shintō shrines. The following is a description by a British traveler in the 1950's of some

A modern Shintō shrine attendant performs a traditional dance.

of the miko, or young women assistants, at Nara shrine.

[3]Richard Cavendish, *The Great Religions* (New York: ARCO Publishing, Inc., 1980), p. 113, and Kidder, *Ancient Japan*, p. 63.

[4]Kidder, *Ancient Japan*, p. 147.

[5]Floyd Hiatt Ross, *Shintō: The Way of Japan* (Boston: Beacon Press, 1965), p. 58.

[6]Louis Frederic, *Daily Life in Japan at the Time of the Samurai, 1185-1603* (London: George Allen and Unwin Ltd., 1972), p. 65.

[7]Ross, *Shintō*, p. 58.

"Almost immediately . . . we saw our first Shintō priestess which came as a lovely surprise for one had heard of the virgin priestesses but not thought much about them. Or for that matter ever before seen living priestesses of any kind. For they are not at all the same as Buddhist nuns. They are young and generally good looking and wear a beautiful and distinctive dress. In fact they are young girls fourteen to twenty years old; seldom if ever older. At that age they leave the shrine and marry; and it is to be noticed that in all the many Shintō temples we were to see there was never a priestess, if, indeed, that is the correct term for them, older than that age, or, so far as one could see, any older woman in charge of them. Their dress, which we much admired, is a wide red divided skirt, of red silk of beautiful color, cut so that it appears as if they are wearing trousers; a white shift or undergarment, and over that a semi-transparent, gauzy cape or mantle. At other shrines, but only rarely, their divided skirts were of green silk . . .

"Their function is really that of dancing girls, the sacred dances they perform are called Kagura . . . [and] the name for the priestesses is Miko which means a maiden serving the gods." [8]

Some women in recent Japanese history have revived the ancient Shintō female shaman tradition. Kotani Kimi, Nagaoka Toshiko, and Kitamura Sayo have founded new sects in modern times.[9] Tenrikyo (Divine Teaching) is a branch of the Shintō religion which has followers in Japan, Korea, and South America. This movement was founded in the 1830's by Nakayama Miki, a country farming woman, who was possessed by kami and became involved in faith healing and helping the poor.[10]

The Shintō religion has allowed for important positions for women and a view which included female kami and important female deities such as Amaterasu. But some elements in Shintōism have been negative for women. Like many of the world's religions, Shintōism has a strong sense of pollution which occurs through having contact with death, disease, excrement, menstruation or spilling of blood. When pollution has occurred, various purification rites are needed for cleansing those that have become polluted. It was thought that women with monthly menstrual cycles could pollute certain ceremonies or hallowed places. Therefore, many sacred areas, such as the top of Mount Fuji as well as shrines, were closed to women.[11] Childbirth, too, was seen as polluting. The sacred island of Itsukushima was kept free from pollution by having any dying

---

[8]Sacheverell Sitwell, *The Bridge of the Brocade Sash* (Cleveland: The World Publishing Co., 1959), p. 129.

[9]Takie Sugiyama Lebra, *Japanese Women: Constraint and Fulfillment* (Honolulu: University of Hawaii Press), p. 19.

[10]Cavendish, *The Great Religions*, p. 122-123.

[11]In the 19th century (October 1867), a British woman, Lady Parkes, broke the tradition and climbed the mountain. Basil Hall Chamberlain, *Things Japanese* (London: John Murray, 1905), p. 194.

person or pregnant woman taken over to the mainland.[12] This emphasis on pollution curtailed women's activities and at times kept them from taking part in Shintō ceremonies. Some observers also feel that the female Shintō shrine attendants in modern times have played only minor parts in the religion.[13] In ancient times, however, it seems that there were Shintō female shamans who acted as powerful religious and political leaders.

Points to Consider

1. What things about the Shintō religion seem especially positive for women? What things are negative?

2. How did the British traveler describe the "Shintō priestesses" she met at Nara? What particularly impressed her? She commented that she had—"for that matter [never] before seen living priestesses of any kind." Why might a British traveler in the 1950's be surprised to observe women as priests?

3. In recent years women have founded and led several new religious sects in Japan. How might ancient Shintō leadership traditions have encouraged women to found new religious sects? Why might Japanese people join these groups?

---

[12]Cavendish, *Great Religions*, p. 113.

[13]Lebra, *Japanese Women*, p. 19.

B. Women and Buddhism Opportunities and Restrictions

The Buddhist religion was founded in India during the 6th century B.C., but although Buddhism spread to Tibet, China, Korea, and Japan, it eventually disappeared from India. Buddhism made its way to Japan in the 6th century A.D., 1000 years after its founding. It was introduced by envoys of the Korean king, sent to the Japanese court. By the time of the reign of Empress Suiko (592-628 A.D.) and her regent, Prince Shōtoku, Buddhism was established as the religion of the Japanese rulers, blended with Shintō ideas of the divinity of the imperial family.

As a religion, Buddhism particularly appealed to upper-class women and empresses. Buddhist convents provided women with an alternative to marriage as religious nuns and a religious leadership role for women as abbesses (heads of convents.) Members of the imperial family — sisters of the emperors, former empresses, or displaced wives — would often leave the court to retire to a Buddhist convent where they might spend their time in prayer or doing charitable works.

As well as providing an alternative to marriage and leadership roles, Buddhist convents sometimes became places of refuge for upper-class women whose fortunes had declined. During the rule of the first shōgun, Minamoto Yoritomo, in the 12th century, one of his waiting-women, Mino-no-Tsubone, founded the Buddhist temple of Tōkeiji. At this time divorce was rare but acceptable for the lower classes but not for women of the upper classes. The wife of a samurai who wanted to divorce her husband without his consent had only one way to do so — by running away.[1] In 1285 an imperial woman, the wife of the regent Tokimune, established the custom of allowing fugitive wives to take refuge in the Tōkeiji temple. If they remained for three years, a divorce became final. Later the Abbess Yodo, the daughter of an emperor, decided that this three-year waiting period was too long and reduced it to two years.[2]

Besides physical refuge, the Buddhist religion offered an outlet for women who wished to help the less fortunate, as Buddhism emphasized the value of charitable works. Empress Kōmyō, who lived in the 8th century, was known for helping the sick and needy. However, these were tasks left to Buddhist monks, and so she was severely criticized for her efforts. After her death, her good works were finally recognized as she was given the title "Empress who shines brightly."[3] The Buddhist god Kannon, in female form, became the sympathetic, concerned, motherly image to whom distressed people might turn for help. In the branch of Japanese Buddhism that worshiped the god Amida, it was thought that women would be equal to men in salvation. The monk Hōnen (1133-1212 A.D.) said that by repeating the Amida name of Buddha, "there will be no distinction, neither between men and women, nor between the good and the bad, the mighty and the weak; all will enter into his [Buddha's] Pure Land merely by invoking [saying] his name, Amida, with complete faith . . . ."[4]

A later reformer-monk, Nichiren, founded the violent, and in many ways intolerant, Lotus sect. Nichiren seems to have been influenced by his affection for his mother and so emphasized a dual view of women and men that valued their separate but complementary roles: "Man is pillar and woman is frame; man is wing and woman is body; if the wing is separated from the body, how can it fly?"[5] In 1300 another monk, Mujū Ichien, wrote a religious pamphlet, *Mirror for Women*, which also had as a theme that a woman could be virtuous and, like a man, strive for salvation by following with diligent concern "the way of the Buddha."[6]

Buddhism also contained some special restrictions on women. Like the Shintō religion, Buddhism had a strong sense that some acts or conditions are purifying, while others are polluting. Menstruation and childbirth were both considered polluting conditions, and because women might be menstruating or have

[1]Louis Frederic, *Daily Life in Japan at the Time of the Samurai* (London: George Allen and Unwin Ltd., 1972), p. 49.

[2]*Ibid.*, p. 49.

[3] Dorothy Robins-Mowry, *The Hidden Sun* (Boulder, Colorado: Westview Press, 1983), p. 11.

[4]Frederic, *Daily Life in Japan at the Time of the Samurai*, p. 198.

[5]Quoted in, Robins-Mowry, *The Hidden Sun*, p. 23.

[6]Robert E. Morrell, "Mirror for Women," *Monumenta Nipponica*, Vol. 35, No. 1, (Spring 1980), p. 75.

The Tōkeiji Temple was founded by Mino-no-Tsubone, of shōgun Minimoto Yoritomo's court. A samurai wife who took refuge here from her husband could obtain a divorce if she remained at the Buddhist temple for a number of years.

just given birth, they were excluded from some religious rites. The Buddhist monk Shinran, who in the 13th century founded an important Buddhist cult, started the idea that women could not, as women, enter paradise, as he claimed that "women by nature are covetous and sinful . . . ."[7] The Chinese Buddhist Tao-Hsüan (596-667 A.D.) had listed what he considered to be the sins of women. Seven sins were particularly thought to be major ones and were repeated in later Japanese Buddhist literature:

1. Women arouse sexual desire in men.

2. Women are jealous.

3. Women are deceitful and smile even when they do not mean it.

4. Women neglect their religious duties and think only of fine clothes.

---

[7]Robins-Mowry, *The Hidden Sun*, p. 23.

27

A Buddhist nun with shaved head escorts Western visitors through a temple in Nara — c. 1960.

5. The honest words of women are few.

6. Women have no shame.

7. The bodies of women are forever unclean.[8]

Since these sins were thought to be so grave, simply being born a woman would keep one out of paradise. A Buddhist belief is in the transmigration of souls — that people live many lives; in each life they try to improve until paradise, or nirvana, is reached. If one was born a woman, it was thought that it was impossible to achieve salvation during that lifetime. A woman would have to be reborn as a male before nirvana could be reached.

The themes of waiting and longing, apparent in some early Japanese women's writing, may be due in part to the sense that they had at least one more life to live — and that this was an inferior one to be lived out as a woman. A Buddhist court lady of the 13th century wrote her daughter as follows:

---

[8] Morrell, ''Mirror for Women,'' p. 67.

28

"The spring flowers and autumn maples you may enjoy or not, but do not forget to contemplate the frostbitten plants of winter . . . . Our life is but a short-lived dream. Study carefully the Buddhist doctrine, and let not worldly pains and troubles torment you." [9]

Buddhism, thus, offered some leadership roles and alternatives for women, as well as the hope for eventual religious salvation. But it also suggested, in this world at least, that women may be inferior and that they must be resigned to that fate.

Points to Consider

1. According to the information given here, what specific things seemed to be beneficial for women in the Buddhist religion that developed in Japan? What things detrimental to women?

2. Why were women sometimes excluded from Buddhist religious rites or ceremonies?

3. There is a sadness about the advice from the "Court Lady" mother to her daughter. Why might she feel that her daughter should "not forget to contemplate the frostbitten plants of winter . . .?"

---

[9]Robins-Mowry, *The Hidden Sun*, p. 23.

C.   Women and Confucian Principles—Triple Obedience and Filial Piety

Buddhism was introduced into Japan from Korea and China in the 6th century A.D. At about this same time, the ideas of Confucianism were introduced into Japan from China. Unlike Buddhism, however, it was not until later, in the Tokugawa period (1603-1867), that Confucianism strongly influenced the Japanese family system.

Confucius was a Chinese scholar who had lived in the 6th-5th centuries B.C. He felt that humans were basically good but needed an orderly system to live by or chaos and corruption would become the rule. His teachings became the basis of a system of morality which later shaped Chinese society and government.
Confucianism, then, was not a religion focusing on how people might achieve salvation in the next world, but was an ethical system which aimed at creating a harmonious society here on earth.

An essential element in Confucianism was that correct behavior would bring order and that the correct way for individuals to behave depended on their position in a hierarchical order. By "hierarchical order" Confucius and his followers meant that there was a clear ranking of positions from superior to inferior; for example, Confucius believed older was superior to younger, male to female, and certain occupations would rank over others. A household would then be run by older members, especially males. Children were to obey their elders and owed respect or "filial piety" to their parents. Young women — particularly outsiders who married into the family — had the lowest status and the least say in household affairs.

Confucian beliefs severely restricted the independence of women because they were taught to follow the "triple obedience" doctrine. This doctrine set forth that a woman was to obey:

- her parents when she was young.

- her husband when she married.

- her son when she was old.

According to Confucianism, there would never be a time when a woman would not be under the control of a male relative. The lot of the young woman who married and moved to her husband's home could be a very hard one. A bride's loyalty was tested by how well she fitted into her new family and how obedient she was to her mother-in-law. She was expected to work extremely hard to win the approval of her parents-in-law. Sons were instructed not to love their wives too much because, "If you love your wife, you spoil your mother's servant."[1] Another saying in the spirit of Confucianism declared, "Even second-best is too good for a daughter-in-law."[2] According to Confucian ideas, a young bride was not really considered a part of her husband's family until she gave birth to a male child, at which time she was accepted as a member of his household. If no children were born, a wife might be sent away or another wife, a concubine, be brought into the family by her husband.

As mentioned earlier, Confucian philosophy strongly opposed women rulers. It was considered to be against the "natural order" to be ruled by a woman since, according to the Confucian hierarchy or ranking system, women were subordinate to men. That women had been in powerful leadership positions in early Japan did not fit Confucian ideals which said that a woman ruling was "like a hen crowing at dawn."

Although Confucianism seems to have been entirely negative for women, there were a few benefits for women within this philosophical system. In theory, at least, a woman's obedience to her father, husband, or son earned her the right to be cared for by family males who were responsible for her welfare. In old age, a mother could expect support and respect from her sons. A widowed mother was supposed to be under the control of her sons. However, since sons had been trained in the ideal of "filial piety" — the ideal of giving absolute obedience and respect to elders — they often obeyed the wishes of their mothers. Furthermore, while the young daughter-in-law's life was often miserable, she could look forward to a time when age might increase her status. As the young bride gave birth to sons, her status rose in the family, especially if she was the wife of the oldest son. Eventually she might gain higher status and more power within the family by arranging marriages for her sons and by having daughters-in-law of her own to do her bidding. Some observers have commented that the requirement of strict self-discipline and obedience in young women by the

[1]William H. Forbis, *Japan Today: People, Places, Power* (New York: Harper & Row, 1975), p. 34.

[2]Sawako Ariyoshi, *The Doctor's Wife* (Tokyo: Kodansha International, 1978), p. 80.

According to Confucianism, the bride's first duty was to care for her mother-in-law, then her husband. In this early 20th century photograph the grandmother holds her grandson with her daughter-in-law and son beside her.

Confucian system actually created strong and responsible women, making them "the stabilizing backbone of Japanese society."[3]

Costs, however, for a young daughter-in-law living under a Confucian family system might be considerable. Families who were particularly concerned about the welfare of their daughters might elect an alternative marriage system called "adopting a son-in-law." The wife of the British ambassador to Japan, Mary Crawford Fraser, described the Confucian family system as it appeared around 1900 and the "adopting a son-in-law" alternative:

[3]Dorothy Robins-Mowry, *The Hidden Sun: Women of Modern Japan* (Boulder, Colorado: Westview Press, 1983), p. 26.

"I know a charming little woman whose husband is a Government official. They are Christians, and devoted to one another; but all his affection could not protect her from a kind of persecution inflicted by the selfishness of his mother. Young Mrs. S____ was in delicate health, and needed all the rest and sleep that she could get; but her mother-in-law would not allow her to go to bed until she herself was ready to retire. Like many elderly people, she slept badly, and sat up regularly, reading Japanese novels till one and two o'clock in the morning. Only when the lights were out, and the venerable [old woman] comfortably rolled up in her futons, might the poor young wife seek her rest; and long before daylight she had to be on her knees by [her mother-in-law's] couch, offering her the early tea. It was she who had to undo the shutters, get hot water, help the old lady to dress, and go through all the services performed for us by our maids, but for the old ladies by daughters-in-law in Japan. Rich or poor, it is the same for all; and if there were an army of servants in the house, it is the weary privilege of the son's wife to attend to these details alone. In this case the result was very nearly fatal. When a son was born, Mrs. S____'s health was so broken down that it seemed unlikely she could survive, and she will all her life be a delicate woman in consequence. Let us hope that she will be merciful to her successors, remembering her own sufferings. Parents of only daughters greatly dread this ordeal for their child, and I am sure it has a great deal to do with the custom of adopting into the family a young man who is willing to take her name and merge his individuality in hers. When this happens, it is done, ostensibly, to carry on the family name and estates; but I believe the dread of a mother-in-law for the petted little daughter has much to do with it, and also the fear in her parents' hearts of having a lonely and uncomforted old age. Although the youth who consents to fill such a position is generally of a class slightly inferior to her own, happy is the girl whose life is run on these lines; her own parents will always be kind and indulgent to her, and her married life is a continuation in a fuller, more perfect sphere, of the sunny years of childhood." [4]

The Confucian system usually made life very difficult for the daughter-in-law in the extended family. At times the Confucian system also led to conflicts of loyalty within the family. In a case from about 1700, during the Tokugawa period, a woman's brother and father killed her husband. When she informed the authorities, they at first arrested the brother and father but then the officials brought the woman to trial. They were going to confiscate her property and sell her into slavery or put her to death for committing the unfilial or disrespectful act of informing on her own father. The judge in the case, however,

---

[4]Mary Crawford Fraser, *A Diplomat's Wife in Japan: Sketches at the Turn of the Century* (New York: Weatherhill, 1982), (1899), p. 145-146.

decided that "a woman cannot obey two masters at the same time," so her first duty was to her husband. The judge was still somewhat uncomfortable with his decision and wished that the wife of the murdered man had acted differently:

"If, on the day that her father's and brother's crime in murdering her husband was revealed, she had killed herself at once, she would have been dutiful to her husband, filial to her father, and sisterly to her elder brother. We would have had to say that she had shown great virtue . . . ." [5]

Since the woman did not commit suicide, as the judge thought she should, his judgment was to send her away to become a nun and have all the family property turned over to the temple. This case, with its emphasis on the wrongdoing of a woman, no matter what she did, and the severe punishments suggested for her "crimes," illustrates something of how severe Confucian principles might be as they were applied to women.

The severe restrictions on women dictated by the Confucian system only came into practice in Japan in medieval times. During the Tokugawa era (1603-1867), the feudal goverment attempted to use the Confucian system to create a strong central authority. Particularly, then, in the Tokugawa period, neo-Confucian principles became a major part of the training of Japanese women.

Points to Consider

1. List specific restrictions for women within the Confucian ethical system.

   List specific advantages for women.

2. According to Mary Crawford Fraser, why did some Chinese families choose the custom of "adopting a son-in-law?"

3. Explain the contradiction toward women in the Confucian system which is indicated in the title of this section. Which women might particularly benefit from the Confucian ideal of filial piety? How was one woman caught in a situation in which it was felt by the man who judged her that her only honorable choice would have been to commit suicide?

4. Thinking over the three religions — or moral systems — covered in this chapter (Shintōism, Buddhism, and Confucianism), how would you rate them on the following women's issues:

---

[5]Joyce Ackroyd, tr., *Told Round A Brushwood Fire* (Princeton, N.J.: Princeton University Press, 1979), p. 202-203.

- Women are acknowledged as spiritual equals to men.

- Leadership roles for women are allowed.

- Women are aided in achieving honored positions in the family and society.

Which of the three religions or moral systems described in this chapter seems to have been the most positive for women? The most negative? Explain your answer.

CHAPTER 3

JAPANESE WOMEN AND THE HEIAN AGE

A. Women Writers of the Heian Age—A "Blazing Fire"

"It could be said that the cultural activity of these passionate women was the blazing fire at the end of the period in which women had free minds and active lives." [1]

The Heian Era is a period in Japanese history recognized for its many literary masterpieces. "Almost every noteworthy author between 950 and 1050 A.D. was a woman."[2] Why women were the major writers during the height of the Heian period puzzles historians. There are several possible explanations for the superiority of women authors.

By Heian times, Chinese culture had come to strongly influence the culture of Japan. Knowing Chinese and being able to write Chinese poetry became status symbols which showed off one's intellectual abilities. The few women educated at all were generally thought to be incapable of learning Chinese and were excluded automatically from being taught this foreign language. The result of their being denied this opportunity was somewhat ironic. The poetry and other writings of Japanese male authors during this period were written in Chinese or in the Chinese writing system. Their writing tended to imitate Chinese literature and thus lacked originality.

---

[1]Tamie Kamiyama, "Ideology and Patterns in Women's Education in Japan," unpublished Ph.D. dissertation, St. Louis University, 1977, p. 5.

[2]Ivan Morris, tr., *The Pillow Book of Sei Shōnagon*, Introduction by Robin Duke (London: The Folio Society, 1979), p. 16.

During the Heian period, the Japanese created their own writing system based on Chinese characters. This made writing much simpler. In the beginning this system was called a women's writing system, and men tended to use the Chinese writing system. In the Heian period, women could take advantage of this Japanese writing system to write more easily and freely. However, these women writers were also well-educated people.[3]

Women writers were generally from the upper classes and were often the daughters of provincial governors and other well-to-do officials. They had the financial resources to be somewhat independent. Although not taught Chinese, these women writers had been educated at home by tutors and could read and write in Japanese. Besides being educated, this particular group of upper-class women had some control over their own time, a condition necessary for a writer. These women authors were not from the poorer classes in which women's time would be taken up with the physical labors necessary for survival, nor were they of the imperial elite whose courtly duties would often interfere with the quiet hours needed for writing. Two of the most famous Heian women writers, Sei Shōnagon and Murasaki Shikibu, were from families which illustrate this pattern. As they came from educated families, they had books and tutors available to them as they grew up. Sei Shōnagon's father and grandfather were eminent poets, and Murasaki Shikibu's great-grandfather, grandfather, and father were poets and scholars of note.

When Murasaki learned more quickly than her brother, her father lamented, "If only you were a boy, how happy I should be!"[4] Even though her father gave her brother a more complete education, he expected his upper-class daughter to be educated. As Murasaki became the most famous family scholar, one historian has noted that her father Tametoki's "chief claim to fame must be his role in the education of his daughter."[5]

Fathers often encouraged their daughters to become educated so they could be placed at one of the imperial Japanese courts.[6] An education was a prerequisite for being selected a courtier. There were several possible advantages for young women living at court.

---

[3]Tamie Kamiyama, Associate Professor of Japanese Language and Literature, Washington University, St. Louis, Missouri, in written discussion with the authors.

[4]Quoted in Ivan Morris, *The World of the Shining Prince* (New York: Alfred A. Knopf, 1964), p. 253.

[5]Richard Bowring, tr., *Murasaki Shikibu: Her Diary and Poetic Memoirs*, (Princeton, N. J.: Princeton University Press, 1982), p. 7.

[6]During Heian times there were numerous imperial courts — of reigning emperors, former emperors, empress dowagers, and empresses. See Morris, p. 49.

They might:

- increase their chances for marrying higher up on the social scale.

- gather valuable career information that would help further the careers of their male relatives.

- develop useful social graces.

The Heian courts, rather like some of the later European Renaissance courts, required both men and women courtiers to give demonstrations of their knowledge as a test for acceptance. A misquoted phrase, an awkwardly constructed poem, poor handwriting (calligraphy), or even an unfortunate selection of clothing could ruin a person's reputation and make the person a laughing stock at court.[7] Therefore, to do well at an imperial court a daughter had to be educated.

These circumstances may explain the appearance of women writers in Heian Japan. But additional factors may have been responsible for these writers composing works of prose as well as writing traditional court poetry. While these women writers often were associated with one of the courts as ladies-in-waiting, they did not necessarily live permanently at court as members of the imperial family would. These writers, as daughters — and then wives — of officials, would periodically leave court to return to their homes for long periods of time. Sometimes their husbands went with them, but frequently they went alone. At home they might have hours alone in which to reflect on their experiences at court. The courts were very structured places where many people observed what was going on

and often gossiped about one another. A diary might provide an outlet for expressing feelings such as loneliness, boredom, or anger, which had to be kept hidden. A Heian court lady, whose name is no longer known, used her diary, called *Gossamer Years*, to release her feelings of jealousy over her husband's other loves.[8] Sei Shōnagon used her diary to make fun of the inadequacies she noticed in her society, particularly those of men of the Heian courts.

Besides a diary, Murasaki Shikibu wrote *The Tale of Genji*, a historical novel of court life. This novel is accepted as one of the major classics of world literature. *The Tale of Genji* has an extensive body of literary criticism written about it, second only to those written about the works of William Shakespeare.[9] What might be called the leisure time of these women was used to create the golden age of Japanese literature.

The women's observations about life at the Japanese courts have made the Heian Age one of the most vividly described eras in world history. Their view was, in reality, a limited one. The world outside the courts was rarely described. In her diary *The Pillow*

---

[7]*Ibid.*, p. 170-198.

[8]See Edward Seidensticker, tr., *The Gossamer Years: The Diary of a Noblewoman of Heian Japan* (Rutland, Vermont: Charles E. Tuttle Company, 1964), Introduction and p. 37-45.

[9]Morris, *The World of the Shining Prince*, p. 276.

Book, Sei Shōnagon showed herself to be something of a snob in the way she described people of the lower classes. She thought that, while court women might have long hair and wear elegant court clothing, serving women should keep their hair "short and neat" and never be allowed to wear scarlet trousers.[10] Nevertheless, she did write about some of the women workers: the women who cleaned toilets, the "brazen" housekeeper, and the women doing rice threshing. Sei Shōnagon particularly admired the bravery of women divers. The following passage shows both her assumption of superiority, when compared with the "common people," and her compassion for the ordinary women who worked as divers:

"The sea is a frightening thing at the best of times. How much more terrifying must it be for those poor women divers who have to plunge into its depths for their livelihood! One wonders what would happen to them if the cord round their waist were to break. I can imagine men doing this sort of work, but for a woman it must take remarkable courage. After the woman has been lowered into the water, the men sit comfortably in their boats, heartily singing songs as they keep an eye on the mulberry-bark cord that floats on the surface. It is an amazing sight, for they do not show the slightest concern about the risks the woman is taking. When finally she wants to come up, she gives a tug on her cord and the men haul her out of the water with a speed that I can well understand. Soon she is clinging to the side of the boat, her breath coming in painful gasps. The sight is enough to make even an outsider feel the brine dripping. I can hardly imagine this is a job that anyone would covet." [11]

The world of the courts, with occasional pilgrimages to religious shrines, was the main focus of these writers' works. As wives of provincial officials it was a world that attracted them, but one in which they never felt completely at ease. They found the rounds of court activities entertaining. There were pageants, dancing processions, *Go* game playing,[12] and flower viewing festivals. There was the fascination of court intrigues — observing which courtiers were gaining favor with the imperial family and which were falling out of favor. Murasaki Shikibu felt particularly sympathetic to those courtiers who seemed outwardly casual and confident but who were "in reality seeking a livelihood in great anxiety."[13] One of the most delightful times, as described by Sei Shōnagon, was when a deep snow made possible the building of a huge snowbank

---

[10]Morris, tr., *The Pillow Book of Sei Shōnagon*, p. 70, 196.

[11]*Ibid.*, p. 242-243. It is unclear what these women are diving for — perhaps sponges or pearls.

[12]*Go* is a popular Japanese board game for two people, somewhat like chess.

[13]Quoted in Annie Shepley Omori and Kochi Doi, trs., Introduction by Amy Lowell, *Diaries of Court Ladies of Old Japan* (Boston and New York: Houghton Mifflin Company, The Riverside Press, Cambridge, 1920), p. 94.

mountain in the palace garden.[14]

Women and men shared in one of the most intense activities at court — the poetry contests that created an atmosphere of "the survival of the wittiest." For members of the Heian courts whose positions were secure, these contests, which involved remembering many lines of poetry and quickly writing new verses, were entertaining. But for those whose status was less secure, the contests were times of anxiety and tension. An emperor or empress might order one of their subjects to supply a new line to an old poem and then make a critical judgment of the courtier's wit, depending on the result. As Sei Shōnagon wrote, "this sort of test can be a terrible ordeal."[15] At times poetry contests which judged courtiers on their ability to memorize and write original poetry, became a cruel game. A man named Tadanobu sent Sei Shōnagon part of a poem, then asked her: "How does the stanza end?" While a messenger waited, she quickly wrote a reply. Tadanobu and his friends were then to supply additions to her lines. They labored all night, but her reply stumped them; they admitted "cudgelling our brains for the right words,"[16] without success. They finally gave up, but Sei Shōnagon's brother related what had happened:

"When the messenger came back the first time empty-handed, I decided that this was in fact a good sign. The next time, when he returned with your answer, I was so curious to know what you had said that my heart was pounding. To tell the truth, it occurred to me that, if

your answer was inadequate, this would reflect on me too as your elder brother. As it turned out, it was not merely adequate; it was outstanding. Everyone in the room praised it warmly, and one of the men told me, 'This is something for you to hear since you're her elder brother.'" [17]

Sei Shōnagon's reactions were both relief, at having stumped the men, and anger; "I was most vexed at the idea that all these men had been sitting in judgment on me without my knowledge." [18]

These rivalries also reached the higher levels of the court. Sei Shōnagon was the most noted poet at the court of the Empress Teishi; Murasaki Shikibu the main writer attending Empress Shoshi. The two empresses were rivals for power. Both urged on their educated ladies-in-waiting partly in their desire for a reputation of having the most cultivated court. These two empresses seemed to have encouraged somewhat different styles and values at their courts. At Empress Teishi's court Sei Shōnagon became noted for her love affairs and perhaps her drinking habits. The court of Shoshi was more stern. Murasaki described "her empress' court":

---

[14]Morris, tr., *The Pillow Book*, p. 99.

[15]*Ibid.*, p. 41.

[16]*Ibid.*, p. 90.

[17]*Ibid.*, p. 89-91.

[18]*Ibid.*, p. 91.

"Her Majesty frowns on any seductive behavior as the height of frivolity, so anyone who wants to get on takes care never to seem too forward. Of course [there are] women who care nothing for being thought flirtatious and lighthearted, and getting a bad name for themselves. The men strike up relationships with this kind of woman because they are such easy game. They must think us either as dull as ditchwater . . . ." [19]

Aside from these rivalries, there were strong ties between the women of the courts. Many of the romances with men seemed shifting and impermanent — affections might change. Women frequently formed a support system for one another within the courts. They wrote each other letters, sent poems, and shared the sorrows and deaths of friends. In the *Sarashina Diary*, the author wrote of the books her aunt gave her, the support of her stepmother in her desire for learning, and concerns for her sister. When the author's sister died, the sister's nurse shared her grief with the words, ''For remembrance of her I wanted to write about her, . . . [but the] ink seems to have frozen up, I cannot write any more.''[20] The diaries of court ladies often mentioned letters or poems exchanged with other women and the pride the women felt in their friendships. Away from Empress Shoshi's court, Murasaki wrote:

"It struck me as a sad truth that the only people I should now miss in the slightest were those of my constant companions at court for whom I felt a certain affection, those with whom

I could exchange secrets, and those with whom I happened to be friendly at the present time. I missed in particular Lady Dainagon, who would often talk to me as she lay close to Her Majesty in the evenings. Had I then indeed succumbed to life at court?

I sent her the following poem:

*My longing for
Those waters at the court
On which we lay
Is keener than the frost
On duck feathers.*

To which she replied:

*Awakening
In the dead of night
To find no friend
To brush away the frost
She longs for her.*

When I saw how elegantly it was written, I realized what an accomplished woman she was." [21]

Murasaki may have been fortunate in her friend because Sei Shōnagon mentioned how much she would like to have had a similar woman friend:

---

[19]Bowring, *Murasaki Shikibu*, p. 125.

[20]Omori and Doi, tr., *Diaries of Court Ladies*, p. 27.

[21]Bowring, *Murasaki Shikibu*, p. 97.

44

"I should like to live in a large, attractive house. My family would of course be staying with me; and in one of the wings I should have a friend, an elegant lady-in-waiting from the Palace, with whom I could converse. Whenever we wished, we should meet to discuss recent poems and other things of interest. When my friend received a letter, we should read it together and write our answer. If someone came to pay my friend a visit, I should receive him in one of our beautifully decorated rooms, and if he was prevented from leaving by a rain-storm or something of the sort, I should warmly invite him to stay. Whenever my friend went to the Palace, I should help her with her preparations and see that she had what was needed during her stay at Court. For everything about well-born people delights me.

"But I suppose this dream of mine is rather absurd." [22]

Women extensively involved in writing and literary criticism, either as friends or rivals, created an unusual situation in Heian Japan. The acceptable roles for upper-class women were limited and the court rules often restrictive, but they did actively participate in the creation of art. Sei Shōnagon, in her outspoken way, may have too readily put down those whose lives differed from hers, but her comments illustrate the freedom of choice present for Heian court women:

"When I make myself imagine what it is like to be one of those women who live at home, faithfully serving their husbands — women who have not a single exciting prospect in life, yet who believe that they are perfectly happy — I am filled with scorn. Often they are of quite good birth, yet have had no opportunity to find out what the world is like. I wish they could live for a while in our society, even if it should mean taking service as Attendants, so that they might come to know the delights it has to offer." [23]

In later years, male Japanese literary critics who believed in the Confucian ideas of women's inferiority, would find it hard to explain — and even an embarrassment — that women wrote the earliest great literature of Japan. They "clutched at any straw," trying to disprove Murasaki Shikibu's authorship of *The Tale of Genji* in order to attribute the book to a male author.[24] The evidence proving her the author was too strong, and the Heian Age is now recognized as both a remarkable age for Japanese culture and for women writers.

---

[22]Morris, *The World of the Shining Prince*, p. 241.

[23]*Ibid.*, p. 43.

[24]*Ibid.*, p. 259.

Points to Consider

1. What explanations are given in this selection for the fact that "almost every noteworthy author [in Japan] between 950 and 1050 A.D. was a woman?"

2. What might some other possible reasons be for this golden age of Japanese women's literature?

3. Why might women have written diaries (and a novel, in the case of Murasaki Shikibu) rather than just court poetry alone?

GROUP EXERCISE:

The Tale of Genji

After reading over the following information about *The Tale of Genji* and the excerpts from the text, discuss the "points to consider" which follow in small groups. Assign a recorder to write down your group's conclusions. Compare answers in large group discussion.

The Tale of Genji by Murasaki Shikibu has received a great deal of scholarly attention over the years. For example:

- The novel has been discussed in more than 10,000 books in Japan alone.

- By the 13th century, about 250 years after the completion of *The Tale of Genji*, a 54-volume commentary was written analyzing the novel.

- A *Tale of Genji Encyclopedia* (1200 pages) was published in 1960.

This continuing interest may seem difficult to explain considering that the novel, *The Tale of Genji*,:

- is over 630,000 words (about three times longer than *Gone With the Wind*, the lengthy American Civil War novel).

- was written in 11th century Japanese which, like Anglo-Saxon English, is no longer easily understood by people in Japan. The novel has been translated into modern Japanese (as well as into English and many other languages).

- was written by a woman of the imperial court at a time when women of the upper classes were often educated — but thought not to be deserving of the finest education.

The following excerpt is from Chapter 9 "Heartvine," of *The Tale of Genji*. In a work of this length, (the newest English translation by Edward Seidensticker is divided into 54 chapters), a single selection can only suggest some of the qualities that have made Murasaki Shikibu's novel a stunning contribution to world literature. One commentator, however, noted that "one need not read the novel in its staggering entirety to enjoy it; the great book is full of short and wonderfully vivid episodes that can be read as self-contained entities."[25]

---

[25]Jonathan Norton Leonard, *Early Japan* (New York: Time Inc., 1968), p. 38.

This monument near Kyōtō is reputed to be the grave site of Murasaki Shikibu, author of *The Tale of Genji*.

BACKGROUND

Genji, favorite son of the emperor who was ruling at the time the story begins, is called the "Shining Prince" because of his extraordinary beauty, grace, and talent. Although married to Aoi (the daughter of a princess and important government official) he is seen in the early chapters as a young man most interested in carrying on numerous affairs with elegant, upper-class women. Heian Japan seems to have accepted these romances between men and women of the upper classes — whether married or not. Murasaki Shikibu, however, describes with great skill and insight the complications and pain which Genji's affairs cause within his family and among his lovers. The following excerpts reveal some of the complications and sorrow caused by Genji's infidelities.

CHARACTERS (In order of their appearance in this excerpt.)

Genji — Son of the emperor who was reigning at the beginning of the book, half-brother to the emperor at the time of the story from Chapter 9 that follows; he is the husband of Aoi, lover of the Rokujō lady and others. Called the "Shining Prince," he now has the title of General.

Rokujō lady — Widow of Genji's uncle (the former crown prince) she is one of Genji's lovers.

High Priestess of Ise — Daughter of the Rokujō Lady.

High Priestess of Kamo — Old emperor's third daughter, half-sister of Genji.

Aoi — Genji's wife, daughter of Princess Ōmiya and an important government official.

Princess Ōmiya — Genji's aunt and mother of Aoi.

"Heartvine"

"With the new reign Genji's career languished, and since he must be the more discreet about his romantic adventures as he rose in rank, he had less to amuse him. Everywhere there were complaints about his aloofness . . .

". . . There was the matter of the lady at Rokujō. With the change of reigns, her daughter, who was also the daughter of the late crown prince, had been appointed high priestess of the Ise Shrine [most sacred of Shintōism, dedicated to Amaterasu]. No longer trusting Genji's affections, the Rokujō lady had been thinking that, making the girl's youth her excuse, she too would go to Ise . . .

". . At Sanjō [home of Genji's wife's family], [Aoi] and her family were even unhappier about [Genji's] infidelities, but, perhaps because he did not lie to them, they for the most part kept their displeasure to themselves. His wife was with child and in considerable distress mentally and physically. For Genji it was a strange and moving time. Everyone was delighted and at the same time filled with apprehension, and all manner of retreats and abstinences were prescribed for the lady. Genji had little time to himself. While he had no particular wish to avoid the Rokujō lady and the others, he rarely visited them.

"At about this time the high priestess of Kamo [shrine on Kano River — Central Japan] resigned. She was replaced by the old

emperor's third daughter ... The new priestess was a favorite of both her brother, the new emperor, and her mother, and it seemed a great pity that she should be shut off from court life; but no other princess was qualified for the position. The installation ceremonies, in the austere Shintō tradition, were of great dignity and solemnity ... Genji was among the attendants, by special command of the new emperor. Courtiers and ladies had readied their carriages far in advance, and Ichijō [town where carriages assembled] was a frightening crush, without space for another vehicle. The stands along the way had been appointed most elaborately. The sleeves that showed beneath the curtains fulfilled in their brightness and variety all the festive promise.

"Genji's wife seldom went forth on sightseeing expeditions and her pregnancy was another reason for staying at home.

"But her young women protested. 'Really, my lady, it won't be much fun sneaking off by ourselves. Why, even complete strangers — why, all the country folk have come in to see our lord! They've brought their wives and families from the farthest provinces. It will be too much if you make us stay away.'

"Her mother, Princess Ōmiya, agreed. 'You seem to be feeling well enough, my dear, and they will be very disappointed if you don't take them.'

"And so carriages were hastily and unostentatiously decked out, and the sun was already high when they set forth. The waysides were by now too crowded to admit the elegant Sanjō procession. Coming upon several fine carriages not attended by grooms and footmen, the Sanjō men commenced clearing a space. Two palm-frond carriages remained, not new ones, obviously belonging to someone who did not wish to attract attention. The curtains and the sleeves and aprons to be glimpsed beneath them, some in the gay colors little girls wear, were in very good taste.

"The men in attendance sought to defend their places against the Sanjō [Aoi's attendants] invaders. 'We aren't the sort of people you push around.'

"There had been too much drink in both parties, and the drunken ones were not responsive to the efforts of their more mature and collected seniors to restrain them.

"The palm-frond carriages were from the Rokujō house of the high priestess of Ise. The Rokujō lady had come quietly to see the procession, hoping that it might make her briefly forget her unhappiness. The men from Sanjō had recognized her, but preferred to make it seem otherwise.

"' They can't tell us who to push and not to push,' said the more intemperate ones to their fellows. 'They have General Genji to make them feel important.'

"Among the newcomers were some of Genji's men. They recognized and felt a little sorry for the Rokujō lady, but, not wishing to become involved, they looked the other way. Presently all the Sanjō carriages were in place.

49

The Rokujō lady, behind the lesser ones, could see almost nothing. Quite aside from her natural distress at the insult, she was filled with the bitterest chagrin that, having refrained from display, she had been recognized. The stools for her carriage shafts had been broken and the shafts propped on the hubs of perfectly strange carriages, a most undignified sight. It was no good asking herself why she had come. She thought of going home without seeing the procession, but there was no room for her to pass; and then came word that the procession was approaching, and she must, after all, see the man who had caused her such unhappiness. . .

". . . He passed without stopping his horse or looking her way; and the unhappiness was greater than if she had stayed at home.

"Genji seemed indifferent to all the grandly decorated carriages and all the gay sleeves, such a flood of them that it was as if ladies were stacked in layers behind the carriage curtains. Now and again, however, he would have a smile and a glance for a carriage he recognized. His face was solemn and respectful as he passed his wife's carriage. His men bowed deeply, and the Rokujō lady was in misery. She had been utterly defeated . . .

"The high courtiers were, after their several ranks, impeccably dressed . . . and many of them were very handsome; but Genji's radiance dimmed the strongest lights. Among his special attendants was a guards officer of the Sixth Rank, though

attendants of such standing were usually reserved for the most splended royal processions. His retinue made such a fine procession itself that every tree and blade of grass along the way seemed to bend forward in admiration.

"It is not on the whole considered good form for veiled ladies of no mean rank and even nuns who have withdrawn from the world to be jostling and shoving one another in the struggle to see, but today no one thought it out of place. Hollow-mouthed women of the lower classes, their hair tucked under their robes, their hands brought respectfully to their foreheads, were hopping about in hopes of catching a glimpse. Plebeian faces were wreathed in smiles which their owners might not have enjoyed seeing in mirrors, and daughters of petty provincial officers of whose existence Genji would scarcely have been aware had set forth in carriages decked out with the most exhaustive care and taken up posts which seemed to offer a chance of seeing him. There were almost as many things by the wayside as in the procession to attract one's attention . . .

"[After the ceremonies] Genji presently heard the story of the competing carriages. He was sorry for the Rokujō lady and angry at his wife. It was a sad fact that, so deliberate and fastidious, she lacked ordinary compassion. There was indeed a tart, forbidding quality about her. She refused to see, though it was probably an unconscious refusal, that ladies who *were to each other as she was to the Rokujō lady should behave with charity and forbearance. It was under her influence that the men in her service flung themselves so violently about. Genji sometimes felt uncomfortable before the proud dignity of the Rokujō lady, and he could imagine her rage and humiliation now.*

"He called upon her. The high priestess, her daughter, was still with her, however, and . . . she declined to receive him.

"She was right, of course. Yet he muttered to himself: 'Why must it be so? Why cannot the two of them be a little less prickly?' . . .

"For the Rokujō lady the pain was unrelieved. She knew that she could expect no lessening of his coldness, and yet to steel herself and go off to Ise with her daughter — she would be lonely, she knew, and people would laugh at her. They would laugh just as heartily if she stayed in the city. Her thoughts were as the fisherman's bob at Ise. Her very soul seemed to jump wildly about, and at last she fell physically ill.

"Genji discounted the possiblity of her going to Ise. 'It is natural that you should have little use for a reprobate like myself and think of discarding me. But to stay with me would be to show admirable depths of feeling.'

"These remarks did not seem very helpful. Her anger and sorrow increased. A hope of relief from this agony of indecision had sent her to the river of lustration [Kamo — where the ceremonies of purification took place], and there she had been subjected to violence . . ." [26]

REVIEWING THE STORY

A. Briefly describe the following: (have recorder note group answers):

- The action which takes place.

- Characters, your impression of them as people, their part in the action:

    Genji

    Rokujō lady

    Aoi

CLOTHING AND THE HEIAN

B. In a recent book, fashion editor and photographer, Leonard Koren, described the clothes of upper-class Heian women in this way:

"In Japan's Heian period [when **The Tale of Genji** *took place] the imperial court lady's costume, popularly known as* **juni-hitoe** *("the twelve-layer dress"), consisted of an outer kimono, an apron extending below the feet, a number of different-colored underkimono (sometimes as many as twenty), and a pleated train. The main focus was the colored strata of underkimono visible at the neckline, sleeve openings, and hems; two hundred different*

---

[26]Murasaki Shikibu, *The Tale of Genji*, Edward G. Seidensticker, tr., New York: Alfred A. Knoph, 1985. p. 158-165.

color combinations were recognized, and an entire household was judged by the skill with which the lady assembled her costume." [27]

What part of the women's costume is mentioned in this excerpt from *The Tale of Genji*? Why? What specific evidence is there in this excerpt of the importance of clothing to the upper classes in Heian times?

THEMES

C. In groups, discuss the following themes — their occurrence, effect on the action, and importance.

- Infidelity
- Jealousy
- Drunkenness
- Shame
- Class system

    Upper-class people
    Lower-class people

- Competition
- Fear
- Sadness

TITLE

D. Discuss the meaning of the title of Chapter 9 "Heartvine," and note down your conclusions.

CONCLUSION

E. In large group discussion compare answers and speculate about why this novel is read today; still admired 1000 years after its appearance.

F. For further discussion: As a homework assignment individual students could convert this story into a modern plot for American television or a popular "Gothic" novel. Compare your results with those of other students in class.

One reason for *The Tale of Genji* being judged a great novel is the psychological insights presented by Murasaki Shikibu or the human reactions of her characters. Looking back over your retelling of her story, how did her insights help you to shape your characters?

[27]Leonard Koren, *New Fashion Japan* (Tokyo: Kodansha International, 1984), p. 44.

B.   The Status of Upper-Class Women of the Heian Age

Murasaki Shikibu, Sei Shōnagon and other women writers vividly described the elegant life of the Heian imperial courts — and offered some glimpses into the condition of more ordinary people. The authors were recognized and honored for their literary abilities; their works have been carefully preserved. The acknowledgment of the intelligence and talent of the Heian women writers was in stark contrast to the suppression of literary works by women in some other cultures. The writing of poetry in ancient China was also considered an essential part of the education and social activities of educated men — but not of women. Poems by early Chinese women which were preserved were shown only to their closest friends. The poetry of Sun Tao-hsüan and Chu Shu-cheñ, 12th century poets, was burned so their clans would not be disgraced by having a female poet in the family.[1] In 19th century England and France, women authors resorted to using male pen names to mask their female identities. Heian Japan, then, was unusual in promoting women writers. In later Japanese history, however, it became increasingly difficult for women to gain public recognition as writers.

Women of Heian Japan enjoyed higher status than later Japanese women in other areas, besides of that artistic recognition. The status of women in this period of Japanese history may have been comparatively high

---

[1]Kenneth Rexroth and Ling Chung, tr., *The Orchid Boat* (New York: McGraw-Hill Book Company, 1972), p. 139.

53

because of:

- the particular marriage system prevalent at that time.

- certain property rights that women were allowed.

- a sense of mutual sexual enjoyment accepted by Heian culture.

- the prestige gained from being a highly literate group of women.

Marriage customs or laws are crucial factors in determining the relationship between individuals in a particular society as well as their status. Under the Chinese Confucian system, for example, marriage customs strongly favored the husband in matters of residence, property ownership, and divorce. The Confucian system was later adopted by the Japanese, but the Heian marriage system, as represented in the diaries of court ladies and Murasaki Shikibu's novel *The Tale of Genji*, was not restricted to the Confucian model. Rather, there seems to have been no one accepted system but a number of possible choices of marriage systems. At least in the area of choice of family residence, historian William McCullough has pointed out that married couples in the Heian upper or courtier classes could choose from among four customary patterns of marital residence:

1. virilocal (or patrilocal): the husband and wife live nearby or with the husband's parents.

2. uxorilocal (or matrilocal): the wife and husband live nearby or with the wife's parents.

3. neolocal: the married couple set up an independent household, not necessarily near to either of their parents.

4. duolocal: the wife lives separately — usually with her parents — and the husband visits her at her home.[2]

Of these four marriage systems, the first represents the Confucian one where the young married couple lived under the control of the oldest male authority in the husband's family. This system was *not* common in Heian times. The other three choices were those usually practiced, with uxorilocal — the couple living near the wife's parents — most common.

Uxorilocal marriage residence had several advantages — and some disadvantages — for women. One advantage for the young wife was that she did not, as under the virilocal system, have to move to the home of strangers where she would have to submit to the frequently harsh authority of her mother-in-law. The married woman who lived near her parents continued to keep strong ties with her male and female relatives. This might cause some difficulties for married couples because husbands did not always feel strongly committed to their wives or even particularly responsible for their welfare. The court diaries testify to the frequency

---

[2]William H. McCullough, "Japanese Marriage Institutions in The Heian Period," *Harvard Journal of Asiatic Studies,* Vol. 27 (1967), p. 105.

of separations, divorces, and jealousies caused by husbands forming new love relationships outside their marriages.

If a husband left or divorced his wife, she was protected by her close ties to her family. In the case of divorce, the wife in a uxorilocal marriage was generally allowed to keep her children. Her children would be raised by her family and she would have a say in their education. Married women were usually provided with some economic security by their own families. Heian women could inherit property. The family residence was commonly inherited by a daughter, and women could also inherit agricultural land and other property. Often all the family property was inherited by a daughter, and property owned by Heian women remained under their control after marriage.[3] Men who were looking for a marriage partner were particularly interested in women who owned their own residence or were likely to inherit one. The following chart illustrates how the residence of one Japanese family was passed down from parents to daughter through a two-hundred-year period.[4]

Succession to the Ononomiya House

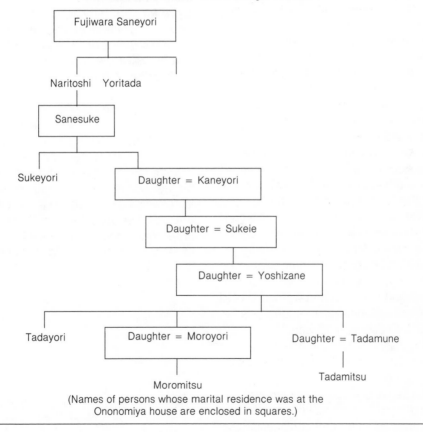

(Names of persons whose marital residence was at the Ononomiya house are enclosed in squares.)

[3]*Ibid.*, p. 122-124.

[4]*Ibid.*, p. 119.

Women in upper-class families often owned their own homes and other property. On both neolocal and uxorilocal marriages there was a strong feeling in Heian times that women *should* be the home owners, and husbands who owned the family residence often gave title to the property to their wives.[5]

In many cultures it is customary that wives who are divorced or widowed are not to remarry and are expected to devote their lives to the care of their children. In virilocal marriages widows are expected to continue to care for their husband's family. Among the Heian upper classes, new marriages or love affairs were not forbidden divorced or widowed women. The diaries of court women suggest the absence of a double sexual standard and even an informal acceptance of love affairs for both men and women. For example, a standard court verse was the "next morning" poem written by the man to the woman in appreciation of their having been together. Later Japanese of the Tokugawa age saw these tokens of affection and love as signs of Heian masculine weakness toward the inferior female sex. Confucian ideals came to be the dominant values after the Heian period. Confucianism stressed that men and women should not show public signs of fondness — even if husband and wife. By Confucian custom the admired widow remained unmarried and chaste, while a widower was expected to remarry. The sense of equality of men and women in their sexual needs, as well as their need for companionship, accepted during Heian times, was lost by the Tokugawa period.

Providing women — at least upper-class women — with an education was another difference between the Heian age and some later periods of Japanese history. During the Heian period it was, however, considered improper for a woman to study Chinese — the scholars' language. They were not expected to become great scholars. The writer Murasaki Shikibu described how upset her maids would become when they found her reading her father's Chinese books:

"My women gather round me and say, 'Madam, if you go on like this, there won't be much happiness in store for you. Why should you read books in Chinese characters? In the old days they wouldn't even let women read the sutras (the sermons of Buddha).'" [6]

Even though Heian women's educations might be more limited than those of men, some fathers instructed their daughters to become learned. Talented women were admired. One brother commented that his sister's success as a poet added to his own prestige. He wrote her that if she answered a poetic challenge inadequately, "this would reflect on me too as your elder brother."[7]

[5]*Ibid.*, p. 118.

[6]Ivan Morris, *The World of the Shining Prince* (New York: Alfred A. Knopf, 1964), p. 257.

[7]Ivan Morris, tr., *The Pillow Book of Sei Shōnagon* (London: The Folio Society, 1979), p. 90.

The golden age of Japanese literature was one result of encouraging women of talent to become educated. A summary of customs of Heian Japan compared to those of neo-Confucian philosophy follows. Confucianism, which originated in China, was introduced into Japan in early times. But after a period of transition following the Heian period, new or neo-Confucianism came to dominate Japanese society during the Tokugawa period.

Heian (794-1184 A.D.)	Tokugawa (Neo-Confucian) (1603-1867 A.D.)
Four types of marriage systems to choose from (the most prevalent is uxorilocal). Most women lived with their relatives.	Only one form of marriage system to choose from — the virilocal. Wives lived under the authority of their mothers-in-law.
Women as daughters and wives could own, control, and inherit property.	Property was controlled by the male head-of-household. Women never inherited land.
Women might be in charge of their own households in case of desertion, divorce, or widowhood. They could operate outside of male authority.	Women were subjected to the "Three Obediences"; in youth they were under the authority of their fathers; in marriage, their husbands; and in widowhood, their sons.
Love between women and men was considered important — a sexual double standard was lessened.	Love was considered unimportant between husbands and wives. Duty of the wife to her husband's family was emphasized.
In case of divorce, a woman usually lived at her natal (parents') home, kept her children, and supervised their education.	In case of divorce, the husband's family kept the children — the divorced woman was forced to leave the family residence.
Education, at least for upper-class women, was limited but encouraged, especially in the arts and poetry.	Education for women was discouraged. The emphasis was on training in household skills only.
Husbands were allowed to have more than one wife,[8] but wives could only have one husband. Divorced and widowed women could remarry.	Husbands were allowed to have more than one wife, but wives could only have one husband. Divorced and widowed women were strongly discouraged from remarrying.

Points to Consider

Beginning in colonial times and continuing after the Revolutionary War, the laws of the United States were based on English Common Law. In his *Commentaries of the Laws of England* (written between 1765-1769), William Blackstone explained the legal position of adult women upon marriage:

[8]Called concubines in China and Japan, they had somewhat lower family status than the official wife.

Male participant in the Kyōtō Festival of the Ages dressed as a Heian noblewoman. As in Kabuki theater productions, it is common for men to impersonate women in this parade.

"But, though our law in general considers man and wife as one person, yet there are some instances in which she is separately considered; as inferior to him,

"and acting by his compulsion. And therefore, all deeds executed and acts done, by her, during her coverture, are void . . ." [9]

The assumption that the husband was head of household and spoke for his wife was continued in the definition of citizenship in the Constitution of the United States. Thomas Jefferson explained women's place:

"Were our state a pure democracy there would still be excluded from our deliberations women, who, to prevent deprivation of morals and ambiguity of issues, should not mix promiscuously in gatherings of men." [10]

1. Compare the position of married upper-class women in the Heian period with that of married women in the United States as defined by English Common Law and continued in the Constitution.

2. Why might upper-class families want to keep married daughters living at their natal home even

"By marriage, the husband and wife are one person in the law: that is, the very being or legal existence of the woman is suspended during the marriage, or at least is incorporated and consolidated into that of the husband: under whose wing, protection, and cover, she performs everything . . .

[9]Quoted in: Susan Moller Okin, *Women in Western Political Thought* (Princeton, N.J.: Princeton University Press, 1979), p. 249-250.

[10]*Ibid*, p. 249.

after marriage in Heian Japan?
(Consider factors such as the
frequency of divorce and
inheritance customs.)

3. During the Tokugawa period
(1603-1867), that followed Heian
period three hundred years later,
the status of women declined and
virilocal marriage became
customary. Why did this form —
and the lack of choice — indicate
a decline in women's status?
What seems to have been the
implied marriage form indicated
by women's status in the early
laws of the United States?

4. What specific indications are
there that upper-class Heian
women did not enjoy complete
equality with Heian men?

C. The Fujiwara Marriage System

Japanese writers have sometimes looked back on the Heian Age as somewhat decadent. Medieval and Tokugawa people found Heian love poems less admirable than samurai swords. But some modern writers have pointed out the comparative peacefulness of the Heian World. News from the provinces sometimes told of ruffians and robbers on the roads in Heian times, but violence seems not to have touched the imperial quarters as described in the diaries of Heian court ladies.[1] In contrast to the peaceful world of the Heian courts, the atmosphere of the Chinese courts was one of intrigues, murders, and rebellions by those seeking to advance their claims to power. Part of the credit for the lack of court violence during the Heian age should go to the Fujiwara family which ruled Japan (without claiming the monarchy) and to the marriage system they created.

One modern scholar described the source of the Fujiwara family's power:

"How did the Fujiwara family manage to acquire supreme power in the Heian period, and how did they retain it for such a long time? Physical force was the least important of their methods. The Fujiwaras themselves never commanded any significant military

---

[1]Edward Seidensticker, "Rough Business in 'Ukifune' and Elsewhere," in, Andrew Pekarik, ed., *Ukifune: Love in The Tale of Genji* (New York: Columbia University Press, 1982), p. 2.

strength — certainly not enough to assure them their long dominance. When they did use violence, it was only as a last resort and, one feels, reluctantly. For, above all, they were consummate politicians, and it was mainly by political methods that they achieved their ends." [2]

Here is the marriage system the Fujiwara developed: the Fujiwara family supplied the young daughters who were married to the young men of the imperial family destined to become emperors. Imperial consorts were all selected from the Fujiwara family. When an imperial couple had a son, the son was appointed crown prince. At age 30 or so, the emperor would resign and the young prince was then made emperor. He was immediately married to a Fujiwara daughter and the cycle would then repeat itself.

Other connections were made between the imperial family and the Fujiwara family which strengthened the ties between them:

- A pregnant empress (always from the Fujiwara family) went to her father's house to give birth.

- The young prince born to the imperial consort was brought up by the Fujiwara family.

- In case of a palace fire, the emperor moved in with the Fujiwara family.

The Fujiwara system essentially meant that each Japanese emperor was raised by the Fujiwara, his mother's relatives would be Fujiwara, and his major advisors would also be Fujiwara. One of the leaders of the Fujiwara, Michinaga, had married four

of his daughters to emperors. He was:

- father-in-law to two emperors.

- grandfather to another emperor.

- grandfather and great-grandfather to a fourth emperor.

- grandfather and father-in-law to a fifth emperor. [3]

By forcing the early abdication of the emperor, the Fujiwara marriage system reduced the emperor's power. The members of the royal family, who might have their own imperial courts, were increased to include, "the reigning emperors, the former emperors, the great empress dowager and the various empresses." [4] The Fujiwara did not put one of their own sons on the imperial throne — they had no need as they already controlled the throne through their daughters and advisors.

How did this Fujiwara marriage system affect women? Daughters were in high demand by the Fujiwaras to act as consorts for the emperor. Sons might be rivals to the emperor, but a daughter could not only become empress but might also be the mother of an emperor. Since the emperors came to the throne at a very young age, their mothers (the empress dowagers) often played major roles.

---

[2]Ivan Morris, *The World of the Shining Prince* (New York: Alfred A. Knopf, 1964), p. 48.

[3]*Ibid.*, p. 48.

[4]*Ibid.*, p. 49.

Empress Dowager Senshi, Michinaga's older sister, was "an exceedingly powerful woman," who made her son give Michinaga his first major appointment.[5]

Families other than the Fujiwara hoped that their daughters could at least become imperial concubines, even if it was impossible to break the Fujiwara monopoly on imperial consorts. Daughters could marry further up on the social scale and so bring fortunes to their families. In the Heian age, during the rule of the Fujiwara, one historian has noted that daughters were more welcome than sons.[6] Daughters may have felt that they were merely pawns in family marriages or they may have seen themselves as useful in family maneuvering for power. The actions of Fujiwara sisters, aunts, and others, in aiding their male relatives, seem to suggest that they did feel some sense of involvement in the system.

It was a system that eventually broke down when the Japanese military became increasingly powerful and important. Warrior sons became more vital than marriageable daughters. But the tradition of intermarriage between the Fujiwara and the imperial family lasted into the 20th century with the present empress of Japan.

Points to Consider

1. How did the Fujiwara marriage system help to make the Heian courts comparatively peaceful ones?

2. Although the sons of the Fujiwara did not become emperors, Fujiwara family members could claim to control the Japanese imperial system. In what specific ways did they gain and maintain their power?

3. In what specific ways did the Fujiwara marriage system affect the status of Fujiwara women? Other women?

4. Why might Fujiwara women have felt like mere pawns in a marriage game? What indications are there that Fujiwara women enjoyed positions of power?

[5]Mildred M. Tahara, "Regent at the Peak of Aristocratic Prosperity," in, Murakami Hyoe and Thomas J. Harper, eds., *Great Historical Figures of Japan* (Tokyo: Japan Culture Institute, 1978), p. 54.

[6]Morris, *The World of the Shining Prince*, p. 207-208.

CHAPTER 4

WOMEN IN MEDIEVAL JAPAN

A.   The Samurai Ideal

By the 13th century a new world was being created in Japan — one led by the military. An emperor was still on the throne who traced his ancestry to the female sun god Amaterasu. There were still imperial courts where courtiers dressed in elegant clothing and poems were written and recited. But the comparatively peaceful Heian Age had passed, ended both by the decline of the Fujiwara family and the civil wars between two other families contending for power — the Taira and Minamoto. The power of Japan had moved from the imperial court to the shōgunate.

The title, shōgun, needs an explanation. Originally the title meant a military chief, but in 1185 Minamoto Yoritomo became military dictator of Japan after the defeat of his rivals, the Taira. He then became the first

shōgun who was virtual ruler of Japan, although the emperor remained as nominal ruler. The office of shōgunate, then, became both that of military chief and ruler.

Following the Heian Age, Japan was rearranged by these warring clans into a feudal system based on personal loyalty and military service. This system, like feudalism in Europe at roughly the same time period, tied peasants to the land as laborers and created a samurai (warrior) class which controlled the land. It also prepared the way for the military dictatorship of Minamoto Yoritomo and the shōguns who followed.

In the early years of Japanese feudalism, the samurai who controlled the land worked alongside peasants in the fields. As time went on, their role became more separate and class distinctions increased. The samurai, as a warrior class of noblemen, developed an unwritten code that emphasized loyalty to the shōgun and personal courage similar to the code of European medieval knights. The samurai code was called bushidō, "the way of the warrior." It demanded that samurai commit themselves absolutely to a military life, accept physical hardship, and believe that a heroic death in battle was the most honorable one.[1] With the ideal being a male warrior, the status of women tended to decline when compared to Heian times. In a curious way, however, the samurai code of bushidō created a parallel ideal for Japanese women of the samurai class.

In the emperor's and the shōgun's courts, upper-class women continued to perform their courtly roles and to take part in the annual festivals as in the past. There were a few women diarists, like Lady Nijō whose diary describes a different way of life than that seen in the Heian court writers. Lady Nijō's diary suggests a ranking of people that included males ruling over females, which was not a common theme of the Heian period:

"I cherished the ambition to leave behind for posterity a travel book such as [the traveler, Saigyo's]. Now that I had found that I could not escape that sad destiny which is the lot of each woman, of obedience to parents when young, to her husband in marriage and to her children when old, I desired all the more to remove myself from the din and bustle of the world, realizing as I did that obedience to my father and my lord and master was not a virtue which had always been in harmony with

the wishes of my inmost heart." [2]

Increasingly, women of the samurai class became less visible and less influential. Exceptional women managed to overcome this decline in influence under the shōgunate, but the widespread networks of intellectual women of the court disappeared. Nonetheless, the daughters of noble families remained important assets in maintaining the often shaky alliance system between the shōgunate and the samurai-nobles. To bring about one peace between three samurai clans — the Hōjō, the Takeda, and the Imagawa — the following marriages were arranged in 1554:

- Imagawa Yoshimoto's daughter married Takeda Shingen's son.

- Takeda Shingen's daughter married Hōjō Ujiyasu's son.

- Hōjō Ujiyasu's daughter married Imagawa Yoshimoto's son.

Already married:

- Imagawa Yoshimoto to Takeda Shingen's sister.

- Imagawa Yoshimoto's sister to Hōjō Ujiyasu.[3]

---

[1]See, Jonathan Norton Leonard, *Early Japan* (New York: Time-Life Books, 1968), p. 59-60, 65-73.

[2]Wilfrid Whitehouse and Eizo Yanagisawa, tr., *Lady Nijo's Own Story* (Rutland, Vermont: Charles E. Tuttle Co., 1974), p. 86.

[3]Mary Elizabeth Berry, *Hideyoshi* (London: Harvard University Press, 1982), p. 36.

A nobleman without marriageable daughters or sisters was clearly at a disadvantage in creating a system of clan allies.

For peasant women, the feudal age seems to have meant an increase in the restrictions placed upon them. Their property rights of inheritance guaranteed in early medieval times declined as land use rights (fief) went to men who could join in military matters. The roles of peasant women as farmers, salt gatherers, weavers, and household workers continued — but with less control over land and other resources.

The lives of women in the middle — between the upper and lower classes — changed the most in medieval Japanese times. Chinese-Confucian ideals of a strict hierarchy or ranking of obligations and obedience were increasingly absorbed into the Japanese religious and warrior ideals. In the world of the samurai, the emphasis was on loyalty to one's daimyō or lord first and on acting in the spirit of bushidō and strict dedication to the military arts. According to the samurai code, emotions were to be controlled, especially emotions of love directed at women considered to be inferiors and who might lead a samurai away from his duty. In Europe, part of the code of the knight involved the ideal of courtly love. The courtly love tradition, which developed in late medieval times, stressed romantic rules of conduct between lovers — usually a knight and his lady, not husband and wife. The code of the samurai did not include these courtly love notions that glorified knights who rescued fair maidens and performed gallant acts to

impress ladies. The ideal samurai woman was expected to be subservient to her lord-husband, just as he was to be subservient to his lord and eventually to the shōgun. Special acts of courtesy were not directed at women. Female hostages were sometimes taken and, in case of treachery, might be killed as was the mother of samurai Akechi Mitsuhide in the 16th century.[4] In another case, the mother of an important samurai, Asai Nagamasa, was finally killed after first suffering removal of her fingers.[5]

A samurai wife was expected not only to take orders, but to take second place to the loyalty the samurai gave to the daimyō, even if this meant giving her life as a hostage. Since a wife was expected to suffer all problems stoically and show absolute loyalty to her lord-husband, a divorce was almost impossible for her to obtain unless it was the husband's choice.

The restrictions and obligations placed on the samurai wife may make it appear as if she were a passive and obedient person. Yet the life of a samurai wife might actually be an active one. With the men away fighting, it was frequently the duty and responsibility of the samurai women to see that the armies were well supplied from the stores left at home. A list of the duties expected of a samurai woman whose husband was away at war might include the following:

---

[4]*Ibid.*, p. 38.

[5]*Ibid.*, p. 47.

- direct the education of the family children and to do much of the teaching.

- supervise the kitchen and food supplies.

- organize the weaving of cloth and sewing of clothing — doing much of it herself.

- supervise the harvesting of rice.

- pay the lesser samurai who guarded the household.

- take over all the financial business of the family in times of disorder.[6]

One historian has described how important it was for a samurai woman to be a good manager:

"Wives of samurai often were the household managers, responsible not only for meeting their husband's needs, but often the needs of his followers and their families, also. Since there was a great deal of mobility among the smaller clans, with warriors switching sides according to how much money they were offered, or how good the 'side benefits' of food, shelter and living conditions were, the ability of the samurai wife to manage an attractive household from these standpoints was a valuable asset to any warrior." [7]

Samurai women had not only to learn to manage the family estates while samurai men were off fighting but to be trained to defend themselves and the family property. At samurai weddings the bride was presented with a dagger which she was expected to learn to use in hand-to-hand combat with an enemy. If an

"honorable death" as a samurai wife was called for she would commit suicide.[8]

It was usual for samurai women to be given some martial or military training, especially in the use of the naginata, a long spear with a curved blade.[9] Also in the early feudal period samurai women were expected to ride horseback well.

One custom for samurai women, which began in medieval times and continued to the 1890's, was that a samurai woman was to keep a "war chest" where her weapons and a male military uniform, to be used as a disguise, were stored. A woman from the United States who traveled in Japan in the 1890's, described what an elderly Japanese woman showed her as they looked through old garments:

"As we turned over the beautiful fabrics, a black broadcloth garment at the bottom of the basket aroused my curiosity, and I pulled it out and held it up for closer inspection. A curious garment it was, bound with

---

[6]Louis Frederic, *Daily Life in Japan at the Time of the Samurai* (London: George Allen and Unwin Ltd., 1972), p. 60-61.

[7]Michael Berger, "Japanese Women — Old Images and New Realities," *The Japan Interpreter*, Vol. 2 (Spring 1976), p. 59.

[8]While samurai men were taught to commit suicide by *seppuku* (cutting their stomachs-bowels), samurai women were taught to use a quick method, slashing their throats.

[9]Elizabeth Powers, "Women in Sports" in, Joyce Lebra, Joy Paulson, and Elizabeth Powers, eds., *Women in Changing Japan* (Stanford: Stanford University Press, 1976), p. 256.

white, and with a great white crest applique on the middle of the back. Curious white stripes gave the coat a military look, and it seemed appropriate rather to the wardrobe of some two-sworded warrior than to that of a gentlewoman of the old type. To the question, How did such a coat come to be in such a place? the older lady of the company — one to whom the old days were still the natural order and the new customs an exotic growth — explained that the garment rightfully belonged in the wardrobe of any lady-in-waiting in a daimyō's house, for it was made to wear in case of fire or attack when the men were away, and the women were expected to guard the premises. Further search among the relics of the past brought to light the rest of the costume: silk hakama, or full kilted trousers; a stiff, manlike black silk cap bound with a white band; and a spear cover of broadcloth, with a great white crest upon it, like the one on the broadcloth coat. These made up the uniform which must be donned in time of need by the ladies of the palace or the castle, for the defense of their lord's property. . .

"The elder lady of the house was wonderfully amused at my interest in these mute memorials of the past, and could never comprehend why I was willing to expend the sum of one dollar for the sake of gaining possession of a set of garments for which I could have no possible use. The uniform had probably never been worn in actual warfare, but its owner had been trained in the use of the long-handled spear, the cover of which she had kept stored away all these years; and had regarded

herself as liable to be called into action at any time as one of the home guard, when the male retainers of her lord were in the field." [10]

The samurai mother was expected to raise her children by strict standards. She was supposed to ingrain in them a strong sense of loyalty to samurai ideals and high courage, as well as assuring that they become physically strong. When Hōjō Masako, a noted woman from feudal times, was sent a message that her small child had killed his first deer on a hunting trip with his father, she replied, "It is what I would expect of the son of a bushi [samurai]. There is no need for the message." [11] A Chinese traveler to Japan in the 1970's was impressed by a statue of another samurai woman, Lady Masaoka, in the Shōgakuji Temple in Tokyo. In about 1620 Lady Masaoka took the young son of her lord into her care. She protected the son of Lord Date from those plotting against his life, even allowing her own son to eat the poisoned sweets given

[10]Alice Mabel Bacon, *Japanese Girls and Women* (Boston: Houghton, Mifflin, 1892), p. 188-190.

[11]Quoted in, Mary R. Beard, *The Force of Women in Japanese History* (Washington, DC: Public Affairs Press, 1953), p. 70.

to the noble boy.[12] The statue is meant to honor her noble and proper dedication to a strict code of loyalty required of samurai women as well as men. Whether or not this incident really happened, the statue does represent the qualities Japanese culture admired in samurai women.

A medieval chronicle tells of a samurai wife who wished to share her husband's fate. The following passage from this chronicle describes a farewell and, despite the code, the strong feelings expressed between the wife and husband of a samurai family:

"Now to his wife Nakatoki the governor of Echigo spoke a word, saying: 'Heretofore I had thought to keep you with me always, even were I perchance to go forth from the capital. Yet I do not believe that it will be easy to escape to the Kanto, since men say that the enemy block up the roads on all sides. No harm will come to you who are a woman, and likewise Matsuji [his son] is still an infant, so that the enemy will not know his lineage, even should they find him. You must go forth secretly in the darkness, hide yourself in a remote place, and wait awhile until the world is quiet. If I come to the Kanto in safety, I shall send men to fetch you quickly. If you should hear that I have perished on the way, you must find another husband, raise up Matsuji, and make him a monk when he reaches the age of understanding, that he may offer prayers on my behalf.'

"So he spoke with fainting spirit, weeping where he stood.

"The lady held his armor-sleeve, lamenting and weeping.

"'Why do you speak these heartless words?' she said. "If I wandered in strange places today with the child, would not all men think, 'She is the kinswoman of one who has fled? And if I were to ask for shelter among our past acquaintance, I would be sought out and put to shame by the enemy, while the child would perish. How bitter that would be! If there is to be an undreamt-of happening on the way, let me die with you there. Even for a time fleeting as a drop of dew in an autumnal gale, I do not wish to linger abandoned beneath a tree which offers no shelter."

"So she spoke, nor could the governor of Echigo bear the grievous parting. Though his heart was the heart of a warrior, he was not made of stone or wood. So for a long time he tarried in that place." [13]

Other endangered samurai women, committed suicide with their husbands rather than be separated.

In later Japanese history, the image of the samurai woman — dutiful, dedicated, brave, and self-controlled — became a part of the cultural ideal for all Japanese women. Japanese women were taught not to cry out in pain, even in childbirth. Daughters

---

[12]Chiang Yee, *The Silent Traveller in Japan* (New York: W. W. Norton & Co., 1972), p. 341.

[13]Helen Craig McCullough, tr., *The Taiheiki* (New York: Columbia University Press, 1959), p. 260-261.

The last shōgun, Prince Tokugawa Keiki, with his family — c. 1867.

were taught to sleep in a stiff, disciplined position.[14] Girls in one school during World War II were not allowed to wear warm coats in the winter so that, like the soldiers in the field, they would feel the cold and share the suffering of the troops.[15] A Japanese man remembered how, when he and his brother, age eight and 11, were sent off to school in the United States, that his mother told them in parting to do well or they would never see her face again. She was not indifferent to her sons' departure — and they were told that she wept after they were gone. But their mother had felt that she had to maintain the samurai ideal of not showing her emotions in front of her young sons.[16] Even into the 19th century, samurai women participated in military actions. During the Satsuma Rebellion, Lady Teru helped to protect her castle in a month-long siege. "Her quiet manner strengthened the hearts of all who came before her."[17] The following account is given of a young woman in 1895, during the Japanese war with Russia, upon receiving the news that her husband, Lieutenant Asada, was killed on the battlefield:

"Even women are found ready to kill themselves for loyalty and duty, but the approved method in their case is cutting the throat. Nowise strange, but admirable according to Japanese ideas, was it that when, in 1895, the tidings of Lieutenant Asada's death on the battlefield, were brought to his young wife, she at once, and with her father's

---

[14]Etsu Inagaki Sugimoto, *A Daughter of the Samurai* (Garden City, New Jersey: Doubleday, 1927), p. 23-24.

[15]Hiroko Nakamoto and Mildred Mastin Pace, *My Japan, 1930-1951* (New York: McGraw-Hill Book Company, 1970), p. 22.

[16]Inazo Nitobe, *Reminiscences of Childhood* (Tokyo: Maruzen Company, Ltd., 1934), p. vi.

[17]Anna C. Hartshorne, *Japan and Her People* (Philadelphia: Henry T. Coates & Co., 1902), p. 333.

**Samurai women watch samurai warriors performing martial arts —
late 16th century screen painting.**

consent, resolved to follow him. Having thoroughly cleansed the house and arrayed herself in her costliest robes, she placed her husband's portrait in the alcove, and prostrating herself before it, cut her throat with a dagger that had been a wedding gift." [18]

Wives joining their husbands in suicide for political reasons was a samurai tradition that continued into the 20th century. Upon the death of the highly respected Meiji emperor in 1912, General and Mrs. Nogi committed suicide.

A 19th century British woman traveler to Japan, described a peaceful visit, when looking at beautiful court dresses her female host pulled out another item:

"She showed me also her sword, which had a beautiful hilt, and on my expressing my surprise that she should be allowed to wear a sword, she replied that all the wives of high officers were permitted to do so, to defend themselves ... She asked me if I would like to see her daughter defend herself. Then suiting the action to the word, she called in a Yakonin and told him to attack her, and that she would defend herself; and so well did she use her weapon that the Yakonin was very glad when she cried out 'Enough.'" [19]

The tradition of the stoical samurai woman — self-sacrificing but strong became a part of the Japanese cultural ideal for women. In some respects it has given Japanese women a strong sense of duty and identity but on the other hand, it has often limited them to a role of serving their husbands and children.

Points to Consider

1. In about 600 B.C. the city-state of Sparta on the southern peninsula of Greece came into being. Sparta was governed as a military dictatorship by a warrior class. A military elite ruled over the majority of the city-state who were peasant-serfs called helots. The military rulers kept these serfs quiet and discouraged foreign enemies. The military claimed that Sparta needed no fortification walls as the Spartan soldiers *were* the walls.

    In order to keep the society functioning, there was need for male soldiers, strong, disciplined, and loyal. There also were requirements for Spartan women of the military elite. The following customs were encouraged for women in Sparta:

    - women were married at 18-20, rather late as compared to most areas of the ancient world where it was customary to marry girls at 14-15.

---

[18]Basil Hall Chamberlain, *Things Japanese* (London: John Murray, 1905), p. 220.

[19]Quoted in, C. Pemberton Hodgson, *A Residence at Nagasaki and Hakodate* (London: Richard Bentley, 1861), p. 214-215.

- women were encouraged to exercise in the nude and to take pride in a physically fit body.

- although women were not allowed to participate in the ancient Olympic games, Spartan women organized their own sports contests.

- if their husbands were off at war for long periods, or were old, women were encouraged to take another husband.

- women could own property; it is estimated that two-fifths of all Spartan property was owned by women.

- mothers were encouraged to be very strict with their sons and to accept their sons' deaths as noble sacrifices for Sparta.

In what specific ways does the code for samurai women seem similar to these customs for Spartan women? In what ways different?

Why might states governed by male military elites adopt these traditions for women?

2. Another possible parallel to the code of the Japanese samurai in the history of western civilization would be that of European medieval times. From what you know of codes of medieval chivalry, what things about the samurai code seem similar? What things seem different? In what ways do the expected roles of women in these cultures seem parallel? How not?

3. In answering question #1., you listed possible reasons for the samurai and Spartan codes for women. One curious reason for Japanese women learning the martial arts of warfare and becoming skilled with swords was described by a Japanese man:

"Mothers gave their sons leave during certain hours to suddenly attack and overwhelm them if they could, at any time and place, whether they were at domestic work or at sewing. Thus they applied their martial training for the education of their sons." [20]

What other reasons are given for Japanese women learning to use swords and daggers?

4. In what ways does the samurai code seem to have restricted women's lives? In what ways provided opportunities?

---

[20]Masuji Miyakawa, *Life of Japan* (New York: The Neale Publishing Co., 1910), p. 36.

B.   Peasant Women—Privileges and Poverty

In some periods of Japanese history, women in the upper classes such as the Heian court women, might lead lives of intellectual engagement. At other times upper-class women seem to have led rather boring lives, given little useful work and few outside stimulations. Glimpses given of peasant women in the diaries of Heian court women show them working at a variety of tasks. By medieval Japanese times (1185-1603 A.D.) their lives are described as a daily round of hard physical labor. The diaries and histories of medieval Japan provide views of lower-class women doing cleaning and cooking chores, planting and harvesting rice, sewing garments, diving to gather seaweed for food, and making salt. A description of this salt-making shows how difficult these tasks might be:

"He watched as the women made salt. Endlessly they trudged from sea to shore, buckets of water straining from a pole over an aching shoulder. They sprayed the water on smooth sand beds to evaporate, raked up the saturated sand, filtered out the salt with more sea water and boiled the concentrate in great iron pots until there remained only the gray, coarse, indispensable crystals which his father sent back to the mountains." [1]

Peasant women worked alongside peasant men — and it is probable that

---

[1]Oliver Statler, *Japanese Inn* (New York: Random House, 1961), p. 15.

their labor was recognized as important for family survival. But no written records have survived to tell how these peasant women and men saw their own lives.

According to official documents from early medieval times, Japanese peasant women had some property rights, including rights of inheritance. The following excerpts are from records of lawsuits from 1232 A.D.:

Question: Whether in consequence of a husband's crime the estate of the wife is to be confiscated or not.

Answer: In cases of serious crime, treason, murder and maiming, also banditry, piracy, night-attacks, robbery and the like, the guilt of the husband extends to the wife also. In cases of murder and maiming, cutting and wounding, arising out of a sudden dispute, however, she is not to be held responsible.

* * * * *

Question: Whether, after transferring a fief [piece of land under feudal obligations used by a peasant] to a daughter, parents may or may not revoke [take back] the transfer on account of a subsequent estrangement [from the daughter].

Answer: A group of legal scholars said that there is no difference between them as regards parental benefactions and that therefore a gift to a daughter is as irrevocable as to a son. If, however, the deed of assignment to a daughter were held to be irrevocable she would be able to rely upon it, and would have no scruples about entering upon an undutiful and reprehensible course

of conduct. And fathers and mothers, on the other hand, forecasting the probability of conflicts of opinion arising, must beware of assigning a fief to a daughter. Once a beginning is made of severing the relation of parent and child, the foundation is laid for disobedience and insubordination. In case a daughter shows any unsteadiness of behavior, the parents ought to be able to exercise their own discretion accordingly.

* * * * *

Question: Whether when a wife or concubine, after getting an assignment from the husband, has been divorced, she can retain the tenure [control] of the fief or not.

Answer: If the wife in question has been repudiated in consequence of having committed some serious transgression [crime or sin], even if she holds a written promise of the by-gone days, she may not hold the fief of her former husband. On the other hand, if the wife in question has a virtuous record and was innocent of any fault and was discarded by reason of the husband's preference for novelty, the fief which had been assigned to her cannot be revoked.

* * * * *

Question: Of the adoption of heirs by women.

Answer: Although the spirit of the ancient laws does not allow adoption by females, yet since the time of the General of the Right down to the present day it has been the invariable rule to allow women who had no children of their own to

Peasant family photographed in about 1900. Until recently peasants lived in much the same way as they had in medieval times.

adopt an heir and transmit the fief to him.[2]

Though upper-class women also had some property rights in medieval times, peasant women may have had advantages in their marriages that upper-class women did not enjoy. The practice of polygyny (a man having more than one wife), which sometimes led to jealousy and loneliness for upper-class women, was not customary for peasant families because of the high cost of maintaining two households. Divorce in the lower classes seems to have been relatively common, but upper-class wives might have to run away to places of sanctuary like the Tōkeiji temple to escape brutal husbands.[3] As

---

[2]As quoted in: David John Lu, *Sources of Japanese History* (New York: McGraw-Hill, 1974), p. 105-107.

[3]Louis Frederic, *Daily Life in Japan at the Time of the Samurai* (London: George Allen and Unwin Ltd., 1972), p. 49.

peasant wives and husbands worked closely together, the wife may have had more say in family decisions than upper-class women who were generally segregated from the activities of their husbands. One modern historian has suggested that peasant women had a major role in family decision-making:

". . . with the common people, if authority was theoretically the father's prerogative, it was the mother who held the casting vote in decisions concerning the well-being of the family; she was both companion and counselor whose advice was frequently followed, and no important decision whatever could be made without asking her opinion." [4]

While upper-class women might be engaged in poetry contests or flower viewing, peasant women had their own social activities. Women took part in festivals, particularly those that celebrated occasions in the agricultural year. Some dances performed by peasant women were described as sexually frank and "they generally do not seem to have led restrained lives as to their opinions."[5]

Although peasant women enjoyed greater freedom and perhaps more equality with peasant men than wealthier women, life for them might be extremely difficult. Peasant women often planted rice all day, with their feet in water, to later watch their landlord take a large share of the harvest. Peasant women might have to plan for times of famine and see family members go without so that some food could be put aside. Their lives were not easy, and the benefits of greater equality might not seem great compared to the luxuries of richer women's lives. One of the poems of the Manyōshū, a collection of poetry written at an earlier age of Japanese history, described a peasant man's feelings about the harshness of his family's life. Though the time is 500 years before the medieval age, it still suggests what life was like for the peasant poor in many ages of Japanese history:

---

[4]*Ibid.*, p. 54.

[5]*Ibid.*, p. 132.

Song of Poverty
By Yamanoue no Okura

On the night when the rain beats,
Driven by the wind,
On the night when the snowflakes
*   mingle*
With the sleety rain,
I feel so helplessly cold . . .

But I shiver still with cold.
I pull up my hempen bedclothes,
Wear what few sleeveless clothes I
*   have,*
But cold and bitter is the night!
As for those poorer than myself,
Their parents must be cold and
*   hungry,*
Their wives and children beg and cry.
Then, how do you struggle through
*   life? . . .*

Here I lie on straw
Spread on bare earth,
With my parents at my pillow,
My wife and children at my feet,
All huddled in grief and tears.
No fire sends up smoke
At the cooking-place,
And in the cauldron
A spider spins its web.
With not a grain to cook, . . .[6]

For peasant women, then, there was
some joy in festivals, some comfort in
their legal rights, with shared family
experiences through hard times and
good ones. But because these
unschooled women left no records like
those of the educated Heian diary
writers, we do not know how they felt
about their lives.

Points to Consider

1. Records remain describing the
    lives of upper-class women in the
    Heian and medieval times. Why
    are there only a few descriptions
    of the activities of peasant
    women? Why are there no
    records left of what they felt about
    their lives?

2. What sources of information are
    there that tell something about the
    lives of peasant men and women?
    Do you think these sources would
    be similar to those describing
    peasants in medieval European
    history of about the same time
    period? Why or why not?

3. Looking back at the title of this
    section, explain what *privileges*
    peasant women seem to have had
    — sometimes in contrast to
    wealthier women. What specific
    things mentioned might seem the
    harshest about the *poverty*
    suffered by peasant women?

---

[6]Lu, *Sources of Japanese History*, p. 39-40.

C.   Exceptional Women

The elite male warrior was considered the ideal person in medieval Japan. But the rivalries and wars of the time created situations in which people of ability — male and female — might possibly break through restrictions of class and gender, therefore, the chronicles of this feudal age frequently mention the exploits of exceptional people, among which are women. These exceptional women appear in a variety of roles, and some held major positions of power.

The best known of these exceptional women is perhaps Hōjō Masako (1157-1225 A.D.) who has been nicknamed in history the "Nun Shōgun." She and her family helped to found the government at Kamakura. The Kamakura government took power away from the emperor's court at Kyōto and gave it instead to a shōgun who handled administrative and military matters. Masako's involvement in the creation of this new government was complex, but it began with her marriage to Minamoto Yoritomo. He managed to bring the warrior groups of Japan under his control. In 1185 Minamoto Yoritomo won a decisive naval battle over his rivals, the Taira family. Minamoto Yoritomo, then, became the first shōgun and Masako began to gain the power she later used to place her family, the Hōjō, in control of the Shōgunate.

In the first years of their marriage, Masako kept to the role of wife and mother. But, with Yoritomo's early death, she became regent for her son Yoriie. In time a series of plots and intrigues began over the succession to the office of shōgun. Various family factions, as well as those surrounding the emperor, fought for power. In the vicious confusion, Yoriie was killed by Masako's own party, and one of Yoriie's sons and Masako's younger son were also killed.[1] When the emperor declared against her, Masako organized both the Minamoto and Hōjō clans to help avenge her. She roused the troops by stating that if anyone thought of joining the emperor, they should kill her first.[2] The warriors supported her and defeated the imperial government, with the result that the new candidate for shōgun was the one Masako proposed and through whom she ruled.[3] Masako's father and brother had supported her efforts, and so their family members — the Hōjō — became the major rulers during early medieval times called the Kamakura period. Although the original source of her power was through her husband and she was supported by both her immediate family and the Hōjō and Minamoto clans, she is still considered to be the founder of the Kamakura government for the following reasons:

"Although [Masako] never personally led the warriors in battle and always operated from a position of assumed deference to her male colleagues . . ., she was ever ready to provide the spirit of direction and relentless dedication to objectives which made the Kamakura feudal system a success. She fully deserves to be remembered as the "Nun Shōgun" of Kamakura, the name by which she was known in the later years of her life." [4]

Masako was not the only exceptional woman of the Kamakura period which followed the Heian. Hino Tomiko

(1440-1496 A.D.) was married to a shōgun and largely ruled through him. The chronicles claim that she declared, "The words of the Shōgun's wife rule from heaven to earth."[5] Eventually she forced her husband out of power and put her son in as shōgun so she could rule through him. Her era was known for heavy taxation but also for government support of the arts and building of temples.

Besides ruling through husbands and sons, some women also became known as samurai-like warriors. Taira Hangaku was known as a skilled archer, better than either her father or brother in "shooting a hundred arrows and hitting a hundred times."[6] She helped to defend her clan's castle until she was wounded and taken prisoner. Her beauty and valor, it was said, were such that one of the opposing samurai asked to marry her.

---

[1]Mary R. Beard, *The Force of Women in Japanese History* (Washington, DC: Public Affairs Press, 1953), p. 71.

[2]Kenneth D. Butler, "Woman of Power Behind the Kamakura Bakufu" in, *Great Historical Figures of Japan*, Murakami Hyoe and Thomas J. Harper, eds. (Tokyo: Japan Culture Institute, 1978), p. 97.

[3]Beard, *The Force of Women in Japanese History*, p. 72.

[4]Butler, "Woman of Power Behind the Kamakura Bakufu," p. 101.

[5]Quoted in Beard, *The Force of Women in Japanese History*, p. 80.

[6]*Ibid.*, p. 72.

This is the temple of Jakkō-in. From the time of Hōjō Masako it has served as a refuge for royal princesses and noblewomen who sought the religious life as Buddhist nuns. The abbess or head nun was always from the royal family.

Another woman warrior was Gozen Tomoe, who rode into battle with her husband. She is said to have told him, "I want to fight with the enemy who is worthy of me and I want to fight the last glorious fight in front of you."[7]

Even women who did not rule or fight might have influence during medieval Japanese times. Toward the end of medieval times, women figured strongly in politics by arranging and maintaining alliances and advising rulers. The military dictatorship of Toyotomi Hideyoshi (1536-1598 A.D.) was a forerunner of the Tokugawa era, which saw the consolidation of Japan as a nation. Many of Toyotomi Hideyoshi's letters remain, so historians have a sense of how this male leader, who was known for his warlike actions, still relied on the support of the women around him.

---

[7]Dorothy Robins-Mowry, *The Hidden Sun* (Boulder, Colorado: Westview Press, 1983), p. 21.

In the tradition of Empress Jingu and Hōjō Masako, these women formed a women's army to oppose the 19th century Meiji emperor in the Satsuma Rebellion.

Four women were particularly important to him, but in different ways. He shared the details of the household life with his wife Yasuko. He wrote her of his plans for the invasion of Korea.[8] To his mother he sent messages expressing concern about her health, giving her advice (to take short trips), and inquiring about her appetite.[9] The concubine Yodo received signs of affection and joy since she bore him the sons his wife did not. Yet, it was finally not to these sons, who met with misfortune, but to his adopted daughter that Hideyoshi felt the most trust and affection. In a letter to his wife, he described how he would have made his adopted daughter his heir — if she had only been a man. He said that if he came home from Korea in triumph, he wished to elevate his daughter to "the first rank."[10] As with many other leaders in the history of Japan, the plans of Hideyoshi were formed and sustained with the women who made up his support circle.

Medieval Japan, then, was a world in which women, as well as men, understood the politics of war and military theory. They acted both as leaders and advisers as well as trustworthy companions.

[8]See, Adriana Boscaro, ed., tr., *101 Letters of Hideyoshi* (Tokyo: Sophia University, 1975), p. 29-30, 35, 53-54.

[9]*Ibid.*, p. 34, 45-46.

[10]*Ibid.*, p. 54.

Points to Consider

1. Who was considered the *ideal* person in medieval Japan? What conditions led to other people breaking through barriers to become powerful and famous?

2. Why is Hōjō Masako called an "exceptional" woman? How did she gain power? Seem to keep it?

3. What is meant by Masako's honorary title "Nun Shōgun?" Why do you think it was considered a compliment?

4. The title of this section uses the term "Exceptional Women." What are these women *exceptions to*? Describe how several of these women were "exceptional."

5. Some women's historians complain that what seems to make these women exceptional is that they behave like male leaders or act in masculine roles. If history was written mainly from the point of view of women, what *men* might be considered exceptional? What roles might be seen as most important and worth writing about?

CHAPTER 5

JAPANESE WOMEN IN THE TOKUGAWA PERIOD

A.   Introduction

A historian recently noted that the "tensions between Japanese and Chinese culture affects the status of women up to the final codification of the female image during the Tokugawa period."[1] In other words, Confucian ideas were introduced into Japan from China in about 700 A.D. However, not until the Tokugawa period (1603-1867 A.D.) was there a rigid acceptance of a neo-Confucian system.[2] Until then there was a wavering between accepting ancient *Japanese* ideals for women or *Chinese* Confucian ones. The following briefly reviews this development:

Ancient Japan *(c. 200 B.C.- 700 A.D.) From earliest Japanese times to the writing down of the Taihō Codes.*

- Amaterasu Ōmikami — female sun god was the supreme god of ancient Japan. The Japanese emperors traced their lineage to her as their original ancestor.

- In the mythology of early Japan, the woman proposed marriage to the man.[3] The Japanese folklore scholar, Tokuzō Ōmachi, claimed

---

[1]Joy Paulson, "Evolution of The Feminine Ideal" in, *Women in Changing Japan*, Joyce Libra, Joy Paulson, and Elizabeth Powers, eds. (Stanford, CA: Stanford University Press, 1978), p. 1-2.

[2]Neo = new, so this was a *new* version of the ancient Confucian philosophical system which had been introduced into Japan in about 700 A.D. but only partly accepted.

[3]Quoted in, Susan J. Pharr, "Japan: Historical and Contemporary Perspectives" in, Janet Zollinger Giele and Audrey Chapman Smock, eds., *Women: Roles and Status in Eight Countries* (New York: John Wiley & Sons, 1977), p. 219.

that "the earliest known form of social organization in Japan was based on . . . matrilocal (or uxorilocal) marriage. A young married couple would live at the home of the bride's parents for a certain period of time . . . [often] for their whole lives — after the wedding ceremony.[4]

- An era of empresses (2nd to 8th centuries A.D.) — saw many women rule as empress dowagers, regents, and as emperors.

- About 250 A.D. a new political system developed in Japan in which family groups ruled. These ruling families were headed by patriarchal chiefs. This system, then, seems to have represented a move away from the earlier matriarchal families.[5]

- Japan's earliest contacts with China started in the 6th century A.D. During the time of the Chinese T'ang dynasty (600 - 900 A.D.), the Japanese contacts with China increased. Chinese culture became much admired in Japan, and many Chinese ideals for women were incorporated into Japanese customs and laws.[6]

Taihō Code and Heian Period (700 A.D.-1185 A.D.)

The Taihō Code of 701 A.D. was supported by Empress Jitō (687 - 697 A.D.). It represented a decline in the status of Japanese women. The new Japanese laws were taken from the Chinese T'ang Code which, in turn, was based on Confucian beliefs. The following is a summary of the Confucian system adopted in the Taihō Code:

- The universe is organized around the principle of Yin/Yang. Yin represents the positive; Yang negative,
  Yin — male / Yang — female,
  Yin — active / Yang — passive,
  Yin — light / Yang — dark.

- In addition to the Yin/Yang view of the universe is the Five Elements analysis of the universe. The combination of these two are the basis of Confucianism:

"One original principle at the root of existence
Two poles, negative and positive, male and female
Three manifestations, Heaven, Earth and Man
Four motions-in space the four cardinal points, in time the four seasons
Five elements-wood, fire, earth, metal, water, which control the rhythm of life
Six kinships-ruler and subject, father and child, husband and wife," [7]

Although the Japanese formally accepted the Confucian doctrine, they adapted it to their own needs.

---

[4]Tokuzō Ōmachi, "Ashiire-kon, Putting-One's-Feet-In Marriage," in Richard M. Dorson, ed., *Studies in Japanese Folklore* (Bloomington, IN: Indiana University Press, 1963), p. 251.

[5]Pharr, "Japan: Historical and Contemporary Perspectives," p. 220.

[6]*Ibid.*, p. 220.

[7]George B. Sansom, *A History of Japan to 1334* (Stanford: Stanford University Press, 1958), p. 72.

- The emperor continued to trace his lineage to the female sun god Amaterasu.

- Aristocratic or upper-class women continued to have fairly high status, including some property rights. Daughters often inherited the family residence. Uxorilocal (or matrilocal) marriage, where the husband moved to the wife's home, was common (see: Chapter 3-B). Under the new Taihō Code, however, women received only two-thirds of land allotted, compared to that available to men.[8]

- Heian court women produced great literary works. They were educated, but it was felt that they should not — or could not — learn the Chinese writing system.

Kamakura Period *(1185-1338 A.D.)*

- Women were often trained in the samurai tradition to use weapons and be skilled in martial arts. Wives of the samurai were expected to defend their castles when their husbands were absent.

- Hōjō Masako, wife of the first shōgun, Minamoto Yoritomo, probably influenced a more liberal law code of 1232 A.D. which guaranteed inheritance, property, and some divorce rights to women.[9]

- The Hōjō family regimes of the 13th and 14th centuries continued customs which encouraged the division of property among all heirs — daughters and sons.[10]

- The ideal person is considered to be the samurai male warrior — loyal, fierce, and courageous.

- In the 13th century the Buddhist monk Nichiren founded a cult which emphasized the dual nature of humans and the value of these separate but complementary roles.

- Another 13th century Buddhist monk, Shinran, started an influential cult which claimed that women were by nature sinful and, therefore, as women they could not achieve paradise — nirvana.

Ashikaga Period *(1338-1500 A.D.) and The Period of The Country at War (1500-1603 A.D.)*

These periods were times of general disruption, civil wars, and generally weak central governments.

- With constant warfare, sons became even more highly valued as soldiers. "Women of the warrior class often became little more than chattel [property] . . . in some cases daughters were [used] to seal feudal military compacts or were given to the heads of enemy clans as hostages." [11]

---

[8]Dorothy Robins-Mowry, *The Hidden Sun* (Boulder, CO: Westview Press, 1983), p. 10.

[9]*Ibid.*, p. 2.

[10]Jonathan Norton Leonard, *Early Japan* (New York: Time, Inc., 1968), p. 104.

[11]See: Pharr, "Japan: Historical and Contemporary Perspectives," p. 224.

- The Zen Buddhist monk Keian returned from China in 1473 and introduced the neo-Confucian ideas of Chinese philosopher Chu-Hsi. The newly interpreted Confucian ideas became increasingly important in Japan over the next two hundred years.[12] The status of women in neo-Confucian philosophy was low.

- 15th century Buddhist Tendai and Shingon sects claimed, like the earlier monk Shinran, that women could not hope to achieve the spiritual existence that men could.[13]

- Beginning in the 14th century, primogeniture became common, with the oldest son inheriting the entire estate. One historian explained that the result was that "girls were increasingly debarred from the rights of succession, for fear that when they married they might take their inheritance as a dowry to another family which could become a rival to their own."[14]

****

The outline above is only meant to suggest some examples of how the status of women tilted from ancient Japanese ideals to those which were mainly based on Chinese Confucianism. The balance might be visualized as a see-saw that fluctuated up and down, with women having more or fewer rights, depending on when they lived and into which class they were born. During the Tokugawa period (1603-1867 A.D.) the see-saw comes to rest, with women's rights in the areas of physical freedom, inheritance and property rights, and marriage privileges sinking to a new low of inequality. The next few sections describe the history of women during this long period called the Tokugawa era.

---

[12]Sansom, *Japan: A Short Cultural History* (New York: Appleton Century Crofts, 1962), p. 380.

[13]Pharr, "Japan: Historical and Contemporary Perspectives," p. 224.

[14]Louis Frederic, *Daily Life in Japan at the Time of the Samurai* (London: George Allen and Unwin Ltd., 1972), p. 63.

B. The Decline in Japanese Women's Rights

"The Tokugawa period was the worst time in the history of Japanese women," concludes one historian — and others agree with her evaluation.[1] What made the Tokugawa era (1603-1867 A.D.) such a bad time for women? It seems that the basic cause was the introduction into Japan of a new Confucian social system whose laws and customs restricted Japanese women's legal rights and even limited their physical freedom of movement.

The Tokugawa shōguns had one major aim for Japan — to create a stable central government under their direction. In order to do so, they put their loyal vassals, or lords, (called daimyō) in strategic areas of the country where they could keep watch over those who had been either neutral or rebellious against their rule. The Tokugawa land system assigned farmers to specific plots that they were not allowed to leave. Mines, cities, and the silk trade came under the control of the Tokugawa government, and the financial resources from these enterprises were used to support their system. This neo-Confucian system of the Tokugawa organized people into set rankings or a hierarchy of classes. At the top of the class pyramid were the soldiers, then farmers, artisans (skilled city crafts workers) and, at the bottom, the merchant-traders. Each group or class was assigned different

---

[1]Tamie Kamiyama, *Ideology and Patterns in Women's Education in Japan*, unpublished Ph.D. dissertation, St. Louis University, 1977, p. 280.

duties, did not intermarry and, by rules of etiquette, were even addressed differently. Increased restrictions on women during the Tokugawa era can be seen as a part of this general tightening of control on all members of society except, as historian George Sansom has put it, "the worst treatment of all was that to which a woman had to submit." [2]

Basic to the neo-Confucianism of the Togukawa period was the belief in the inferiority of women. The influential neo-Confucian writer, Kaibara Ekken, described the general nature of women in his "Greater Learning for Women," written in 1672:

"The five worst maladies [illnesses] that afflict the female mind are: indocility, discontent, slander, jealousy, and silliness. Without any doubt, these five maladies infest seven or eight out of every ten women, and it is from these that arises the inferiority of women to men. A woman should cure them by self-inspection and self-reproach. The worst of them all, and the parent of the other four, is silliness.

"Woman's nature is passive. This passiveness, being of the nature of the night, is dark. Hence, as viewed from the standard of man's nature, the foolishness of woman fails to understand the duties that lie before her very eyes, perceives not the actions that will bring down blame upon her own head, and comprehends not even the things that will bring down calamities on the heads of her husband and children. Neither when she blames and accuses and curses innocent persons, nor when, in her jealousy of

others, she thinks to set up herself alone, does she see that she is her own enemy . . . Again, in the education of her children, her blind affection induces an erroneous system. Such is the stupidity of her character that it is incumbent on her, in every particular, to distrust herself and to obey her husband." [3]

As this passage shows, the assumption was that women were so stupid and "silly" that they always needed outside direction from men. This direction, as the Chinese philosopher Confucius had said, must come first from the woman's father, then her husband and, finally, her son. Particularly, a wife was supposed to look upon her husband as her "lord," according to Kaibara Ekken:

"A woman has no particular lord. She must look to her husband as her lord, and must serve him with all worship and reverence, not despising or thinking lightly of him. The great life-long duty of a woman is obedience. In her dealings with her husband, both the expression of her countenance and the style of her address should be courteous, humble, and conciliatory, never peevish and intractable, never rude and arrogant: — that should be a

---

[2]George Sansom, *A History of Japan 1615-1867* (Stanford: Stanford University Press, 1963), p. 89.

[3]Basil Hall Chamberlain, *Things Japanese* (London: John Murray, 1905), p. 507.

Nijō Castle — Built in 1603 as the home of Tokugawa Ieyasu and the Tokugawa shōguns who followed him.

woman's first and chiefest care. When the husband issues his instructions, the wife must never disobey them. In doubtful cases, she should enquire of her husband, and obediently follow his commands. If ever her husband should enquire of her, she should answer to the point; — to answer in a careless fashion were a mark of rudeness. Should her husband be roused at any time to anger, she must obey him with fear and trembling, and not set herself up against him in anger and forwardness. A woman should look on her husband as if he were Heaven itself, and never weary of thinking how she may yield to her husband, and thus escape celestial castigation. . . .

"Let her never even dream of jealousy. If her husband be dissolute, she must expostulate with him, but never either nurse or vent her anger. If her jealousy be extreme, it will render her countenance frightful and her accents repulsive, and can only result in completely *alienating her husband from her, and making her intolerable in his eyes. Should her husband act ill and unreasonably, she must compose her countenance and soften her voice to remonstrate with him; and if he be angry and listen not to the remonstrance, she must wait over a season, and then expostulate with him again when his heart is softened. Never set thyself up against thy husband with harsh features and a boisterous voice!"* [4]

It was therefore thought by some that women were so silly and stupid that educating them would only lead to trouble. One 18th century shōgun wrote:

"It is well that women should be unlettered. To cultivate women's skills would be harmful. They have no need of learning." [5]

Left without the firm control and guidance of men, the picture given of women was a frightening one to these Tokugawa philosophers. It was thought that, as a bride, a spoiled daughter could potentially "hate and decry" her new father-in-law and create "domestic dissensions." [6] The Tokugawa, however, had a vested interest in seeing that the lower classes and women "behaved" themselves. Rebellion was especially feared. To prevent rebellion Tokugawa legal codes and social customs aimed at keeping each group in line and hard at work.

A document that illustrates this attempt to make others work for the central Tokugawa government is one issued in 1649 to all Japanese villages. The major instructions were for the peasants to be frugal and hard-working, but notice the fear expressed of the "rambling" wife:

"Farm work must be done with the greatest diligence. Planting must be neat, all weeds must be removed, and on the borders of both wet and dry fields beans or similar foodstuffs are to be grown, however small the space.

Peasants must rise early and cut grass before cultivating the fields. In the evening they are to make straw rope or straw bags, all such work to be done with great care.

They must not buy tea or sake to drink, nor must their wives.

Men must plant bamboo or trees round the farmhouse and must use the fallen leaves for fuel so as to save expense.

Peasants are people without sense or forethought. Therefore they must not give rice to their wives and children at harvest time, but must save food for the future. They should eat millet, vegetables, and other coarse food instead of rice. Even the fallen leaves of plants should be saved as food against famine . . . During the seasons of planting and

---

[4]*Ibid*, p. 504-505.

[5]Herbert Passin, *Society and Education in Japan* (New York: Teachers College, Columbia University, 1965), p. 46.

[6]Chamberlain, *Things Japanese*, p. 502.

Princess Tokugawa Aya, one of the descendants of the Tokugawa family, dressed in traditional costume — early 20th century photograph.

harvesting, however, when the labor is arduous, the food taken may be a little better than usual.

The husband must work in the fields, the wife must work at the loom. Both must do night work. However good-looking a wife may be, if she neglects her household duties by drinking tea or sightseeing or rambling on the hillsides, she must be divorced.

Peasants must wear only cotton or hemp — no silk. They may not smoke tobacco. It is harmful to health, it takes up time, and costs money. It also creates a risk of fire." [7]

Attractions of the wife — her beauty or laughter — were supposed to be seen as unimportant compared with her household duties. Since one of these "duties" was to have a son, some writers crudely wrote, "the womb is a borrowed thing." [8] Love between husband and wife was not particularly encouraged lest the men be "led astray by the folly of their wives." [9] Rebellion against the Tokugawa overlords might be one way husbands could be "led astray." Ironically, then, all these restrictions on women suggest a fear of the power of women. Their "silliness" or "stupidity" was generally seen not as really doing "dumb" things (like burning meals or sewing clothes upside down), but in fostering rebellion or refusing to work for the lord.

It seems that women, for the Tokugawa, had to be restricted for the safety of the state. This was done in a variety of ways. One was through physical restrictions on the movements of women — and a

common use of hostages. When the local noblemen went to their home districts, their wives and children were required to stay at Edo (Tōkyō), the shōgun's capital. If the nobleman rebelled against the shōgun, his family would be executed. A 19th century traveler described the guard post that made sure no women escaped from the capital to go home:

"Half-way between the two capitals is a shallow lake, on the Miyako shore of which stands the town of Aray, the station of the Great Edo guard. So important is this post esteemed, that the prince in whose dominions it lies, and whose troops furnish the guard, is almost invariably a member of the Council of State. No one may pass Aray towards Edo without the grand judge's passport. No woman can pass without the most especial permission; and, therefore, besides the examination of their papers and baggage to guard against the introduction of contraband goods, travelers are obliged to submit to a personal inquest, lest a woman should be smuggled through in male attire; a crime, the perpetration of

---

[7]Quoted in, Sansom, *A History of Japan 1615-1867*, p. 99.

[8]*Ibid.*, p. 90.

[9]R. P. Dore, *Education in Tokugawa Japan* (Berkeley: University of California Press, 1965), p. 65.

which would infallibly cost the lives of the offending woman, of her male companions, and of the guards whose watchfulness should have been thus deceived." [10]

The physical freedom of women to move about — and even to journey home with their husbands — came to be strictly regulated during the Tokugawa era. Another way used to control women was through changes made in their property rights. Before the 15th century, Japanese women had clearly defined inheritance rights. During the Heian period uxorilocal marriage (in which the husband came to live at his wife's home) was common, and generally the family residence was inherited by a daughter. Therefore, whether a woman was married, widowed, or divorced, she had the security of property ownership in her own right. During the Tokugawa era women experienced a severe decline in their right to inherit the family home. This decline was related to other changes. During later medieval times the household became more important than the individual. A household was seen as a unit which paid taxes and was subject to the shōgun's rules. All household property was controlled by the head of the household, who was responsible for its members. The "head" was to be a male. It was difficult for widows to inherit their residence, as all property went to the nearest male relative's estate. A woman's economic support — whether as daughter, wife, or widow — was dependent upon her male relatives.

Unlike the usual uxorilocal marriages of Heian times, during the medieval period the usual marriage arrangement was virilocal (where the wife moved to the home of her husband.) A wife's rights within her marriage were now dependent upon the will of her husband's family. Trial marriages occurred in which the marriage was not registered until the birth of a son. If no son was born, the wife could be sent back to her family — or sent away without any provision for her support. This view that a wife was on trial until a son was born continued, in some cases, until recently. In 1945 a young woman, Kofumi, described her life as a "trial wife," or "woman with one foot in the door:"

"After World War II, in 1945, Kofumi was a soft, solemn twenty-year-old, intent only upon pleasing Yamamoto Masatsune, the handsome eldest son of Tsuya-Giku's true mother, Eiko. Kofumi was married to Masatsune and yet she was not married. She was a 'trial wife,' a 'woman with one foot in the door.' In Yoshino, as a trial wife you are literally on trial. You move into the home of your man and his parents, and assume all the duties and obligations of a true wife. Under the tutelage and surveillance of your mother-in-law, you perform the chores your man's household demands. You sweep the floor and get the food ready and light the fire, and, after you are done at home you go out to the fields to labor side by

---

[10]*Manners and Customs of the Japanese* (London: John Murray, 1841), p. 100. (Anonymous).

Education for women during the Tokugawa period was often limited to learning skills such as brush painting.

side with your man and his father. And all you do you must do with courtesy, being careful always not to give umbrage [annoyance] to your mother-in-law. When night comes, you must also indulge your man, entering into the spirit of his lovemaking, while being certain at the same time that you are not agitating the green in your mother-in-law's eyes. If, after six months, your trial husband's family is content with you, you may remain in his home. If not, you will be driven out." [11]

Even after a boy child was born, a wife's position was not secure under this marriage system that developed in later medieval times and continued during the Tokugawa period. She could be divorced for any of the following reasons:

- disobedience.
- lewdness.
- jealousy.
- leprosy.
- talking too much.
- stealing.

The husband could decide when these conditions had been met and could

[11]Sara Harris, *House of The 10,000 Pleasures* (New York: E. P. Dutton, 1962), p. 193.

simply hand his wife a three and one-half line written notice — she would have to leave.[12] She was not allowed to take her children with her. These Japanese women had no grounds for divorcing their husbands. In cases of abuse, the best a wife might do was to escape to a Buddhist convent.

These inheritance, marriage, and divorce laws contrasted bleakly with earlier law codes; for example, the "Formulary of the Jōei era of 1232," were laws meant to be followed in the early medieval courts. These laws reflected the views of Minamoto Yoritomo, the first shōgun, but no doubt were, heavily influenced by his powerful wife Hōjō Masako. They provided upper-class women with equal inheritance rights with brothers, rights to control property in marriage, power to control peasants, and some divorce rights.[13]

Under the restrictive Tokugawa code, adultery committed by a wife was punishable by death, while a husband might keep women as concubines in his own home — and have other sexual affairs without restrictions. The constant advice to young girls to grow up to be obedient wives might be seen as teaching future wives a necessary survival skill for the time they entered a world that denied them essential marriage rights.

Women of the Tokugawa were limited in their physical movements, right to property, and marital rights. They were also restricted in their most basic right — that of being allowed an education to become a complete adult person. The debate over whether or not women should be educated at all was a lively one in this era. On one side of the debate were those who thought

women too "silly" to be educated. On the other side were those who thought women could be taught something and should have some sort of training. No one in this era supported the idea that women should be as highly educated as men. The earlier ideal for court women of the Heian period of educated, witty, literate women was lost. It was thought, however, that a completely uneducated woman might have her own opinions and lead her sons and husband "astray." Therefore, some education of women in clan or small local schools did take place during the Tokugawa era. The following chart suggests how many girls and young women these small "terakoya" schools may have educated toward the end of the Tokugawa period:

[12]Nakagawa Zennosuke, "A Century of Marriage Law," *Japan Quarterly*, Vol. 10, No. 2 (April-June 1963), p. 184.

[13]Dorothy Robins-Mowry, *The Hidden Sun* (Boulder, Colorado: Westview Press, 1983), p. 27.

Social Group	Estimated Literacy	Proportion in Total Population*
Samurai men	almost 100%)	
Samurai women	50%)	7%
Merchants in large cities	70-80%)	
Their women folk — perhaps	)	
somewhat higher than	)	
samurai women	)	3%
Merchants in smaller towns	)	
and rural areas	50-60%)	
Artisan classes (skilled workers) in large cities	50-60%)	
Artisan classes in smaller	)	2%
towns and rural areas	40-50%)	
Village notables	almost 100%)	
Village middle layers	50-60%)	
Lower peasant levels	30-40%)	87%
Peasants in the more	)	
isolated areas	20%)	

(Men — bracket spanning Merchants in smaller towns through Peasants in the more isolated areas)

*Based on Irene Taueber, *The Population of Japan* (Princeton: Princeton University Press, 1958), pp. 26-28.[14]

Training for women was largely in basic reading and mathematical skills, household arts, and "moral education" aimed at encouraging them to become submissive, obedient wives. Even the classics of Japanese literature by women such as Murasaki Shikibu's *The Tale of Genji* and Sei Shōnagon's *Pillow Book* were considered too risque and corrupting for the Tokugawa young women.[15] While young women were encouraged in the gentle artistic skills of calligraphy and flower arranging, they were not encouraged in self-expressive, personal writing such as was seen in Heian court diaries. Creative writing might lead to independent thought — and even rebellion. In 1629 female actresses were banned from participation in theatrical productions called Kabuki dramas, as they were considered too distracting and dangerous, causing a decline in public morals. Male actors were substituted in Kabuki dramas, even in female parts.[16]

[14]Quoted in, Passin, *Society and Education in Japan*, p. 57.

[15]Dore, *Education in Tokugawa Japan*, p. 66.

[16]Kabuki: A type of drama developed in 17th century Japan. Highly stylized or artificial plays, melodramatic and traditional — featuring colorful costumes and dancing. These traditional plays are still performed in Japan. See: Jonathan Norton Leonard, *Early Japan* (New York: Time, Inc., 1968), p. 169-181.

Although Tokugawa regulations severely limited all Japanese women, perhaps the restrictions fell most heavily on women of the samurai class. Merchant marriages seem to have been more equal, perhaps because both partners were needed to tend shops and carry on trade. As their property could be more easily divided, they could provide daughters with respectable dowries that gave them status in the groom's family.[17] The custom of adopting a son-in-law, rather than always giving up one's daughter to her husband's family, was still practiced by merchants. In the countryside older wives might be respected household leaders. The general trend, however, of the long Tokugawa period from 1603 to 1867, was a decline in women's rights. Along with this decline came the idea that women were inferior and did not need nor deserve personal rights. The regaining of rights for women — their physical freedom, marital equality, educational privileges, personal dignity, and a sense of self-worth would be among the important themes of modern Japanese times following the Tokugawa.

Points to Consider

1. The *Introduction*, Chapter 5-A, lists a few indicators of the status of women before the Tokugawa period. What specific evidence is there that women's status was higher before the Tokugawa era? What things might indicate that it was not as high as that of men?

2. During the Tokugawa period, women's freedoms were restricted in several important ways. Explain how women were restricted in the following areas:

   • physical mobility
   • property rights
   • equality in marriage
   • educational opportunities

3. It seems from the *Introduction* that the status of women in Japan before the Tokugawa period was often in balance between forces that would lower it and ancient traditions that assigned women higher status. The major force for changes that lowered women's status came from the Confucian ideas imported from China to Japan over a long period of time.

What specific things about the Confucian system contributed to the lowering of the status of women?

The following are the grounds for divorce in traditional China. After reading them over, compare them to the Japanese divorce code of the Tokugawa era. How are they the same? Are they different in any way? How did the Tokugawa code differ from earlier Japanese divorce codes?

---

[17]See, Susan J. Pharr, "Japan: Historical and Contemporary Perspectives" in, Janet Zollinger Giele and Audrey Chapman Smock, eds., *Women: Roles and Status in Eight Countries* (New York: John Wiley & Sons, 1977), p. 226.

"According to tradition, the Chinese scholar Confucius (c. 55-497) laid down seven reasons for which a man could "put away" (divorce) his wife. These grounds were a part of the legal code of the empire until the fall of the Manchu Dynasty and final revision of the codes in the early 20th century.

"The seven grounds on which the husband could divorce his wife:

- *She is rebellious or unfilial toward her parents-in-law.*

- *She has failed to produce a son.*

- *She has been unfaithful to her husband.*

- *She has shown jealousy toward her husband's other woman.*

- *She has a repulsive and incurable disease (such as leprosy).*

- *She is given to hurtful talk, talebearing and talking too much.*

- *She is a thief.*

The three grounds on which a wife can prevent her husband from putting her away (divorcing her):

- *She has mourned three years for her husband's parents.*

- *She has no family to which to return.*

- *She married her husband when he was poor, and now he is rich.*

The grounds on which a wife can put away (divorce) her husband:

None." [18]

4. At various times in the history of the world there have been periods when *misogyny* — hatred or fear of women — has been particularly common in literature and public speech. One such period was late medieval Europe. A few quotations from European medieval documents of the 14th and 15th centuries, are representative of the misogynous thinking of the time. After looking over these statements, compare them to those of Kaibara Ekken from 17th century Japan. In what specific ways are the complaints about women similar? How different?

From a 14th century Italian writer, Paolo da Certalds, in his *Handbook of Good Customs*:

"The female is an empty thing and easily swayed: she runs great risks when she is away from her husband. Therefore, keep females in the house, keep them as close to yourself as you can, and come home often to keep an eye on your affairs and to keep them in fear and trembling. Make sure they always have work to do in the house and never allow them to

---

[18]Quoted in, Susan Gross and Marjorie Bingham, *Women in Traditional China*, p. 102.

be idle, for idleness
is a great danger to both man
and woman, but more to the
woman . . . ." [19]

15th century Roman Catholic Inquisitors (investigators of heresy), Heinrich Kramer and Jacob Sprenger in their book on witchcraft, *Malleus Maleficarum* or *Hammer of Witches*:

"All wickedness is but little to the wickedness of a woman. What else is woman but a foe to friendship, an unescapable punishment, a necessary evil, a natural temptation, a desirable calamity, a domestic danger, a delectable detriment, an evil of nature, painted with fair color!

"The second reason is that women are naturally more impressionable and more ready to receive the influence of a disembodied spirit; and that when they use this quality well they are very good, but when they use it ill they are very evil.

"The third reason is that they have slippery tongues, and are unable to conceal from their fellow-women those things which by evil arts they know; and, since they are weak, they find an easy and secret manner of vindicating themselves by witchcraft . . .

"It should be noted that there was a defect in the formation of the first woman, since she was formed from a bent rib, that is, a rib of the breast, which is bent as it were in a contrary direction

to a man. And since through this defect she is an imperfect animal, she always deceives.

"Therefore a wicked woman is by her nature quicker to waver in her faith which is the root of witchcraft." [20]

Renaissance humanist and philosopher Juan Luis Vives wrote a book of advice for the daughter of Catherine of Aragon, who became Queen Mary I of England. Called *Christian Woman*, the reason given for educating women was that they might become more pious and submissive to their husbands:

"Nature has given unto man a noble, a high and a diligent mind to be busy and occupied abroad. To gain and to bring home to their wives and family, to rule them and their children and also all their household. And to the woman nature has given a fearful, a covetous and humble mind to be subject unto man." [21]

---

[19]Julia O'Faolain and Laura Martines, eds., *Not in God's Image: Women in History from the Greeks to the Victorians* (New York: Harper & Row, 1973), p. 169.

[20]Quoted in, Alan C. Kors and Edward Peters, eds., *Witchcraft in Europe 110-1700* (Philadelphia: University of Pennsylvania Press, 1972), p. 114-121.

[21]Quoted in Ruth Kelso, *Doctrine for the Lady of the Renaissance* (Urbana: University of Illinois Press, 1956), p. 17-18.

5. The Tokugawa government had its own reasons for suppressing the rights of women. Why did they fear educated and independent women? Physically active women?

6. Once the status of women had suffered the serious setbacks in a number of areas in the Tokugawa period, why might it be difficult for women — or men — to regain these rights for women?

C.   The Geisha

To keep an eye on daimyō or feudal lords who might become too independent, the Tokugawa government required them to spend part of their time in Edo (later Tōkyō) the capital of the shōgunate. As members of the privileged upper classes, the samurai lords were allowed to display their wealth; they competed with each other in building the most elegant mansions and maintaining the largest staffs of servants. Their luxurious city lifestyle required large amounts of cash. They borrowed heavily from the city merchants who became rich on speculation in rice — and from lending money to the samurai. Unlike the samurai lords, the merchants ranked low on the hierarchy of social classes. The Tokugawa shōgunate refused them the privilege of displaying their wealth by wearing elegant clothes in public or by giving lavish entertainments. But they had become wealthy by catering to the needs of the high-class samurai — and desired to spend their money. To satisfy the needs of this wealthy yet low-ranking class, a special area of Edo and other cities was set aside for their entertainments. This was called the ukiyo or Floating World.

Life, according to Buddhist thought, was sad and painful. Fortunately for Buddhists, however, reality was not to be found in this world, but in the final achievement of the state of nirvana. This early Buddhist idea was changed in Tokugawa times. Wealthy city dwellers agreed that life was often miserable and short but, as this was the case, it might as well be enjoyed to the fullest.[1] The Floating World, then, was the name for a subculture of worldly pleasures as well as being a specific area of Edo and other cities.

The Tokugawa government aimed at an orderly, stable society and demanded that the Floating World be regulated and supervised. To achieve this, certain parts of each city were set aside where women "entertainers," especially prostitutes, were fenced into walled areas where they were licensed to work.[2] The area of Edo was called Yoshiwara; Kyōto, called Shimabara. One group of entertainers who were not ordinary prostitutes, but were also found in these walled quarters, were the geisha.

The geisha are part of an exotic image that many outsiders have formed of Japanese culture, but they are also a part of the internal cultural heritage of Japan. The question of what has been the reality of the lives of the women who have made up the geisha has been the center of controversy among historians and other observers. Much has been written about the geisha, but perhaps the following four views are representative ways of looking at these women geisha. They:

- represent "an elegant form of slavery."[3]

- have primarily been artists and have filled a notable, distinct role for Japanese women.

- have had a rich cultural heritage and have acted as a bridge between the normally segregated worlds of Japanese women and men. They have created a public space or meeting place for men where they could carry on serious discussions.

- have been business women with their own networks, organizations and enterprises.

In some ways these views conflict with each other — and in others they overlap. The variety of views, however, suggests the complexity of the role of the geisha. Perhaps one reason that it has been a long-lasting one in Japanese history is because the geisha fulfills many purposes.

* * * * * * * * * * * * * * * * *

The first theory, that geisha were elegant slaves, sees the geisha tradition beginning in early medieval Japan. This view traces its beginnings to the time when the Minamoto clan defeated the Taira clan in 1185 A.D. and the victors forced some of the captive women to dance before them. Later, these chambermaids of the Taira were supposed to have gone into a "miserable life" of serving at inns near ports.[4] They are said to have appeared before customers in their old uniforms that they had worn when they served the noble Taira women. Since these maids had served nobles,

---

[1]Liza Crihfield Dalby, *Geisha* (Berkeley: University of California Press, 1983), p. 269.

[2]*Ibid.*, p. 54.

[3]Ihara Saikaku, *The Life of An Amorous Woman* (New York: New Directions Publishing Corp., 1963), p. 10.

[4]T. Fujimoto, *The Story of The Geisha Girl* (London: T. Werner Laurie, Ltd., n.d.), p. 11.

they were well trained and somewhat educated. They could recite poetry, sing, and play musical instruments. As the warriors during medieval times were often away from home fighting, these women became camp followers and entertainers for the armies.

The geisha tradition, according to this first theory, started with a defeated group of women who used their entertainment skills to survive. This view of the geisha can also be found in the documents which record the buying and selling of little girls into the geisha houses — and also into houses of prostitution. The practice of selling unwanted village girls to brokers who took them to the cities for further sale, continued in Japan until the 1930's. A reporter visited a family who had sold a daughter in 1934 and described the interview:

"As I entered the house, an old woman past seventy, the parents of the girl who was sold, and a little girl of about five were huddled around a smoky fireplace. The little girl seemed to have a cold and was wailing away. After her older sister was sold and left home, the child had turned into a crybaby, they said. 'Why did you sell your daughter,' I asked. The old woman blinked her eyes, which had been damaged by the charcoal smoke and afflicted with trachoma [eye disease], and said, 'Sumie has been sold and is leading a hard life. I don't care if I die. I would like to see my grandchildren have an easy life.' Tears poured out of her red, festering eyes.

"This family had lost their house because of debts that they had

incurred, and had been living with neighbors. They then sold their fourteen-year-old daughter Sumie to a brothel in Nagoya and used the money to buy this house. They got 450 yen on a five-year contract. [After deducting commissions and expenses] they got 150 yen. Seventy yen was used to pay off the debts, 40 yen was used to build this house, and the remaining 40 yen quickly vanished.

"The father did not sell his daughter willingly. But the family had no rice to eat because of the crop failure. On top of that his wife was pregnant and was afflicted with beriberi, and the money lenders pestered him every day . . . So he finally sold his daughter. Now all he has left is one tiny thatched hut. His daughter wrote: 'My boss says that I must start taking customers after New Year's. I don't want to become a prostitute. I am so miserable.' A fourteen-year-old girl from Tsugaru is waiting for the arrival of New Year's Day with terror." [5]

Most families sold their daughters because of famine, but a woman justified the selling of her 23-year-old daughter as follows:

"In order to pay our debts and reduce the size of our family, even by one, we sold our oldest daughter.

---

[5]Quoted in, Mikiso Hane, *Peasants, Rebels, and Outcastes* (New York: Pantheon Books, 1982), p. 211-212.

The money we got for her was 800 yen for six years' service. Twenty percent was taken by the middleman. In addition, the cost of getting her ready [clothing] and other expenses were deducted, so we received in hand 500 yen. I don't think it's wrong to sell our own daughter, whom we raised ourselves. Other people use the money they get to go on excursions to famous sites. Some even go to hot springs to enjoy themselves. On the other hand, we sold her in order to pay our debts, so we feel we needn't be ashamed." [6]

In these 20th century examples, the young girls or women were sold into lives of prostitution. Geisha were not considered to be prostitutes but have been seen primarily as elegant entertainers of men. In the Floating World of the Yoshiwara and other entertainment areas, the major focus was on theater, social conversation, showing off fancy clothing, dancing, singing, and eating.[7] The geisha were a central part of that world of pleasure. Girls were also bought as young children from brokers to be raised as geisha. Their fate might not be as harsh as those sold to brothels where, in open cages, they were inspected for men to make their choice. Still, one anthropologist described the often bleak lives of young girls in the early part of the 20th century when the "geisha population of Japan soared:"

"Early in this century, a geisha might have lived in a variety of circumstances ranging from complete independence (jimae) to a state of virtual captivity (kakae).

Young girls shepherded in from the countryside usually found themselves in the latter situation. They would live in the okiya (geisha house), first as maids and then, if the mistress of the house thought they showed promise, as apprentices. At last, they would earn their keep as full geisha. After this, everything they had, from the food that went into their mouths to the kimono on their backs, was sold or leased to them by the okiya.

"The owners of the geisha houses were then in a position to reap some profit from their investment in the once scared and unpolished rustic child; therefore the house felt entitled to receive all the woman's wages as a geisha. The geisha houses that routinely recruited members in this way were often managed by unscrupulous owners who charged the inmates exorbitant rates for room and board, intentionally keeping them in a state of dependence . . .

"I met a few older geisha who told pitiful stories of a childhood of near-slavery. The ones who had had such bitter experiences were not from the better geisha areas." [8]

[6]*Ibid.*, p. 212.

[7]Dalby, *Geisha*, p. 55.

[8]*Ibid.*, p. 221-224.

Future geisha were trained as young girls to entertain men with singing, dancing, games, and diverting conversation. Yet, this theory that emphasized the geisha as slave points out that when these young women were finally trained and ready for the geisha life, men would pay their owner huge sums to be with them the first night. Financial arrangements with the women continued until they paid their owners the original price of their purchase as well as the cost of their training and upkeep since childhood. If a geisha was fortunate, she might find a patron who would buy up her contract and then marry her or keep her in comfort.

Geisha pose in recent photograph.

Contemporary Japanese law forbids legal prostitution and the purchase of young girls, but some critics see the geisha as an expensive status symbol for Japanese males. It may be the sense of artificial romance that the geisha creates that led one Japanese author to write, "I have never been to a geisha party where I have not felt an undercurrent of sadness."[9]

The second theory does not see the geisha as pathetic, but as occupying one of the few roles for women that allowed for creativity and a certain amount of freedom. This theory sees the origin of geisha in Tokugawa times as being modeled after the tradition in China of having public women hosts who entertained official visitors with their graciousness and fine poetry. Both men and women entertainers became known as "geisha," or "accomplished people" in Japan. Women slowly took over the field, and by 1779 the Tokugawa government was registering them and telling them what to wear.[10] According to this view

of geisha as artist, what should be emphasized is the long hours of lessons and practice needed for the women to become fine singers, players of the samisen, dancers, and story tellers. Rigorous training and talent needed to become professional entertainers is stressed. In the past, for example, geisha went through winter training where they practiced outside or dipped their hands in cold

[9]Kimpei Sheba, *I Cover Japan* (Tokyo: Tokyo News Service, Ltd., n.d.), p. 98.

[10]Liza Crihfield, "The Institution of the Geisha in Modern Japanese Society," unpublished Ph.D. dissertation, Stanford University, 1978, p. 43.

water to toughen them.[11] In modern Japan the geisha have maintained these artistic traditions of study and the performance of customary dances and music. When geisha perform in annual public programs, the present and the past are linked.

Some observers have seen the role of the geisha as not only that of artist but as offering one of the few times in which Japanese males and females share social equality. Though the duty of a geisha was to flatter her male clients, she might have several rivals for her attention. In the wit of her conversation and the romances that occurred, the geisha might have more chance at the "romantic freedom to love" denied women in traditional, arranged marriages.[12] A top ranked geisha, thus, had more freedom of choice and economic independence than other women. She was also seen in Tokugawa days as a fashion leader and respected for the grace of her appearance — the movie star of her time. Of course the numbers of women who achieved this were few, but, so the second theory goes, geisha did lead creative lives. According to a recent survey, modern geisha seem to have been attracted to their life for the economic independence it brings and pride in their art.[13]

A third theory concerning the geisha looks at the social function they fulfilled. Westerners have been somewhat startled by the custom of a geisha visiting one of her clients' wives or of a wife paying the geisha's bills. The geisha, this theory would say, has generally fulfilled the role of public hostess which started long ago in China. In Japan the male world has been sharply segregated from the female world in all but the peasant class. Where men and women rarely socialized together, geisha provided a gracious setting where men could meet socially with female company present. It was felt that men socializing with other men might lead to a brawl; geisha could move social events along smoothly and still allow the men some release from the strictly regulated Tokugawa life. To his wife, the Tokugawa male was supposed to be a distant authority, but, with a geisha, the man might laugh and even play what (to Western observers) seemed rather silly games. Therefore, the geisha came to fulfill a useful function to both the wife and husband by allowing the release of tensions outside the marriage. As this theory suggests, however, the wife was expected to hide any feelings of jealousy she might have. Today there seems to be an assumption by some Japanese wives that when a husband is socializing away from home he is safer with a geisha than with a bar hostess or other non-family woman.[14]

Geisha entertained men with music and games, but geisha teahouses also became "public spaces" where serious discussions have gone on. The

[11]Sara Harris, *House of The 10,000 Pleasures* (New York: E. P. Dutton & Co., 1962), p. 64-65.

[12]Crihfield, "The Institution of the Geisha in Modern Japanese Society," p. 95.

[13]*Ibid.*, p. 242.

[14]Dalby, *Geisha*, p. 171.

downfall of the Tokugawa regime in the 19th century and the reinstatement of the Meiji emperor as the central power was led by a group of reformers who had strong ties with the geisha quarter of Kyōto. Since the geisha had a strong code that forbade them revealing guests' conversations, these Meiji reformers had a place in which to begin plotting against the Tokugawa government. Their involvement with the leaders of the restoration of the imperial government enhanced a geisha's reputation.[15] Several statesmen of the era married geisha:

- Count Koin Kido — married Kumatsu of Kyōto

- Marquis Kaoru Inoue — married Kayoko of Shinbashi

- Count Shojiro Goto — married Konaka of Kyōto[16]

Other Meiji reformers were involved with geisha, even though they did not marry them; for example, the Marquis of Saionji, Japanese ambassador to the Versailles Treaty Conference in France in 1919, brought his geisha/concubine with him, although his daughter acted as his official hostess.

This tradition of well-known officials being involved with geisha continued through World War II. The admirals Yamamoto Isoroku and Yonai Mitsumasa were particularly known for their geisha contacts. Admiral Yamamoto's wife, Reiko, was so traditional that she reported, ''I never so much as went for a walk with my husband;''[17] the geisha Chiyoko shared many of his hours. At the present time, Japanese male politicians are still known to use the geisha setting for serious policy discussions. This third theory would claim that geisha have provided a culturally useful institution in creating public spaces for political and other serious discussions.

The fourth theory emphasizes the business element in a geisha's life. According to this theory, money is basic to their role. A successful geisha would be one who was self-supporting, bought her own way out of her contract, and perhaps set up her own teahouse to train other geisha. To become a noted geisha required that a woman spend a good bit of money on her training and, particularly, on clothes. Currently, a year's wardrobe may run into the thousands of dollars.[18] Besides these costs, the geisha has household and elaborate hairdressing expenses as well as travel expenses to the various teahouses. She also must pay fees to a central registry office. In the past, without a patron, it would be unlikely for a geisha to be able to pay back her debts and her expenses. She would then continue to be under the control of the person holding her contract.

Even now, for a geisha to pay off her debts and her expenses requires a

---

[15]A. C. Scott, *The Flower and Willow World* (London: William Heinemann Ltd., 1959), p. 121.

[16]*Ibid.*, p. 121.

[17]Hiroyuki Agawa, *The Reluctant Admiral* (Tokyo: Kodansha International, 1979), p. 66.

[18]Crihfield, ''The Institution of the Geisha in Modern Japanese Society,'' p. 120.

good business head. Geisha have to be able to size up men as clients and figure out how best to tie them into becoming regular customers. They also need to be able to judge whether or not a man has money or is just being wildly extravagant.[19] The wrong choice of one patron or another — if others are thus excluded — could lead to a decline into poverty. Many romantic stories in Japanese folklore tell of a geisha sacrificing all for the love of a young, impoverished student. Others saved their money and viewed the role of a geisha primarily as an economic opportunity.

Whatever theory may be developed about them, the geisha role for women established in the Tokugawa period exists today in Japan. The primary role of today's geisha is to entertain at very expensive parties given for men. Their former role of entertaining specific clients at teahouses has been replaced by the bar hostesses of modern Japan. Because the geisha are now so expensive to have at parties, only men with business expense accounts or great wealth can afford to hire them as entertainers. Nevertheless, the tradition of the geisha exists, with its rigorous training, accepted set of codes, and separate entertainment world which places women and men together outside the main culture. A woman from the United States, Liza Crihfield, trained as a geisha as a way of conducting scholarly research of their lives. She grew to have great admiration for the talents and training of the women currently living as geisha. One of her final comments after conducting her study was, "Everyone's life is rocked from time to time by the waves of fortune, but the geisha live in rougher waters than most."[20] Looking back at the four theories about geisha, it would seem that all four would agree with this statement.

Points to Consider

1. Why were the wealthy merchants of Edo not allowed to display their wealth in Tokugawa times? How did they come by their riches? Where did they find an outlet where they were allowed to enjoy their wealth?

2. As a group, geisha have frequently been observed, studied, and written about. They form a institution unique to Japanese culture. In what specific ways have they been outside the mainstream of accepted Japanese culture in their:

   • family life.

   • female/male socializing.

   • female conduct.

3. Briefly list the four basic views historians and other observers have had of the role and condition of geisha:

---

[19]Fujimoto, *The Story of The Geisha Girl*, p. 93.

[20]Dalby, *Geisha*, p. 312.

In what ways are these views different? Where do they overlap? How might you account for the differences in views?

4. What seems to have been the bleakest fate for young girls sold to "brokers?" What reasons did families give for selling their daughters? Why do you think daughters usually were sold and not sons?

5. What evidence is there that geisha did not necessarily suffer under the stigma of having "bad reputations?" How might they achieve some fame?

6. Why do you think Liza Crihfield, who trained as a geisha, claimed that "the geisha live in rougher waters than most [other people]"?

D.   Early Contacts With the West

During the century before the Tokugawa era, the Japanese first came in contact with people from Europe through dealings with Portuguese traders. Silk and porcelain, available in Japan, had become highly prized in Europe. The Japanese leader Oda Nobunaga wished to "bring Japan under one sword," using the guns brought for trade by the foreigners.[1] The Portuguese not only brought guns but also Christianity to Japan. Francis Xavier, a founder of the Roman Catholic Society of Jesus (Jesuits), with two other priests, landed at Kagoshima in southern Kyūshū in 1549. They soon had converted 150 people to Christianity. In the early years, they convinced many to become Christians. Their rapid progress in converting Japanese to Christianity may have been partly due to the language barrier, as some Japanese seemed to have thought that they were preaching a form of Buddhism, with the gentle Virgin Mary having a religious role similar to that of the female god of mercy, Kannon.[2]

The various local rulers in Japan came to have mixed emotions about Christianity — at times encouraging conversions and other times ordering missionaries to leave the feudal

---

[1]Quoted in Bradley Smith, *Japan — A History in Art* (Garden City, NY: Doubleday & Company, Inc., 1964), p. 156.

[2]George B. Sansom, *Japan, A Short Cultural History* (New York: Appleton Century Crofts, Inc., 1962), p. 415.

Kannon female god of mercy. This statue of her at Sanjusangen-do temple, Kyōtō is a famous one. Richard Cocks visited the temple in 1616 and commented in his diary on this extraordinary "Thousand-Armed" statue of Kannon.

territories of the Japanese rulers. The foreigners brought wealth and guns through trade, but the missionaries turned out to be intolerant of Buddhism and even preached that long-dead Japanese ancestors would burn in hell because they had died unconverted. As Japanese became better acquainted with Christianity, they noted that Christian doctrines often contradicted those of Buddhism and Confucianism about the proper roles of the lower classes, and particularly, of women.

The Roman Catholic Church, which sought Christian converts in Japan, was organized as a male hierarchy which ranked church leaders from the pope down to the local priest. But the Christian religion included beliefs that all souls female and male — might achieve salvation and were equal in the eyes of God. The Catholic Church

stressed the importance of the Virgin Mary as the female image of the loving mother with the power to intercede for sinners. These doctrines might appeal to women because they could not achieve nirvana as *women* according to Buddhist ideas of the time, and because women ranked low on the Confucian hierarchy. By 1582 the Jesuits reported 150,000 converts.[3] Although not a huge number, considering the size of the Japanese population, it did represent a challenge to the feudal system of the shōgunate. That system insisted on a strict Confucian ranking of people according to their importance. Christianity insisted that individuals were equal in the sight of God and that their loyalty should be given to God, not to the daimyō or lord. Roman Catholicism was a foreign religion that looked to the authority of the pope in Rome for direction instead of to the local ruler. This new religion disapproved of the Japanese custom of taking concubines and challenged late medieval Japanese ideas about the inferiority of women. In consolidating their power during the 17th century, the Tokugawa leaders insisted that they be the supreme authority in Japan. They saw the ranking of women as inferiors to be an important element in their system of control over the feudal lords who might challenge their authority. The doctrines of Christianity were a direct threat to their imposed system.

[3]*Ibid.*, p. 417.

As a result when the Tokugawa shōgun, Ieyasu, came to power in 1603, he renewed earlier anti-Christian policies. This eventually eliminated the Japanese Christians except for a few who practiced their religion in secrecy.[4] In 1623 there began a period of persecution called the "Great Martyrdom" by the Roman Catholic Church. Dutch Protestants who had also come to trade in Japan, had sowed seeds of distrust against the Jesuits and other Catholic missionaries, which added to the growing suspicions of the Japanese. Probably only a few thousand Christians lost their lives during the persecutions, but men, women, and children were included in this number. An English trader, Richard Cocks, who, as a Protestant, was unsympathetic to these Roman Catholic converts, nevertheless was moved by executions he witnessed in 1623:

"I saw fifty-five of them martyred at one time at Miyako. Among them were little children of five or six years, burned alive in the arms of their mothers, who cried, 'Jesus, receive their souls!' There are many in prison who hourly await death, for very few return to their idolatry." [5]

Being a woman was not an excuse to escape martyrdom. One noted Christian woman who died for her religion was Hosokawa Gracia Tamako who "remained in her flaming home rather than be captured and forced to betray her Catholic religion." [6] Another Christian woman, Hashimoto Tenkuru, was burned to death along with her husband and five children. According to a Japanese Christian writer:

"'the martyrs were seen all looking up to the sky, showing no sign of pain at all on their faces, just as though they had been gazing on the blessed sight of an angel visiting our terrestrial world, bringing with him the heavenly prize.' It is also written: 'Though the mother clucked softly to soothe the crying little ones, patting them on their heads, the older children calmly and bravely faced their death, even with smiling looks, much to the wonder and admiration of all the spectators.'" [7]

After the persecutions, the Christian religion was outlawed and the Portuguese forced to leave Japan. However, some Dutch traders were allowed to remain. Since the Dutch were Protestants who did not believe in what they called the "idols" held in reverence by Catholics, they were willing to stamp on the crucifix or on pictures of the Virgin Mary to show they were not believers like the earlier missionaries. The Tokugawa government allowed the Dutch to set up a small trading center at Nagasaki, but the Dutch were almost imprisoned

---

[4]*Ibid.*, p. 449.

[5]George Sansom, *A History of Japan 1615-1867* (Stanford: Stanford University Press, 1963), p. 41.

[6]Quoted in, Dorothy Robins-Mowry, *The Hidden Sun: Women of Modern Japan* (Boulder, Colorado: Westview Press, 1983), p. 22.

[7]Quoted in, Mary Beard, *The Force of Women in Japanese History* (Washington, DC: Public Affairs Press, 1953), p. 93.

121

A family portrait of the Blomhoff family from 1817 includes a Javanese servant at the right.

there.[8] The Dutch traders were permitted to mix only with lower-class Japanese women, and Dutch women were refused entry. When a Dutch trader, Jan Blomhoff, brought his wife and child to Nagasaki in 1817 — two hundred years after Christianity was outlawed — the Japanese government allowed them to land, but then refused their petition to settle. Unless shipwrecked, no foreign woman entered Japan during the long Tokugawa period.[9] The family was separated, and Mrs. Blomhoff and child went back to Holland. Whether the Tokugawa government wanted to keep down the number of foreigners in Japan or particularly wished to exclude foreign women is unclear. With their views about how women might lead men astray, and with fears that Christians might undermine their regime, the Tokugawa leaders may have seen the presence of Mrs.

Blomhoff as a potentially dangerous one.

When Japan was opened to foreigners in the 19th century and Christian missionaries returned, one of their major accomplishments was the girls' schools they founded. Western influences, as the Tokugawa understood, might challenge some of their own views of women — to be kept out of Japan as long as possible.

---

[8]Sansom, *Japan, A Short Cultural History,* p. 451.

[9]*Manners and Customs of the Japanese* (London: John Murray, 1841), p. 16-19. (Anonymous)

122

Points to Consider

1. What did the Japanese want from Portuguese (and later Dutch) traders? What did Europeans want from the Japanese?

2. Why do you think local rulers in Japan came to have mixed emotions about Christianity?

3. From this selection, why does it seem that some Japanese converted to Christianity? Why do you think women may have been particularly attracted to the Christian religion?

4. For what specific reasons was Christianity seen as a threat by the Tokugawa government?

5. Who were Hosokawa Gracia Tamako and Hashimoto Tenkuru? Why do you think comparatively few Japanese converted to Christianity? Why might some have stuck with their new faith even when faced with death?

6. It is unclear whether Mrs. Blomhoff was sent home because the Japanese wished to exclude foreign women or just wanted to severely limit the number of foreigners of their sex. Why do you think they might have wished to exclude *all* European women?

CHAPTER 6

JAPANESE WOMEN AND THE WESTERN WORLD

A.   Western Travelers' Views

Portuguese sailors and missionaries journeyed to Japan in the 1500's for trade — and to bring the Christian religion to the Japanese. The Dutch arrived somewhat later and were allowed to stay in very limited numbers after other Europeans were expelled in 1638. For 265 years the Tokugawa governments severely limited all Japanese contacts with the West — Europe and the United States. Whaling ships from the United States that sailed near Japan were attacked, and shipwrecked crews seeking aid were imprisoned and often executed by the anti-foreign Japanese government. Great Britain, Russia, and the United States all tried unsuccessfully to make treaties with the Tokugawa shōgun.

By the middle of the 19th century it was becoming obvious that the old Tokugawa military system was no longer able to keep out Western ships. In 1853 an American fleet of four ships under Commodore Matthew C. Perry anchored in the Japanese harbor of Uraga. After sending a letter asking for changes in Japanese isolationist policy to the shōgun, Perry departed but returned and negotiated a treaty with the Japanese the following year. Other Western countries followed the United States example making treaties and sending ambassadors, traders, and visitors to Japan. These Western travelers brought with them a curiosity about Japanese customs fed by the two and one-half centuries of isolation. Much misinformation about Japan had circulated in the West. Maps showed an exotic country of one-eyed monsters or dwarfs and, in one case, a nation of female Amazons.[1] Many 19th century travelers, then, made comments and wrote down their observations about Japan, particularly, Japanese women.

In observing Japanese women, most of these Western travelers came to realize that there were clear distinctions in Japanese culture between the way of life for upper-class and lower-class Japanese women. The early visitors to Japan saw very few upper-class women. These women lived secluded lives and were expected to stay within the walled inner courts of their homes. The Americans and Europeans were used to women taking part in social gatherings and found Japanese all-male banquets rather dull. The secretary of the United States Legation in Japan in 1857 commented on the absence of women:

"This absence of man's angel of mercy gives a sort of emptiness, a certain sadness to the Governors' dinner. Had some noble Japanese matron been hostess at the table, had we been able to dance a polka with the Governors' daughters, what a good time we would have had." [2]

Sometimes negotiators might hear women's whispers behind screens and know that these secluded women were curious about the "barbarians," as Westerners were called. But, as one American sailor described Perry's first visit, "You are followed every where by Japanese Police who follow you and keep all the Women Shut up and their houses closed." [3]

Although upper-class women were

usually hidden from Western male visitors, lower-class women went about their work in public and could be observed. One striking feature of 19th century travel accounts is the descriptions of the numerous occupations filled by Japanese women and how hard they worked. One of the officers with Perry's expedition wrote of the working women he saw:

"We walked over to [the town of] Shimoda, situated in the bight [bay] of the harbor; on the way I saw a woman carrying a bundle that would have been weight enough to founder a man and a boy — I saw a woman carrying water enough for twenty men and twenty boys: I saw a woman splitting wood as hard as flint, that would have been enough to bake a dozen men and a dozen boys. I saw a woman pounding rice with a big mallet, that would have broken the heart of twenty men and any number of boys. I saw a woman smoke pipes enough to stupefy four men and many boys, in fine I have not paper enough to tell what the women I saw were doing." [4]

---

[1]Bradley Smith, *Japan — A History In Art* (Garden City, NJ: Doubleday & Company, 1964), p. 224.

[2]Henry Heusken, *Japan Journal 1855-1861* (New Brunswick, NJ: Rutgers University Press, 1964), p. 92.

[3]Henry F. Graff, *Bluejackets with Perry in Japan* (New York: The New York Public Library, 1952), p. 160.

[4]Allan B. Cole, ed., *With Perry in Japan: The Diary of Edward Yorke McCauley* (Princeton, NJ: Princeton University Press, 1942), p. 105-106.

Pickle sellers, c. 1890

Later visitors would find similarly tough working women. One described the "pathetic sights" of women tea workers trudging home at sunset after a long day's labor, with their babies on their backs.[5]

Some European males, perhaps forgetting the plight of English women who worked in coal mines and factories, became indignant at what they saw as unchivalrous attitudes of Japanese males toward these women laborers:

"Often, as I returned toward the sea-beach, I was met by groups of fishermen, with their wives and children — the wife suckling her baby and carrying the fish; the father loaded only with some light fishing-tackle." [6]

Western travelers witnessed the usual household duties carried out by women such as cooking, carrying water, getting firewood, cleaning,

---

[5]Eliza Ruhamah Scidmore, *Jinrikisha Days in Japan* (New York: Harper & Brothers, 1891), p. 356.

[6]Rutherford Alcock, *The Capital of The Tycoon* (New York: Harper & Brothers, 1877), p. 393.

Women picking tea leaves — c. 1900.

caring for children, nursing the sick, and sewing. Besides these more expected household chores, Japanese women were seen working as:

- tea pickers
- silk worm caretakers
- spinners of silk
- teachers in small elementary schools
- innkeepers
- seaweed gatherers
- traveling musicians
- farmers working in rice fields
- threshers of rice
- shop saleswomen
- fisherwomen
- servants in hotels
- nursemaids
- miners
- caretakers of Shintō temples
- Buddhist nuns
- geisha entertainers

Another occupation described was, "grimy women and young girls carrying baskets of coal swung on poles across their shoulders, [shuffling] along between the moored junks in the water and the coaling-sheds."[7] This long list of occupations held by Japanese women before industrialization suggests, perhaps, why Japanese women were used so extensively in industry at a later period. There already was a long tradition of hard-working women in Japan.

Despite the fact that they worked hard, travelers also noted that the lower-class women actually seemed happier than those of the upper class. Once European and American women began coming to Japan, they became acquainted with both classes. Unlike foreign men, they were allowed to meet upper-class, secluded women and, because they were allowed to move about in public, they also observed women from the lower classes. These female visitors began to make comparisons between groups of Japanese women. An American woman wrote:

"My impression is, that, according to our notions, the Japanese wife is happier in the poorer than in the richer classes. She works hard, but it is rather as the partner than the drudge of her husband. Nor, in the same class, are the unmarried girls secluded, but, within certain limits, they possess complete freedom." [8]

A Dutch doctor noted that he saw more of what seemed to be real love marriages among the lower classes than among the upper classes where women struggled with a "great sense of duty" since "no love remained."[9] Travelers also saw lower-class women as more likely to tease, laugh, drink, and, to the horror of some Westerners, make sexual jokes and be unabashed by nudity.[10]

In contrast to the freedom of lower-class women, the condition of most upper-class women was seen as dull and restricted. As one author put it, "the higher the rank of the family into which she entered by marriage, the more difficult would be her position."[11] Travelers generally found upper-class women in arranged marriages in which they were restricted to their households and lived lives of obedience to their husbands' wishes.

"Japanese women are most womanly, — kind, gentle, faithful, pretty. But the way in which they are treated by the men has hitherto been such as might cause a pang to any generous European heart. No wonder that some of them are at last endeavoring to emancipate themselves. A woman's lot is summed up in what are termed 'the three obediences,' — obedience, while yet unmarried, to a father; obedience, when married, to a husband and that husband's parents; obedience, when widowed,

---

[7]Pat Barr, *The Deer Cry Pavilion* (London: Macmillan and Co., 1968), p. 187.

[8]Isabella L. Bird, *Unbeaten Tracks in Japan* (New York: G. P. Putnam's Sons, 1889), p. 304.

[9]J.L.C. Pampe Van Meedervoort, *Doctor in Desima* (Tokyo: Sophia University, 1970) (1867), p. 48.

[10]Cole, *With Perry in Japan*, p. 108.

[11]Lafcadio Hearn, *Japan: An Attempt at Interpretation* (New York: The Macmillan Company, 1904), p. 84.

to a son. At the present moment, the greatest lady in the land may have to be her husband's drudge, to fetch and carry for him, to bow down humbly in the hall when my lord sallies forth on his walks abroad, to wait upon him at meals, to be divorced almost at his good pleasure. 'Society,' in our sense of the word, scarcely exists ... Probably such acts of courtesy do not extend to the home, where there is no one by to see; for most Japanese men, even in this very year of grace 1904, make no secret of their disdain for the female sex." [12]

Western women also agreed that upper-class Japanese women were graceful, self-controlled, and impressive. One woman, visiting a princess of the royal family, felt an earthquake:

"While I was sitting with Princess Komatsu we were favored with a shock of earthquake. This was a rather alarming occurrence, as earlier in the morning we had been treated to a very sharp shock. The Princess, however, showed the greatest composure and dignity, never moving from her seat. I felt, therefore, with this splendid example before me of courage and sangfroid *[icy nerves], the least I could do was to act likewise, but nevertheless my feelings on this occasion, glued as I was to my chair, are more easily imagined than expressed!"* [13]

Some European women felt that many upper-class Japanese women were rather poorly educated and had limited world views. They admired, however, the moral strength and gracious

manners of these Japanese women:

"Manners! If they were — as in a measure they may be — the passport to heaven, the Japanese women would certainly have reserved places, and many a 'smart' European would have to take a back seat. Kindness and modesty, a wakeful, real consideration for the feelings of others — surely these make up for a little unwilling ignorance of the higher subjects which most interest us." [14]

Despite the respect Americans and Europeans had for upper-class Japanese women, it was a respect often tinged with sadness. In Japan, travelers did not see customs such as Chinese foot-binding or Middle Eastern veiling that severely restricted women's movements and clearly distinguished women's limits. Japanese traditions, as one author put it, seemed to treat women with more respect and allow them better educations than any other country in Asia.[15] Yet, as he admitted, these

---

[12]Basil Hall Chamberlain, *Things Japanese* (London: John Murray, 1905), p. 500.

[13]Baroness Albert d'Anethan, *Fourteen Years of Diplomatic Life in Japan* (London: Stanley Paul & Co., 1912), p. 294.

[14]Mary Crawford Fraser, *A Diplomat's Wife in Japan* (New York: John Weatherhill, Inc., 1982), p. 99.

[15]William Elliot Griffis, *The Mikado's Empire* (New York: Harper & Brothers, 1876), p. 551-552.

privileges were still a "gray light" compared to the equality of a "far-off full day." [16]

One American woman was particularly struck by how bright and attractive young Japanese women were, but then found that:

"Just at the time when her mind broadens, and the desire for knowledge and self-improvement develops, the restraints and checks upon her become more severe. Her sphere seems to grow narrower, difficulties one by one increase, and the young girl, who sees life before her as something broad and expansive, who looks to the future with expectant joy, becomes, in a few years, the weary, disheartened woman." [17]

Whether or not the picture that Westerners got of Japanese women's lives was accurate may be questioned. They were viewing — and judging — Japanese women's lives as outsiders coming from different value systems and cultures. In the accounts that they wrote about lower and upper-class women, travelers were generally impressed with the hard-working and dutiful Japanese women they had seen and met.

Fisherwoman collected driftwood for fuel — c. 1900.

Group or Individual Exercises

Read the following and then answer the problems that follow, in small groups or as individuals.

3. "The Victorian Period" describes the historical time of 19th century

Points to Consider

1. What specific differences did travelers observe between the lives of upper-class and lower-class women?

2. Which class seemed to have more freedom? Why do you think that this was the case?

[16]*Ibid.*, p. 552.

[17]Alice Mabel Bacon, *Japanese Girls and Women* (Boston, Houghton, Mifflin and Company, 1892), p. 36.

133

England whose values became accepted in France, the United States, and other Western countries. Queen Victoria reigned from 1837 until 1901 and she set the tone for this time period. Values and conditions that applied to women during Victorian times included these:

- Women were to uphold (and be judged by) four primary virtues: piety, purity, submissiveness, and domesticity.[18]

- Men were in charge of the public world — women the private world of the home.

- Men were to get ahead and make money by hard work in the public world of commerce and business. Women ideally were to lead lives of leisure, as this showed off their husbands' ability to support them. Servants were to do the housework.

- Legally, upon marriage a man and woman became one person — and he (the husband) was the person. The wife was under the protection and supervision of her husband. She had no legal rights to property or to the custody of her own children. She was expected to focus her attention on pleasing her husband.

- One English woman, commenting on education for women, wrote in 1866 that as "girls [after marriage] are to dwell in quiet homes, . . . to be submissive and retiring," their educations should be restricted, as "any strain upon a girl's intellect is to be dreaded, and any attempt to bring women into competition with men can scarcely escape failure." [19]

- During the 19th century some property laws slowly changed and reform movements for women's education and suffrage were developing in the United States, England, and other European countries. Both women and men were active in these movements for reform. However, the ideal of the pious, submissive, and dependent woman who focused her attention on husband and home continued into the 20th century.

A. On one side of a divided piece of paper list specific *similarities* between this ideal for Western, Victorian women and those for upper-class Japanese women. On the other side list *differences* between the two ideals.

B. Write down things you notice about your lists of

---

[18]See, Barbara Welter, "The Cult of True Womanhood: 1820-1860," *American Quarterly*, Vol. 18 (Summer 1966), p. 151-166.

[19]Quoted in, *Victorian Women*, Erna Olafson Hellerstein, Leslie Parker Hume, and Karen M. Offen, eds. (Stanford: Stanford University Press, 1981), p. 69-70.

similarities and differences on the bottom or back of the sheet of paper.

C. Why do you think Europeans and Americans observed and commented on restrictions on the freedoms of Japanese upper-class women while not seeing restrictions on women in their own cultures? What groups of women might have had more freedom in Western cultures? Why?

4. Madame Butterfly, an opera by Giacomo Puccini, was first presented in 1905. After a failed first performance, it quickly became popular and is still frequently performed. The story of Madam Butterfly is based on a novel written in 1888 by Pierre Loti, a Frenchman who had traveled to Japan as a naval officer.[20] Both the novel and the opera appealed to the European and American interest in then recently opened Japan. The romantic story has also continued to have wide appeal.

Here is a brief summary of the plot:

A handsome but unscrupulous American naval officer named Pinkerton arranges through a go-between to marry the beautiful, innocent and childlike geisha, Butterfly. Pinkerton has no intention of making Butterfly his permanent wife, but, at first, their marriage is one of mutual passion. Pinkerton leaves Japan.

Butterfly gives birth to their son and awaits Pinkerton's return with complete faith. Three years pass, and Butterfly sinks into poverty but continues to look for Pinkerton on each American ship. Finally he arrives bringing his American wife. When this situation is finally made clear to the faithful Butterfly, she decides to give up her son to Pinkerton's new wife and then commits suicide with her father's dagger.

One tradition for Japanese women has been a set of values sometimes called the "Madame Butterfly" tradition. These have included ideals for women such as:

- a willingness to suffer in silence.

- a complete devotion and faith toward their husbands.

- quietly accepting personal insult.

- continuing to love the man involved even when wronged and abandoned.

Considering what you know thus far of conditions for Japanese women, why do you think a long-suffering woman is a seemingly common type?

_____

[20]Puccini probably based his opera on the play Madame Butterfly by American author John Lather Longs, which was based on Pierre Loti's novel.

Do you think there is a similar
type of woman in Western
cultures? Until 1880 it was legal
for a Japanese man to take
concubines as additional wives.
How might this have been a factor
that led to the Butterfly tradition
being more common in Japanese
history than in the West?

B. An Exercise on Points of View

When the culture of the Western world met that of Japan the customs that each assumed were correct and appropriate were often seen as shocking to the other culture. The following are lists of brief descriptions of Japanese and Western customs from the late 19th century.

In groups of four to six students, read over the list of customs. Assign a recorder.

- For each of the categories, decide which view of each custom seems to make the most sense to your group.

- Give a short explanation of why your group selected the particular custom as the reasonable one.

In some cases you may decide that *neither* custom is particularly reasonable. In that case suggest an alternative.

After making your group decisions, compare your answers and explanations with the other groups in a class discussion. (A bibliography of the sources used follows the exercise.)

Comparisons of two cultures from the late 19th century

JAPANESE CULTURE	WESTERN CULTURE

I. Appearance and Concepts of Beauty

1. Teeth were to be blackened when a woman was married. White teeth were thought to be ugly.[1]

1. Teeth were left unadorned.

2. If a woman was married, eyebrows should be shaved off or, if she was not yet married, they were to be bushy like a "caterpillar."

2. Eyebrows were plucked to shape around the eyes — often rather thin.

3. White powder should be used to make a woman's face very *white* — an American woman was asked if she painted hers white.[2]

3. Powder was used and the face was protected from becoming tan, except for slight rouge to give rosy cheeks.

4. Thick obi, or waistband, was worn around the waist and tied tightly.

4. Corset was worn, tied tightly, to make a small waist.

5. Kimono were worn. The back of a woman's neck was considered the "intriguing spot."

5. High-collared dresses were worn, except for evening gowns which were cut low to show off the bosom. Some Japanese males thought this was indecent.[3]

6. Elaborate hairdos were worn by upper-class women, but no hats were used.

6. Bonnets were always worn outdoors (one woman was asked if she slept in it.)[4]

II. Social Life

1. Only male guests attended banquets. Sometimes geisha were present as hostesses.

1. Dinners and balls were attended by both men and women. Japanese visitors were astonished at "the curious spectacle of ladies and gentlemen dancing."[5]

2. Men were expected to walk in front of their wives, eat first, and have their needs taken care of first. Women knelt before men when serving them.

2. Men were expected to be chivalrous, stand when women came into a room, and care for them. One Western visitor found it disgusting to have women kneel before him.[6]

3. A Japanese mother described kissing, with disgust, to her daughter: "it is the custom for foreign people to lick each other like dogs do."[7]

3. Kissing was an important way to show mutual affection.

4. Public baths were common with separate areas for men and women. Bathing was an important Japanese ritual, and there was no false modesty.

4. Modesty was highly emphasized — showing a woman's ankle was considered immodest. Baths were private and, even for the sea, women were completely covered. A British woman was asked by a Japanese why she dressed up to go swimming.[8]

5. The oldest males of the household entertained visitors.

5. The wife of the host took the lead in entertaining visitors. Japanese visitors to the United States were especially dismayed when bachelor President Buchanan's young niece acted as his official White House hostess.[9]

6. Japanese women were expected to be quiet when with strangers. One visitor said they were like a "sphinx."[10]

6. In Western culture women were expected to be gracious, witty, and to move conversation along.

III. Political Life

1. Japanese women were excluded from politics. They could not vote and generally concentrated their energies on their households.

2. Women leaders had been excluded from politics since medieval times. The empress was revered and had important ceremonial roles.

3. There was no movement for women's voting rights in late 19th century Japan. There were reformers interested in women's issues.

1. Women in Western societies could not vote, but they were expected to be involved in charitable community activities.

2. Women politicians were excluded, but Britain was ruled by a queen, Victoria. (Japanese men burst out laughing when British officers told them they were led by a queen).[11]

3. Some states in the United States had given women the right to vote by the late 19th century; the suffrage movement was not yet a large scale popular cause.

[1] Rutherford Alcock, *The Capital of The Tycoon* (New York: Harper & Brothers, 1877), p. 90.

[2] Clara A. N. Whitney, *Clara's Diary* (Tokyo: Kodansha International Ltd., 1979), p. 35.

[3] Alice Mabel Bacon, *Japanese Girls and Women* (Boston: Houghton Mifflin and Company, 1892), p. 259.

[4] C. Pemberton Hodgson, *A Residence at Nagasaki and Hakodate* (London: Richard Bentley, 1861), p. 214.

[5] Carmen Blacker, *The Japanese Enlightenment* (Cambridge: Cambridge University Press, 1964), p. 6.

[6] Henry Heusken, *Japan Journal 1855-1861* (New Brunswick, NJ: Rutgers University Press, 1964), p. 135.

[7] Etsu Inagaki Sugimoto, *A Daughter of the Samurai* (Garden City, NY: Doubleday, 1927), p. 193.

[8] Marie C. Stopes, *A Journal from Japan* (London: Blackie & Son, 1910), p. 193.

[9] Sharon L. Sievers, *Flowers in Salt* (Stanford: Stanford University Press, 1983), p. 1-2.

[10] Mrs. Hugh Fraser, *Letters From Japan*, Vol. I (New York: Macmillan, 1899), p. 198.

[11] R. Mounteney Jephson and Edward Pennell Elmhirst, *Our Life in Japan* (London: Chapman and Hall, 1869), p. 74.

Bibliography

Alcock, Sir Rutherford. *The Capital of the Tycoon*. N.Y.: Harper & Brothers, 1877.

Bacon, Alice Mabel. *A Japanese Interior*. Boston: Houghton Mifflin & Co., 1900.

Bacon, Alice Mabel. *Japanese Girls and Women*. Boston: Houghton Mifflin & Co., 1892.

Bird, Isabella L. *Unbeaten Tracks in Japan*. N.Y.: G. P. Putnam's Sons, n.d.

Blacker, Carmen. *The Japanese Enlightenment*. Cambridge: Cambridge University Press, 1964.

Dixon, William Gray. *The Land of the Morning*. Edinburgh: James Gemmell, 1882.

Fraser, Mrs. Hugh. *Letters from Japan*. N.Y.: The Macmillan Company, 1899.

Fraser, Mary Crawford. *A Diplomat's Wife in Japan*, Hugh Cortazzi, ed. N.Y.: Weatherhill, 1982 (Abridged version).

Heusken, Henry. *Japan Journal 1855-1861*. New Brunswick: Rutgers University Press, 1964.

Hodgson, C. Pemberton. *A Residence at Nagasaki and Hakodate*. London: Richard Bentley, 1861.

Jephson, R. Mounteney and Edward Pennell Elmhirst. *Our Life in Japan*. London: Chapman and Hall, 1869.

Sievers, Sharon L. *Flowers in Salt*. Stanford: Stanford University Press, 1983.

Stopes, Marie C. *A Journal from Japan*. London: Blackie & Son, 1910.

Sugimoto, Etsu Inagaki. *A Daughter of the Samurai*. Garden City, NY: Doubleday, 1927.

Whitney, Clara A. N. *Clara's Diary: An American Girl in Meiji Japan*. Tokyo: Kodansha International, 1979.

C. Rokumeikan—The Deer Cry Pavilion

By the mid-19th century it had become obvious to Japanese leaders that the Western societies of Europe and the United States had superiority in technology and industrial manufacturing. Japan began a process of rapid industrialization spurred on by the progressive Meiji Emperor who came to power in 1868. The Japanese feared the fate of China which had been cut up into spheres of influence, each controlled by a European power. The Japanese leaders realized that Western societies judged other areas according to their own ideas of what they considered "civilized." The Japanese government encouraged the view that Japan could absorb and make use of Western customs, science, and technology. Male government officials discarded Japanese dress and wore the long

trousers and high collars expected in diplomatic circles of the 19th century. For a brief period, upper-class Japanese women were also expected to become Westernized. It was not a long time period, but it had some lasting results for Japanese women.

This period — roughly the decade of the 1880's — has been called the Rokumeikan Era. The name was taken from a Victorian style building in Tōkyō in which dances, dinners, and Western style entertainments were held. In English the name is translated as the "Deer Cry Pavilion." The pavilion was built in 1883, and, four years later, in 1887, a costume ball was held there that scandalized conservative Japanese. At the ball, Japanese social leaders wore, in European style, fancy dress or costumes and, even more shocking to conservatives, men and women danced together. Shortly after

141

Japanese woman in Western dress c. 1880.

*velvet and bugles [glass beads]
which would persist in tumbling
backwards, though sternly tied under
the chin, and a wrinkled European
gown . . . When she got up a spasm
of pain crossed her face at the
torture of high-heeled narrow shoes
. . . [and] her gloves, poor dear, were
at least three sizes too large."* [2]

Some American women traveling in
Japan were interested in the dress
reform movement in the United States
which advocated more practical and
comfortable clothing for women. They
tried to warn Japanese women of the
health problems created by the tight
Western style corsets and the lack of
mobility caused by long, heavy skirts.[3]
Other European women thought the
Japanese switch to Western clothes
an artistic mistake. The wife of a
foreign ambassador wrote in her diary,

*"I sat just behind pretty Princess
Kan-in; and near by was an old lady
with an interesting and expressive
face, who I was told was Madame
Atsuko, the poetess and friend of
the Empress. She was dressed in a
lovely kimono and brocaded obi.
This gathering of people was by far
the most Japanese thing we had yet
seen, and we could not but help*

the costume ball the Rokumeikan was
closed down. For this brief time,
upper-class women had been
expected to become like Westerners.[1]

One of the ways in which this was
supposed to happen was through the
adoption of European style clothes.
The Empress took the lead in dressing
in European clothes and did so in
elegant fashion. For other women, the
tight corsets, multiple undergarments,
heavy skirts, and low-necked evening
dress must have proven
uncomfortable and awkward. Since
Western clothing styles were
unfamiliar, ladies' bonnets were
sometimes placed at strange angles
that might appear a bit comical. Lewis
Wingfield, a Western diplomat,
described the result in a rather
patronizing manner:

"She had a fearsome bonnet of

[1]George B. Sansom, *The Western World and
Japan* (New York: Alfred A. Knopf, 1958),
p. 270-271.

[2]Quoted in, Pat Barr, *The Deer Cry Pavilion*
(London: Macmillan, 1968), p. 178-179.

[3]Basil Hall Chamberlain, *Things Japanese*
(London: John Murray, 1905), p. 126.

regretting more than ever, on admiring the beauty of the national costume ... the present fashion of wearing European clothes, which can never have the charm or artistic beauty of the Japanese ladies' own lovely garments. It was a picturesque sight, watching these dainty personages in their bright-colored and graceful raiment glistening in the sunlight, appearing like butterflies from the seclusion of groves of feathery bamboos." [4]

Even school girls changed their clothing style during this decade. Pictures of classes in one girls' school showed all the students wearing:

- 1882 — traditional kimono.

- 1890 — Western dress for graduation ceremonies.

- 1891 — traditional kimono for graduation.[5]

The girls at the school, like other Japanese women, had started "dressing up" in Western style clothes. Japanese women, however, were expected to change in other ways besides their dress. They were now expected to eat at Western style banquets with men. What seemed to them complex etiquette rules were to be followed. They had to learn to cut up food at the table (considered barbaric by traditional Japanese standards) and to use the proper fork for each of the many dinner courses. An American woman was impressed at how quickly the upper-class women became skilled at following the new rules:

"Japanese matrons, who, a few years ago, led the most quiet and

Young women attending teachers' college in Japan in 1886 wore western style uniform.

secluded existence, now preside with ease and grace over large establishments, built and maintained like the official residences of London or Berlin. Their struggles with the difficulties of a new language, dress, and etiquette were heroic. Mothers and daughters studied together with the same English governess, and princesses and diplomats' wives, returning from abroad, gave new

[4]Baroness Albert d'Anethan, *Fourteen Years of Diplomatic Life in Japan* (London: Stanley Paul & Co., 1912), p. 38.

[5]Tamie Kamiyama, "Ideology and Patterns in Women's Education in Japan," unpublished Ph.D. dissertation, St. Louis University, 1977, p. 83.

143

The Rokumeikan or Deer Cry Pavilion built in 1883 in Tokyo and used for Western style entertainments.

ideas to their friends at home." [6]

One result of the new mix of Japanese and Europeans was an increase in the number of intermarriages, with some of the leading male diplomats from both cultures marrying women from the other. These women, like the Japanese Lady Arnold and the British Baroness Sannomiya, often acted as social links between Westerners and Japanese that helped to tie new, international groups together.

These groups included organizations which encouraged new community activities for Japanese women. Among these were the creation of a chapter of the International Red Cross, for which the imperial family acted as sponsors. A "Monday Club" was sponsored by the British

ambassador's wife, Mary Crawford Fraser. After a paper was presented on Jane Austen by the Belgian ambassador's wife, Japanese women were invited to comment, and the Europeans found, "It is somewhat remarkable how very many appear, not only to have read, but to be well grounded in Jane Austen's works." [7] The International Temperance Society had a Japanese branch. A flag was embroidered for them by members of

---

[6]Eliza Ruhamah Scidmore, *Jinrikisha Days in Japan* (New York: Harper & Brothers, 1891), p. 132.

[7]d'Anethan, *Fourteen Years of Diplomatic Life in Japan*, p. 276.

An artist's sketch of the costume ball at the Rokumeikan pavilion in 1887 that scandalized conservative Japanese.

the imperial family.[8] Both Japanese and European women, as members of these international organizations, helped to arrange fund-raising bazaars for hospitals, orphanages and schools. Joint English and Japanese language classes were held. Women's education was encouraged by these groups. One sign of Westernization was when girls at the imperial school acted on *stage* — something utterly forbidden in traditional Kabuki and Nō theater where men dressed as women to take the female roles.

"The freedom that women seemed to obtain in the Rokumeikan period . . . disappeared very quickly. . . ."[9] For a variety of reasons, but centered on a feeling by the Japanese government that it did not have the respect of the European powers, the attitude of Japanese leaders changed. By 1900 the new approach was no longer to try *merging* with the West. Instead, the government emphasized *selecting*

from Western cultures things that seemed most necessary to make Japan a great world power. Western views of the proper roles for women were increasingly seen by Japanese leaders as an alien threat to Japanese society. Japanese men might still wear Western clothes, but women were to go back to wearing obi and kimono. Rokumeikan balls and banquets were no longer held.

Although women's clothing was again Japanese and traditional customs once more practiced, the women's organizations did not entirely fade away. The international links, particularly in women's education,

---

[8]Barr, *The Deer Cry Pavilion*, p. 259.

[9]Kamiyama, "Ideology and Patterns in Women's Education in Japan," p. 96.

145

temperance, and charitable reforms remained. The "Deer Cry Pavilion" had, perhaps, tried to move Japanese women too fast into artificial, foreign ways. The time of the Rokumeikan did, however, start trends which would surface again and again in Japanese life — and influence the future for Japanese women.

Points to Consider

1. In what specific ways did the adoption of Western ways for women in the Rokumeikan period seem to offer more freedoms or opportunities to Japanese women?

2. In what specific ways did the adoption of Western ways for women in the Rokumeikan period seem to offer less freedoms for women than traditional Japanese customs?

3. In 1979 the Shah of Iran was overthrown in the Iranian Revolution and replaced by the Ayatollah Khomeini. One of the first acts of the new Islamic Republic led by Khomeini was to reinstate the traditional woman's costume — the chador — and traditional customs that restricted women's freedoms such as their right to work outside the home. It has been said that one reason for the Shah's downfall was that he moved too fast to reform and Westernize roles for Iranian women. In Algeria after the revolution of the 1960's, women were again asked to wear veils and coverings, which they had discarded during the war with France.

This pattern of areas first imitating Western ways — and then drawing back to more traditional values — has become a common one. It does seem, however, that often the *drawing back* involves customs that affect *women* more than those that affect *men*.

Why do you think that it is sometimes seen as more important to keep traditional values and customs which involve women than those that involve men?

Do you see any signs of this drawing back in the United States to more traditional values for women of the 1980's? Explain your answer and give examples.

CHAPTER 7

WOMEN AND THE MEIJI RESTORATION — 1868-1912

A. Education for Women

The Meiji era takes its name from the Emperor whom reformers put into central power in 1868.[1] During the Tokugawa era the shōgun actually ruled Japan while the emperor became a mere figurehead. In the 19th century a group of reformers set about to create a new Japan. They hoped to modernize the Japanese political, economic, and education systems to allow Japan to stand up to the Western powers. They also hoped, however, to maintain traditional Japanese values and customs. As part of this modernization process, the possibility of introducing Western-style women's education was to be explored. Foreign advisers, like the American educator David Murray, as well as Japanese men who had been to the United States such as Kuroda Kiyotaka, encouraged Meiji reformers to include women in the new educational system being proposed.[2] One step toward advancing women's education was to send five very young Japanese girls to the United States with an official Japanese government trade mission. These girls, ranging in age from eight to 15, were left in the United States as students.[3] What happened to these girls became symbolic of the Meiji mixed view of women's education.

---

[1]For explanation of *Meiji*, see glossary.

[2]Sharon L. Sievers, *Flowers in Salt* (Stanford: Stanford University Press, 1983), p. 11-12.

[3]*Ibid.*, p. 12.

These five Japanese girls, ages eight to 15, photographed with their chaperone, were sent to study in the United States in 1871. Tsuda Umeko, the eight-year-old child in the center, graduated from Vassar and Bryn Mawr Colleges and later founded a women's college in Japan.

On November 10, 1871, five girls were presented to the Empress and given the charge of going to the United States to learn how women were educated there. The girls chosen were:

- Yoshimatsu Ryōko — 15 years
- Ueda Sadako — 15 years
- Yamakawa Sutematsu — 12 years
- Nagai Shigeko — 9 years
- Tsuda Umeko — 8 years

The Empress gave them instructions as they left:

"I congratulate your willingness to study abroad. Study hard in order to be able to become the models for Japanese women upon your return from the completion of your study abroad." [4]

Although it might seem that the youngest girls would have the hardest time adjusting to the United States, it was the two 15-year-olds who became sick after a year or so. The three other

[4]Quoted in, Tamie Kamiyama, "Ideology and Patterns in Women's Education in Japan," unpublished Ph.D. dissertation, St. Louis University, 1977, p. 54.

girls finished their educations and two graduated from Vassar College. These three girls fulfilled honorably the duty that had been given them by the Empress.[5]

When the young women returned to Japan ten years later, they found that the Japanese government had virtually forgotten them and their mission to bring Western ideas of women's education to Japanese women. During the decade that the girls had lived in the United States — between the early 1870's and the middle 1880's — some shifts had occurred in the way the Meiji reformers saw women's education. In the early 1870's, when the girls left for America, the major idea was to create a curriculum that would be roughly the same for girl and boy students, even when schools were segregated by sex.[6] Japanese schools (the terakoya) before the Meiji Restoration had educated some samurai and merchant daughters, but the emphasis had been on making them obedient wives and good housekeepers. In 1872 the government created the Tōkyō Girls' School which had a demanding curriculum including English, history, biology, and contemporary affairs.[7] After a brief five-year existence, that school was closed in 1877 — supposedly for financial reasons.

The Meiji period gave a double message to young Japanese women. More grammar schools were opened for girls and, in the early years, opportunities for higher education for women were encouraged. In 1872 the Japanese government declared in the Fundamental Code of Education,'' . . . in the future, there shall be no community with an illiterate family, nor

a family with an illiterate person.'' All should be educated,'' . . . every one— nobles, samurai, farmers, artisans, merchants, women and girls. . . .'' [8] The following chart suggests the change that occurred in attitudes towards women's education:

Enrollment of Students in Elementary Schools (percentages): 1875-1930

Year	Total	Girls	Boys
1875	35.8	18.6	50.5
1880	41.1	21.9	58.7
1885	49.6	32.1	65.8
1890	48.9	31.1	65.1
1895	61.2	43.9	65.1
1900	81.5	71.7	90.6
1905	95.6	93.3	97.7
1910	98.1	97.4	98.3
1920	99.0	98.8	99.2
1930	99.5	99.5	99.5

Source: Kaigo Tokiomi, *Japanese Education*: Its Past and Present (Tokyo: Kokusai Bunka Shinkokai, 1968), p. 65.[9]

There was some opposition to girls being educated, particularly because of the financial burden to the family caused by school fees and productive labor lost. There was, however, a gradual acceptance of the government's plan to have all Japanese people become literate.

---

[5]*Ibid.*, p. 54.

[6]Fujii Harue, ''Education for Women,'' *Japan Quarterly*, Vol. 24, No. 3 (July-September 1982), p. 301.

[7]Sievers, *Flowers in Salt*, p. 1.

[8]Quoted in, Kamiyama, ''Ideology and Patterns in Women's Education in Japan,'' p. 34.

[9]Elizabeth Knipe Mouer, ''Women in Teaching'' in, *Women in Changing Japan*, Joyce Lebra, Joy Paulson, and Elizabeth Powers, eds. (Stanford: Stanford University Press, 1976), p. 161.

The idea of literacy for women was accepted, but the notion of women being equally educated with men became a different question. The Japanese government, faced with the huge expenses of universal education, generally decided to fund only male education beyond the elementary school level. While secondary schools and universities were being created for male students in the 1870's, institutions like the Tōkyō Girls' School were briefly attempted — and then shut down. One school for girls of the nobility was the Peeresses' School, started by the Empress. Even with her backing, the Peeresses' School had to compete for limited funds with the comparable boys' school, the Peers' School. The following is an excerpt from a letter of an American teacher at the Peeresses' School during one of their financial conflicts:

"I do not think I have written you that a beautiful new brick building has been in process of construction for some time past, to be occupied, as soon as finished, by our school. It is quite near here, . . . and I have watched its growth all winter with great interest, as we thought how pleasant and comfortable the new building would seem after the ramshackle old one that we now occupy. It is all finished now, and workmen are engaged in laying out the grounds, and in taking up the trees and shrubs from our present school-yard to plant them in the new place; for here in Japan, when you move, you carry with you not only your furniture, but your garden as well, shade trees, turf, and all. For months the school authorities have been busy choosing carpets,
curtains, and furniture, and the plan was, after the examinations were over, for us to move into the new building for our graduating exercises. We were to have a fine time, and the Empress was to make us a speech in person. Such were our hopes and expectations, but at present they seem likely to suffer an untimely blight.

"There is another school beside our own under the management of the Imperial Household. It is a school for boys, corresponding in rank with that of our girls, and is called the Peers' School. Last fall it was moved into the buildings of the old Engineering College, and because they were so fine and large a new building was planned for us, that we might be equally well housed. Now, just as our new school-house is finished, the authorities of the boys' school discover that their accommodations are too large, and sent in a petition to the Imperial Household Department requesting to be removed to our new building. Of course when I heard of it I simply smiled at the audacity of such a demand, and inquired why they should trouble themselves to make so useless and ridiculous a request, but I am assured that this is no laughing matter, and that there is quite a strong probability that the request will be granted, especially as it is a question of girls' right against boys' wishes. I am fairly boiling over with wrath, but the worst of it is that there is nothing to do but boil, for our school authorities are as utterly powerless to do anything in the matter as they would be to avert a typhoon or an earthquake that

Classmates from the Peeresses school meet for a reunion — c. 1917.

threatened to destroy the building. They cannot even say anything, or write up their wrongs for the newspapers and get public sympathy on their side; they must just smile and submit, and thank the Peers for leaving them the old building instead of trying to grab that too." [10]

In this case the young women were protected by the intervention of the Empress behind the scenes, the influence of their upper-class families, and the threat of resignation by all the teachers. The girls got their school, which lasted until it was bombed in World War II.

Financial reasons were given for limiting educational opportunities for Japanese girls. Another reason given was a fear expressed that Western-style educations would make daughters more rebellious — and less marriageable. One of the schools for girls, Kōtō Jyo Gakko, where some American and European women taught, came under attack for threatening Japanese "morals" or traditional values. Alice Bacon, an American teaching at the Peeresses' School, described the attack on Kōtō Jyo Gakko:

"[There has been] an attack on one of the finest girls' schools in the city, an attack that has been so

[10]Alice Mabel Bacon, *A Japanese Interior* (Boston: Houghton, Mifflin and Company, 1900), p. 212-214.

successful that they say that there is not a single application for admission to the school this summer where there were hundreds last year at this time. The school is the Kōtō Jyo Gakko, where the Misses Prince teach, with whom I stayed when I first came to Tōkyō. The attack began in a low paper that makes its living by publishing lies of just the kind that were told about the school and its teachers. The stories once started, other low papers took them up, and added to them until they became big enough, and began to look enough like truth, for the more respectable papers to comment on them. Soon the scandal was in the mouths of all Tōkyō. When the school gates were opened in the morning, scurrilous placards were found posted upon them, and as the girls went to school they were insulted by school-boys and students on the street, and all this because of stories which had no foundation, except that one of the teachers had once delivered before the girls a rather foolish and ill-advised lecture on the choice of husbands, in which he had viewed marriage from the somewhat sentimental standpoint of Europe and America, instead of taking the purely business view of it common in Japan. The teacher has been turned off, and possibly the president of the school may be also, as a sacrifice to the public feeling that has been aroused about the matter, and to save the school itself from complete collapse. That this was intended for an attack not simply on the one school, but on female education in general." [11]

The attack on the girls' school for being too Western was part of the return to Japanese values that began in the 1880's. By 1890 an "Imperial Rescript on Education" was issued that limited the education taught. It emphasized a return to Confucian values such as children giving filial piety or absolute obedience to parents and elders. Moral training was of primary importance, and it declared that "in the teaching of girls, special stress must be laid on the virtues of chastity and modesty." [12] The moral training given girls was again to prepare them to be "good wives and wise mothers." The ideal woman was to devote herself to her family's welfare and be obedient to her husband's wishes; for example, it was all right, one official said, for women to learn foreign languages if it helped them as wives to read their husbands' book titles so they could dust them properly and put them on the shelves in order! [13]

Some young women, given a chance for an academic education, were not satisfied with the Japanese school system and curriculum planned for girls. Tsuda Umeko, one of the five girls to be sent to the United States, who attended the colleges of Vassar and Bryn Mawr, rebelled against an arranged marriage and fought to

---

[11]*Ibid.*, p. 221-222.

[12]Quoted in, Kamiyama, "Ideology and Patterns in Women's Education in Japan," p. 141.

[13]*Ibid.*, p. 111.

establish more rigorous educational opportunities for women. She founded a women's college and created a network of Japanese and American women to help support it. She contrasted what she saw as the "old training" for Japanese girls with the "real training":

"The Japanese girls are capable, have good minds, and some of them are very talented. But as the result of the old training they lack self-confidence and initiative and, above all, strength of will. Yet to encourage these, as some would do, without the development of mind and the reasoning powers, brings in elements of great danger. What is needed is a chance for the growth of the spiritual life, a real training of the understanding, moral teachings that fit the new conditions of life in modern Japan, and which will develop a realization of the possibilities that come with freedom — in a word, Christian education on higher lines." [14]

Families of young women who wished them to have a more varied and academic education often sent them to Christian schools. The contribution of these Christian mission schools to women's education in Japan, one historian has said, has been "great" both in the past and present.[15]

Many young women made considerable sacrifices to receive an education. One girl disguised herself as a boy to enter a Christian upper-level boys' school because it was the only way to go on with her schooling.[16] Another young woman was teased but remained the only girl in the class.[17]

One family enrolled a daughter in school under her mother's name so the family would not bear the shame of having a studious daughter.[18] Some of the first nurses in Japan risked being disowned by their families who thought this profession unsuitable for their samurai daughters.[19] Other women found they could find the education they wanted only by leaving Japan. Of the "pioneer women leaders" of the Meiji Restoration it has been found that fifty percent studied, traveled, or lived abroad.[20] Coming back, these women often found that they did not fit into the old patterns; that arranged marriages were uncomfortable, that their movements were seen as too Western and ungraceful, and that they felt confined being Japanese wives. As one observer wrote, "The first generation or two of educated women must

[14]Quoted in, Al Hoshino, "The Education of Women" in, Inazo Nitobe, *Western Influences in Modern Japan* (Chicago: The University of Chicago Press, 1931), p. 226.

[15]Kamiyama, "Ideology and Patterns in Women's Education in Japan," p. 76.

[16]*Ibid.*, p. 76.

[17]Hani Motoko, "Stories of My Life," in, *The Japan Interpreter*, Vol. 12, No. 3-4 (Summer 1979), p. 332.

[18]Mouer, "Women in Teaching," p. 162.

[19]Takie Sugiyama Lebra, *Japanese Women: Constraint and Fulfillment* (Honolulu: University of Hawaii Press, 1984), p. 60.

[20]Dorothy Robins-Mowry, *The Hidden Sun: Women of Modern Japan* (Boulder, CO: Westview Press, 1983), p. 49.

endure much for the sake of those who come after.'' [21]

For these young women seeking educations it was not only a matter of *enduring.* It was also a matter of *achieving*, as did Dr. Yoshioka, a Japanese woman doctor who founded the Tōkyō Women's Medical College. Hani Motoko, who later founded a magazine and a major progressive school, realized the problems of having an education before it became normal for girls, but also realized the benefits. For modern students, Hani Motoko's life at the Christian Meiji Women's School must seem to have been very regimented. Hani sacrificed much to work her way through the school but remembered it fondly:

"About one hundred students lived in the dormitory of Meiji Women's School. At seven in the evening, we would gather in the auditorium for a prayer service and stay on to study until nine o'clock. I worked on manuscripts during this period. Fairly well-read for my age, I could handle my job, but it was only through the sheer kindness of Mr. Iwamoto that I was given a job which could have been done easily by a regular employee. Now I find myself in a position similar to Mr. Iwamoto's, managing a school and a journal simultaneously, and appreciate more than ever the extra consideration extended to me when I needed it most.

"At the school I learned of the benefits for mind and body of a regimented daily routine. For a country girl like myself, it was not easy at first to get up early in the morning, to wash in a crowded washroom, and to eat and bathe expeditiously. I took up the challenge and reaped an unexpected dividend: stubborn headaches I had suffered throughout my First Women's Higher School days from constant, indiscriminate reading late into the night stopped. I was cured, moreover, of the bad habit of snacking ingrained as a child growing up in the countryside, where constant nibbling was a way of life . . .

"One of the dormitory supervisors, a Mrs. Kuroyanagi, was a widow who combined the graciousness of her native Kyōto with the high spirit worthy of a Tōkyōite. Her competent management and creative imagination contributed immensely to our health and enjoyment. The chief maid was a stocky authoritative woman; under her direction, rice for one hundred boarders was cooked to perfection three times daily. The term 'maid' has since been replaced by a more respectable word 'helper.' In our day, though, it did not occur to anyone to attach the honorific '-san' to our maids' names; yet we enjoyed a good rapport with them. They were kind and attentive, remembering which girls liked the crispy browned rice from the bottom of the pot or which disliked raw fish. (I was

---

[21]Alice Mabel Bacon, *Japanese Girls and Women* (Boston: Houghton, Mifflin and Company, 1892), p. 80.

among the latter and they would give me fish cakes instead.) The most popular dishes included beef vegetable stew and dumpling soup.

"How clearly I recall the old handyman carrying a large cloth bundle on his back. Every Saturday, he would come hurrying down the dormitory hallway delivering the sweets we had ordered. We were allowed to buy three sen's worth of snacks per week. On Saturday mornings, we could each make out a list including such favorites as roasted sweet potatoes, rice cakes, sweet rolls and salted beans. The room leader would collect and submit our orders to the supervisor, who would send the old man off to fill them. Wednesdays and Saturdays were our bath days, and it was one of our greatest pleasures to gather in our rooms after bathing, to nibble at our sweets and let forth volleys of girlish chatter." [22]

The Meiji Restoration period was a mixed one in the area of women's education. It included laughter in girls' school dormitories and strict hours of kneeling to learn moral precepts. It was an attempt to preserve the past while nevertheless creating a literate society that included educated women. Finally, the government seemed to retreat to the earlier Tokugawa ideals for women of "good wife, wise mother." But those who had been encouraged to study and influences from abroad created an environment that continued to encourage and demand higher education for women. This era was,

then, a beginning which eventually led to an acceptance of educational opportunities for Japanese women.

Points to Consider

After each student has read over the information below, decide on answers to the Points to Consider in class discussion.

* * * * *

In the 19th century, formal education for women became a major focus of reformers in many parts of the world, yet education was also considered a controversial subject in many world areas. It seemed that women often had to fight similar kinds of prejudices to achieve the right to an education. The following are views of women's education commonly held by Europeans and Americans in the 1800's:

- Women's brains were smaller than those of men and this caused women to be intellectually inferior.

- Women would be driven mad if they studied higher mathematics.

- Women *could* learn but *should* learn only things that would make them good wives and mothers.

- Women should be taught to be pious and particularly to be subservient to their husbands — the husbands were in charge of the family.

---

[22]Hani Motoko, "Stories of My Life," p. 341-342.

Although these and other similar ideas were common ones, the emphasis on the need for women's education grew during the 19th century. "Female seminaries" and girls' schools beyond grammar school were opened in the United States and Europe. The first college for women in the United States was founded in 1837. Reformers like Domingo Faustino Sarmiento of Argentina, Madadev Govinda Ranade of India, and N. G. Chernyshevsky of Russia stressed the importance of women's education in their countries. Therefore, by the end of the 19th century there was strong pressure *for* and *against* equal education for women:

- Notions of women's intellectual inferiority and the idea that curriculum for girls should ready them specifically for their roles as wives and mothers continued in the West and elsewhere.

- A growing emphasis on women's abilities and potential included the argument that women needed to be as fully educated as men to meet the demands of the modern world.

1. Considering this section and the above information, why do you think that Japanese reformers during the Meiji contemplated including women's education in their modernized education system?

2. Why do you think they backed away from a goal which encouraged equal educational opportunities for girls and women?

3. List specific examples of prejudices and fears in Japan about fully educating girls similar to those in the Western World. Were there fears about girls' education that seem to have been unique to Japanese culture?

4. What evidence is there in this selection that at least some girls were changed by their educations and might have then rejected some traditional Japanese customs or values?

5. List Westerners mentioned who worked in Japan for women's education. With similar problems at home, why do you think they chose to work for reforms in Japan? What might make it easier to change things in a country foreign to one's own? More difficult? (When forming your answers you might think of the *Peace Corps* and other recent voluntary groups as well as these 19th century missionaries and reformers.

6. Do you think that some of these arguments about educating girls and women are still given? Do you feel girls are equally encouraged to be educated? Should they be?

B.   The Role of Empress

In the previous selection the Meiji Empress was mentioned several times. She supported women's education, saw the five girls off to study in the United States, and supported the Peeresses' School for girls.

The Empress was named Haruko during her lifetime and, from all accounts of the era, managed to be an effective model for women in a particularly difficult age. The role of empress had declined in importance during the Tokugawa era as power was focused on the shōgun. During the Meiji Restoration the Empress Haruko began to assume a more public and active role in Japanese affairs. After her reign, the empresses again became rather isolated from society until the present time, when Empress Nagako is seen in various social and charitable activities.

In the 1870's the Meiji Reformers and the newly empowered imperial family had some major decisions to make about the roles of the emperor and empress; for example, they might follow the model of the Chinese imperial family. The Chinese had tended to keep their imperial court isolated from foreigners. The Chinese Empress-Dowager Ci Xi (1860-1908), who ruled as regent, had worn Manchu dress[1] and made no secret of

---

[1] The Manchu conquered China in the 17th century and continued to rule until the 20th century. They kept themselves apart from the Han Chinese. Empress-Dowager Ci Xi was also contemptuous of foreigners. She encouraged the Boxer Rebellion, in which foreigners living in China were attacked by gangs of Chinese.

her disdain for foreigners. The Japanese Empress-Dowager (the mother of the Emperor Meiji) was a traditionalist who also held herself aloof from foreigners. The wife of the British ambassador in the 1890's described the Empress-Dowager as follows:

Empress Haruko wears the costume of a 19th century Western monarch in this photograph taken in 1874.

"I was much amused a little while ago to hear that the Empress-Dowager was leaving Tōkyō, and taking a journey of several hours' duration, so as to enjoy some good — mushroom-hunting! The Empress-Dowager does not show herself in public, and is, I believe, an ardent adherent of the old modes of life and thought in Japan. I cannot find any foreigner who has seen more than the outside of her norimono, or closed palanquin [covered sedan chair]; I know her Grand Master of Ceremonies, and one or two Japanese who belong to her especial Court, and they wear an habitual expression of disapproving reserve, of patient deprecation, which has the effect of a dumb protest against changes of any sort, and more especially against the admission of the stultus vulgus, the profane foreigner, into the sacred precincts of Japanese life. Perhaps they are chosen for their dignified offices because their peculiar views harmonize with those of the royal lady; perhaps they have imbibed them through intercourse with her, for I have often noticed that the opinions of great personages are extremely contagious. Be that as it may, a high wall of conservative precedent is built round the Empress-Dowager; and when one expresses a desire to see her, one is met by a mournful shake of the head

and dead silence, as if to make the hopeless temerity of the wish. She must be kind and benevolent; for when we had our charity concert for the Leper Hospital and the new chapel, she took thirty tickets, and a message came with the contribution to the effect that her Majesty was much interested to hear of the Leper Hospital, and wished it all success." [2]

An American woman, however, found that the Empress-Dowager appreciated her interest in sacred Japanese dances and arranged a special seat for her at their performance.[3] The Empress-Dowager

[2]Mary Crawford Fraser, *A Diplomat's Wife in Japan* (New York: John Weatherhill, Inc., 1982), p. 106-107.

[3]Mrs. Robert C. Morris, *Dragons and Cherry Blossoms* (New York: Dodd, Mead & Company, 1896), p. 199-200.

was not entirely unsympathetic to Western women, but her court kept the old etiquette as well as its distance from Western influences.

The Meiji reformers were more sensitive to Western opinion than the older court of the Empress-Dowager. They set out to prove that their imperial court was not mysteriously "oriental," but was as "civilized" as the European courts. In order to appear more Western, Empress Haruko took the lead with a graciousness that impressed all those around her. These were some of the precedents she established.

- She appeared in public in 1876 — something former empresses had not done — to see the Emperor off on a trip.

- In 1889 the Emperor and Empress rode together in an open carriage, breaking the tradition of her following him in a separate, closed carriage.

- The Emperor and Empress jointly greeted guests at receptions instead of the Emperor alone meeting visitors.

- She stopped the court practice of blacking the teeth and shaving off women's eyebrows.

- She helped start the Peeresses' School for girls and wrote its school song.

- She was one of the first supporters of the Japanese Red Cross.

- She dressed in Western clothes and set court styles.

- She communicated directly with Western visitors and wrote

European heads of state.

- She made personal visits to hospitals and schools indicating her interest.

Empress Haruko was so involved in social causes and in encouraging the reception of more modern views toward women, that one writer thought she might have done more to change Japanese society than the ancient empress, Jingu, who was said to have conquered Korea.[4]

Although Empress Haruko led the way in changing many Japanese customs she was not living in a Westernized world. Many Japanese court traditions were still followed. Poetry writing contests dating from early Heian times continued. Haruko was known for her fine poetry.[5] President Grant and Mrs. Grant came to visit Japan following his term as president of the United States. At that time there was a Western custom of a man offering his arm to escort a lady into dinner. The person of the Empress, like the Emperor's, was not supposed to be touched. A court official was ready with a dagger

---

[4]William Elliot Griffis, *The Mikado's Empire* (New York: Harper & Brothers, 1876), p. 80.

[5]Hiroyuki Agawa, *The Reluctant Admiral* (Tokyo: Kodansha, International, 1979), p. 358. The famous Japanese Admiral Yamamoto, who was shot down in World War II, was found to be carrying on his body some of her poems.

Woodcut block print of the visit of former President Grant to Japan in 1879. Empress Haruko, Emperor Meiji, Mrs. Grant, and ex-President Grant watch entertainment at a reception.

to kill President Grant if he touched the Empress. Fortunately, for all concerned, he did not.[6]

Empress Haruko kept some traditional Japanese court customs and helped to change others. Descriptions of her by Europeans and Americans were almost uniform in praising her courtesy, dignity, and self-control:

"I was charmed with Her Majesty's appearance. She was dressed in a fabrication evidently straight from Paris, of lovely mauve satin, ... and she wore as ornaments one large diamond brooch, and the star of her country. During the whole time of our interview she never moved a muscle of her face, keeping her *small and beautifully shaped mouth partly open, and speaking in a whisper. She never seemed even to blink an eye. Her interpreter repeated all her remarks and mine also in a whisper. To speak in a whisper is, I am told, Court etiquette in Japan."* [7]

[6]Kimura Ki, *Japanese Literature, Manners and Customs in the Meiji-Taisho Era* (Tokyo: Obunsha, 1957), p. 98.

[7]Baroness Albert d'Anethan, *Fourteen Years of Diplomatic Life in Japan* (London: Stanley Paul & Co., 1912), p. 26.

Besides self-control, the Empress conveyed a sense of sadness and resignation. Mary Fraser, wife of the British ambassador, described a conversation she had with the Empress:

"In a voice so low that even in that hushed atmosphere I could hardly catch its tones, she said many kind things, which were translated to me in the same key by the lady-in-waiting, who acted as interpreter. First the Empress asked after the Queen's health; and then, when she had welcomed me to Japan, said she had been told that I had two sons whom I had been obliged to leave in England, and added that she thought that must have been a great grief to me. Her eyes lighted up, and then took on a rather a wistful expression as she spoke of my children. The heir to the throne is not her son, for she has never had children of her own, and has, I believe, felt the deprivation keenly; but perhaps the nation has gained by her loss, since all of her life which is not given up to public duties is devoted to the sick and suffering, for whom her love and pity seem to be boundless.

"When at last the little hand was held out in farewell, I went away with one of my pet theories crystallized into a conviction; namely, that it is a religion in itself to be a good woman, and that a sovereign who, surrounded by every temptation to selfishness and luxury, never turns a deaf ear to the cry of the poor, and constantly denies herself, as the Empress does, to help them, comes near being a saint." [8]

A Japanese woman, Kishida Toshiko, who had been Empress Haruko's lady-in-waiting, described the court system surrounding the Empress more bitterly as "an enchanted land, far from the real world, filled with a sense of ennui [boredom] and beautiful women."[9] Part of the sadness in the Empress' eyes was said to stem from the Emperor's concubines who were part of the court and her lack of a living son. Haruko might dress in European fashions and encourage Western ideas at court, but her family life remained similar to that of other upper-class Japanese women of her day.

In 1912 the Meiji Emperor died, and two years later, before the formal enthronement of Emperor Taishō, Empress Haruko died. One historian felt that she was thereby spared the pain of seeing the son of one of the emperor's concubines become emperor.[10] With the death of the Emperor Meiji, the imperial court returned to seclusion. Part of the reason was that the heir to the throne, Taishō, was mentally ill. His wife, the Empress Sadako, had a difficult marriage since Emperor Taishō was dissolute and suffered periods of

---

[8]Fraser, *A Diplomat's Wife in Japan*, p. 19-20.

[9]Quoted in, Sharon L. Sievers, *Flowers in Salt* (Stanford: Stanford University Press, 1983), p. 34.

[10]Leonard Mosley, *Hirohito, Emperor of Japan* (Englewood Cliffs, NJ: Prentice-Hall, Inc., 1966), p. 26-27.

When Crown Prince Akihito, married after World War II, he broke with tradition by marrying a commoner, Shoda Michiko.

mental disturbance. Nevertheless, she seems to have tried to continue the modernizing of the court that was started by Empress Haruko. Empress Sadako, for example, insisted that her son, Hirohito, be allowed to marry outside the Fujiwara family. Even some government officials tried to prevent this marriage by circulating the false rumor that Nagako, the chosen bride, was from a family in which color blindness was common. Sadako supported her son's choice, however, and Hirohito and Nagako were married.[11]

After the death of Taishō, the Empress-Dowager Sadako and the Empress Nagako continued to encourage visits to the court by Western women. The American ambassador to Japan in the 1930's described the Empress Nagako in terms similar to those used by earlier Western travelers to describe Empress Haruko. He described Empress Nagako's interest in people and her gracious charm.[12]

---

[11]*Ibid.*, p. 38-46.

[12]Joseph C. Grew, *Ten Years in Japan* (New York: Simon and Schuster, 1944), p. 16-17.

After World War II a tutor for Crown Prince Akihito was needed. Perhaps one can see the influence of the Empresses Sadako[13] and Nagako in the choice. An American woman, Elizabeth Vining, a Quaker from Bryn Mawr College was selected. Bryn Mawr had been one of the early supporters of Tsuda College for Japanese Women. Empress Haruko had seen Tsuda Umeko off to America in 1871, and now later Empresses would again try to bring some Western views of women to the imperial family and to their country.

Points to Consider

1. Until the Meiji empress Haruko, how were Tokugawa empresses suppose to behave? What roles did they fulfill as empress or empress-dowager?

2. What customs changed with Haruko as empress? What traditions were kept by her?

3. Why might Haruko have conveyed a sadness to visitors?

4. Why might Empress Sadako have had a difficult life?

5. What things seem to you to be the most interesting about being the Empress Haruko, Sadako or Nagako?

   What things described here would seem to you to be the most difficult about being these empresses?

[13]After the Emperor's death, Empress Sadako's official name became Empress-Dowager Teimei. To avoid confusion, we have left her name as Sadako.

C. The First Feminists of Japan The Two Waves

Empress Haruko and the Meiji emperor, looking to Western models, encouraged changes in the Japanese imperial court. The empress wore Western clothes and supported the Peeresses' School for girls. The emperor and empress received guests at receptions and appeared together in public, which broke with the tradition of the seclusion of the empress. While the court and imperial family did westernize some customs, the concept of equal rights and privileges for women was without support. The Meiji reformers' interest in the West, however, brought certain Japanese women into contact with women's groups outside of Japan, particularly in the United States and Great Britain. Some Japanese women's organizations worked for women's suffrage (the vote) as well as for women's rights in employment, education, and family law (marriage, divorce, and child custody.)

The beginnings of a women's rights movement began in Japan in the 1880's. Kishida Toshiko, the young lady-in-waiting who had described the world of the court as boring and "far from the real world,"[1] began making speeches in the early 1880's that strongly criticized the lack of women's right to divorce, the concubine system, and inadequate educational opportunities for girls. She attacked

---

[1] Quoted in, Sharon L. Sievers, *Flowers in Salt* (Stanford: Stanford University Press, 1983), p. 34.

167

Kishida Toshiko, lady-in-waiting to Empress Haruko, spoke out for women's rights in the late 19th century.

the notion of the three obediences in which women were to be under the control of their fathers, husbands, or sons throughout their lives. "In this country, as in the past," she declared, "men continue to be respected as masters and husbands while women are held in contempt as maids or serving women."[2] She and other women, such as Fukuda Hideko, began to organize women's discussion groups and lecture societies where speakers spoke up for women's rights. Some of these women joined political parties like the Liberal Party, which were working for reforms. Kishida Toshiko and others were sometimes arrested for speaking out. They were seen as a potentially dangerous threat to the social and political order particularly when they attacked the Japanese family system.

Fukuda Hideko

Ten years before Kishida Toshiko began her campaign of speaking on women's issues, a widow had called attention to the unfair voting laws of the newly reformed Meiji Japan. Kita Kusunose had become a taxpayer and head of household upon her husband's death, and her angry letter complaining of injustice to the authorities was widely publicized:

"We women who are heads of households must respond to the demands of the government just as other ordinary heads of households, but because we are women, we do not enjoy equal rights. We have the right neither to vote for district assembly representatives nor to act as legal guarantors in matters of property, even though we hold legal instruments for that purpose. This is an enormous infringement of our rights! . . .

"If it is reasonable to assume that rights and duties go together, then we should make that widely held assumption that they are in fact corresponding responsibilities a reality. . . . I do not have the right to vote. I do not have the right to act as guarantor. My rights, compared with those of male heads of households, are totally ignored. Most reprehensible of all, the only equality I share with men who are heads of their households is the onerous duty of paying taxes. . . .

[2]Quoted in, *Ibid.*, p. 38.

"Officials to whom I complained tell me that men have greater rights than women because they bear the additional burden of military service ... but my protest stands, since it is well known that men are routinely excused from military service precisely because they are heads of their households." [3]

These political moves by women in the 1870's and 1880's to achieve some rights and equality for women were severely limited by the Meiji Constitution adopted in 1889. In the new constitution, not only were women not permitted to vote, but they were excluded from inheriting the throne for the first time in Japanese history.[4] Harsher restrictions were still to come. Article 5 of the 1890 Police Security Regulations made it illegal for any woman to:

- join a political party.

- organize a political association.

- attend a political meeting.[5]

The intent of these regulations was to prevent any women's protests. The first wave of Japanese feminists was silenced.

The "second wave"[6] of Meiji feminist reformers began in 1910. These women were still severely restricted in their political activities by legislation and police regulations, so they began to voice their criticisms through journalism. One journal particularly notable for its stand on women's rights was *Seitō*, or *Bluestocking*, named after an 18th century British women's intellectual organization. *Seitō* deliberately set about to criticize Japan's discrimination against women. Hiratsuka Raichō, one of its editors,

opened the publication of the first issue with the following quotation:

"In the beginning, woman was the sun.
An authentic person.
Today, she is the moon.
Living through others.
Reflecting the brilliance of others. . . .
And now, **Bluestocking,** *a journal created for the first time with the brains and hands of today's Japanese women, raises its voice."*
Hiratsuka Raichō, September 1, 1911[7]

Although Hiratsuka Raichō was an organizer and writer of the magazine (which her mother helped to finance with money intended for Raichō's wedding), other women also wrote for the magazine. These included:

- Yosano Akiko, one of Japan's leading poets.

- Tamura Toshiko, an author of short stories.

- Itō Noe, a government critic who was later arrested and then strangled by a police officer.

- Fukuda Hideko, a socialist and feminist reformer.

---

[3]Quoted in, *Ibid.*, p. 29.

[4]*Ibid.*, p. 51.

[5]*Ibid.*, p. 52.

[6]*Ibid.*, p. 165.

[7]Quoted in, *Ibid.*, p. 163.

Hiratsuko Raichō was a founder of the feminist magazine, *Seitō*.

The articles and stories in *Seitō* ranged from poems about erotic love, to birth control debates, to Marxian communist views of women.

Publication of the journal was often made difficult by harassment from postal officials. A number of issues of the magazine were banned by the government when the authorities considered the content too controversial. Money for publication was always short and, after Hiratsuka Raichō finally left the journal, Itō Noe described the difficulties of trying to carry on by herself:

"There is no one to consult. There is no one to whom I can turn for assistance. Recently I have been getting upset and cross even when my good friend Kobayashi Katsu comes to visit me. Somehow I am unable to get used to going out constantly to pick up advertisements and take care of other business, and I always return home completely exhausted. The child is always waiting for me to feed him. Whenever there's a free moment, I find laundry to do. And then the proofreading. . . . Nevertheless, the thought that I have perhaps helped some other young people encourages me to continue." [8]

The magazine finally became dangerous to support and publication ended with the beginning of World War I.

Some of the women who had worked on *Seitō*, such as Yosano and Raichō, continued their interest in women's issues. Raichō, joined by Ichikawa Fusae and others, formed a New Women's Society and a Women's League in 1920 and 1921. They also began a women's suffrage party. Even though this magazine from the Meiji period, *Seitō*, failed financially and the government had banned some of its issues, the quality of the writing and the network of feminist women formed made a lasting impact which would eventually lead to the "third wave."

[8]Quoted in, Miyamoto Ken, "Itō Noe and the Bluestockings," *Japan Interpreter*, Vol. 10, No. 2 (Autumn 1975), p. 198.

Points to Consider

Feminism is generally defined as a broad reform movement that aims at the emancipation of women from special restrictions imposed on them. The *Feminist Movement* has called for the acceptance of woman's:

- equal worth to that of man.

- right to her own conscience and her own judgments.

- right to make decisions concerning her own individual destiny.

The *Women's Rights Movement* may be considered a part of this broader feminist movement. The women's rights movement made specific demands for changes to benefit women in areas such as education, suffrage, family law, and work privileges.[9]

Both movements have their roots far back in history. People have worked for rights for women — and fought against the idea that women were inferior — in many times and countries. The modern Western (United States and Europe) feminist movement dates from the Enlightenment period of the 18th century. The first wave of the Western women's rights movement started in the 1830's and faded out as women received the vote. The second wave may be dated from the late 1950's to the present time. Feminism may have subsided after suffrage was achieved, but World War II provided unusual opportunities for women, which may be one root cause of the modern feminist and women's rights movements in the West.

1. What specific changes were encouraged by the Meiji court and Meiji reformers that might be said to be part of the demands of a women's rights movement? What ways *not* supportive of a feminist movement?

2. What things did Kishida Toshiko, Kusunose Kita, and Hiratsuka Raichō advocate that supported the concept of a women's rights movement?
    Were all three part of a feminist movement? Explain your answer.

3. What ended the First Wave feminist movement in Japan?

4. What was the focus of the second wave of Japanese feminism? What specific things brought the second wave to an end.

5. Considering the time periods of the feminist movement in the West, give one reason why the "first wave" of Japanese feminism began in the 1880's.

6. What women's rights issues that concerned Japanese women do you think would have been similar to those in Western countries? What issues do you think would be specifically important to Japanese women?

7. Why do you think the manifesto (public declaration of intensions) of *Seito* began with "In the beginning, woman was the sun?"

---

[9]For a discussion of definitions, see: Barbara J. Berg, *The Remembered Gate: Origins of American Feminism* (New York: Oxford University Press, 1978), p. 5; Richard J. Evans, *The Feminists* (New York: Barnes and Noble Books, 1977), p. 39; Gerda Lerner, *The Majority Finds Its Past: Placing Women in History* (New York: Oxford University Press, 1979), p. 48-62.

D. Visionaries or Moderate Reformers—Men Who Worked for Women's Rights

Westerners who visited or worked in Japan were sometimes critical of the treatment of Japanese women. It seemed to Europeans and Americans that Japanese women were unfairly restricted by being secluded at home and demeaned by walking behind their husbands when in public. They observed that, although education for girls had become the norm in the West by the late 19th century, opportunities for a Japanese girl to seek a higher education were limited. Some Meiji reformers seemed to have been interested only in making token reforms for women's rights, perhaps intended to prevent these Western criticisms. There were, however, some Japanese men during the Meiji Period who became deeply involved in issues of women's rights. These male reformers were not necessarily advocates of absolute equality for women. Instead they argued for a "separate sphere" for women within which they could achieve success and be given recognition for accomplishments. The following diagram suggests three views of the ideal place for women in Japanese society:

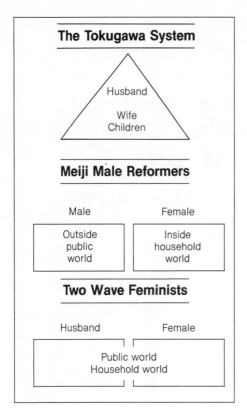

The Tokugawa System

Husband

Wife
Children

Meiji Male Reformers

Male · Female

Outside public world	Inside household world

Two Wave Feminists

Husband · Female

Public world Household world

He felt that women got all the pain and men all the pleasure in the traditional Tokugawa marriage system.[2] Fukuzawa Yukichi favored a more equal marriage arrangement:

"The foundation of human morality," [he wrote as early as 1870], *"lies in the relation between husband and wife. Both men and women are human beings living between heaven and earth, and there is no reason to suppose that one is more important than the other."* [3]

Educator Fukuzawa Yukichi was one of a group of male writers referred to as the "Meiji Six." They published a journal which included debates over women's issues. Mōri Arinori — another member of the Meiji Six and a colleague of Fukuzawa — was also a critic of the Japanese marriage system. The focus of his criticism was on the concubine system in which a married man could bring additional secondary wives into his household:

"The child of a concubine is commonly made heir to the house. . . . The heir treats his real mother like a nurse and looks up to his father's unrelated wife as his mother. . . . To adopt a child from outside the family may not be as shameful for the wife, but for her to

With one exception, these Japanese male reformers of the Meiji Era did not support women getting the right to vote. The writer Ueki Emori stood out as the sole advocate for complete equal rights for women. Male reformers also did not support women's equality within marriage yet they strongly criticized the Tokugawa system of absolute obedience of the wife to her husband. Fukuzawa Yukichi, Japanese educator and reformer, felt that the idea "that a woman should regard her husband as Heaven was almost too stupid to deserve serious criticism." [1] Fukuzawa further criticized the whole system of Japanese marriage that preached *duty* to the woman — and allowed the man complete freedom.

[1]Carmen Blacker, *The Japanese Enlightenment* (Cambridge: Cambridge University Press, 1964), p. 82.

[2]*Ibid.*, p. 82.

[3]*Ibid.*, p. 78.

be forced to recognize the son of her husband's concubine as her son is indeed cruel and unjust." [4]

Fukuzawa agreed with Mōri's criticism of the concubine system and answered those who tried to justify it:

"Someone may counter that if a man supports a number of mistresses, there will be no violation of human nature if he treats them properly. This is the opinion of the man himself. . . . If . . . true, a woman should be allowed to support a number of husbands. She should be able to call them male concubines, and give them lower ranking positions in the household. . . ." [5]

The Meiji Six criticized the Tokugawa family system but also the Tokugawa system of education. Mōri had encouraged the trade mission to take the five Japanese girls to study in the United States in 1871. Other men of this era such as Mitsukuri Shuhei, Naruse Jinzo and Kuroda Kiyotaka thought it was important for women to be educated. Mitsukuri wrote in favor of education for girls, Naruse founded Japan Women's College, and Kuroda suggested that girls be sent to the United States for an education. Fukuzawa Yukichi, referring to the small sword given to samurai brides, said that a Western-style education would be "the civilized girl's dagger" with which to protect herself.[6]

Fukuzawa Yukichi seems to have wanted an education for women roughly equal to that for men. Other members of the Meiji Six wanted women educated but only towards a specific goal. Nakamura Masanao, for example, wanted a woman's

Fukuzawa Yukichi

education to produce a "good wife, wise mother."[7] Wives needed educations to be able to converse with their husbands on a more equal level and to direct their children's early educations. Mōri Arinori also described the education of women as

---

[4]Quoted in, Sharon L. Sievers, *Flowers in Salt* (Stanford: Stanford University Press, 1983), p. 19.

[5]*Ibid.*, p. 19.

[6]Blacker, *The Japanese Enlightenment*, p. 88.

[7]Sievers, *Flowers in Salt*, p. 22.

important for the family but also the country.[8]

Women's education, then, was not seen by these reformers as a way for individual women to benefit. In another society education might aim at having an individual's curiosity satisfied or aiding a career. The goal of women's education in Japan — as with that of men — should be to fit them into society's idea of their proper place — within the family and state.

The limits these reformers set on their aspirations for women can also be seen in their actions. As minister of education, Mori did not push for strong high schools for young women as he did not favor intellectual programs for them. Although Fukuzawa founded a major university, it did not admit women. One Japanese male educator writing in the 1930's, wondered "why [Fukuzawa] did not found a school for girls, as he did for boys, and try to produce women who could make themselves economically independent, or at least who would fight for these rights themselves."[9] Even Fukazawa's own daughter was raised in the old-fashioned manner with a limited education and an arranged marriage.[10]

The Meiji Six, as perhaps was typical of the era of the Meiji Restoration, gave double messages to women of the time. On the one hand, some changes occurred for women:

- Public education for young girls was encouraged.

- Some higher education, most often provided by outsiders in Christian schools, was available to women.

- Family laws were amended allowing women the option of divorce.

But on the other hand:

- Educational curriculum was limited to that which would make a woman a "good wife, wise mother."

- Family laws were still unequal. Adultery was not grounds for divorce for a wife but was for a husband. Child custody went to the father in case of a divorce. Concubinage remained legal.

- Property in marriage was controlled by the husband.

- Women were excluded from the throne.

- Short hair was made illegal for women in 1872 as it was considered radical and Western.

Yet the Meiji Six and other male reformers set in motion changes for women. Mōri Arinori may not have realized that his encouragement of eight-year-old Tsuda Umeko's schooling in the United States, would later lead her to found a major English school for women in Japan.

---

[8]Quoted in, Tamie Kamiyama, "Ideology and Patterns in Women's Education in Japan" unpublished Ph.D. dissertation, St. Louis University, 1977, p. 63.

[9]Ai Hoshino, "The Education of Women," in Inazo Nitobe, *Western Influences in Modern Japan* (Chicago: The University of Chicago Press, 1931), p. 223.

[10]Blacker, *The Japanese Enlightenment*, p. 157.

Ueki Emori, photographed with Ishida Taka, Tominaga Raku — who were active in the women's movement — and the young Shimizu Toyoko, on the right, who later wrote supporting women's causes.

Fukuzawa's daughter may have been confined, but his writings encouraged other women.[11] In recognizing that women had abilities that could be respected, these men were speaking for a new kind of dignity for the Japanese women of their day.

Points to Consider

Men were active in many world areas in the 19th century in seeking legal, educational, and political rights for women. They were also active in reform movements which advocated changes in social customs that restricted women's lives. The following chart represents just a few of the many active "male feminists" who called for reforms:

---

[11]*Ibid.*, p. 158.

Name/Occupation	Cultural Area/Country	Reforms Advocated
Li Ruzhen (1763-1830) *Writer*	China	Anti-footbinding: Wrote *Flowers in the Mirror* in which he satirized footbinding by having a fictional character, Merchant Lin, travel to a women's kingdom where he is captured and made a concubine to the king (a woman); his ears are pierced and his feet are bound.
Kang Youwei (1855-1927) *Teacher/Writer*	China	Organized an anti-footbinding society in 1883 and with his pupil, the emperor of China, Guang Xu, started reforms called the Hundred Days. Those for women included: equal education, equal government and professional job opportunities; all social customs and rules would be the same for men and women; clothes would be the same and women would keep their own names.
John Stuart Mill (1806-1873) *Philosopher/Writer*	Europe/Great Britain	In Mill's book, *The Subjection of Women*, he strongly advocated women's rights. When he married Harriet Taylor he refused all the legal powers that were allowed him over his wife under the British law of that time. He and Harriet both continued to advocate the emancipation of women and both wrote extensively on the subject of the equality of the sexes.
D.K. Karve (1858-1940) *Reformer/Political Organizer*	India	After his first wife's death, Karve decided to marry a widow. This was a dramatic move for a high caste Brahman, for by custom, remarriage was prohibited for widows. Since child marriage was common in 19th century India, many widows had never lived with their husbands and would have no chance for children or a family of their own. Karve continued to work for widow remarriage, although he was strongly condemned and persecuted for his own marriage.
Madadev Govinda Ranade (c. 1841-1901) *Educator/Reformer*	India	As a young man in his late 20's, Ranade was married by family arrangement to an 11-year-old illiterate girl. He started teaching her to read and write, over the strong opposition of family members. Madadev and his wife Ramabai continued to work for reforms for women and were especially active in encouraging education for women.
Domingo Faustino Sarmiento (1811-1888) *Educator-later President of Argentina*	Latin America/ Argentina	Sarmiento was known as a defender of education for women. He traveled to the United States and met educators Mary and Horace Mann. Mary Mann helped him recruit about 65-70 women teachers, who went to Argentina to help set up schools for girls. Later, as President of Argentina, Sarmiento instigated more public education — even public co-educational schools.

Qasim Amin (1865-c. 1915) *Judge/Lawyer/Writer*	The Middle East	In Amin's book *The Emancipation of Women* published in 1891 and another in 1901 called *The New Woman* he advocated basic education, more physical freedom (although not outlawing the veiling of women) and changes in the divorce laws. Although these suggestions seem quite tame by today's standard, the book caused a great outcry in Egypt. Amin gained followers and is credited with beginning the Egyptian movement for rights for women.
M.L. Mikhailov (1826-1865) *Writer*	Russia/USSR	Mikhailov stressed the need for education for women. He was the first Russian to speak out strongly for women's rights. His stand for co-education was considered radical at the time.
N.G. Chernyshevsky (1828-1889) *Political activist/Writer*	Russia/USSR	Chernyshevsky wrote for *The Contemporary*. He was arrested by the Tsar's government for his political ideas. While in prison he wrote a novel *What Is To Be Done?* (1863), an influential book that advocated radical changes for women such as no forced marriages, open professional and educational opportunities and equal political rights.
Frederick Douglass (1817-1895) *Journalist/Political activist*	United States	Douglass was born a slave and escaped to the north. He edited an anti-slavery newspaper *The North Star*, which had on its masthead: "Right is of No Sex — Truth is of No Color." Douglass was the only man to take part in the Seneca Falls Convention of 1848 called to discuss rights for women, marking the beginning of the women's suffrage movement in the United States.
Henry Brown Blackwell (1825-1909) *Reformer/Political activist/ Lecturer*	United States	Brother of the first American woman to become a doctor, Elizabeth Blackwell, Henry Blackwell was active in the anti-slavery movement before the Civil War. He married Lucy Stone, an outspoken feminist. They both worked for women's rights but particularly for women's suffrage.

---

1. After reading the article and looking over the chart, list things that you notice about the reforms for women that most concerned these men. What factors might have influenced the reforms that they felt were important to improve the condition of women in their cultural area?

2. Looking at the occupations or positions these men held, how might their position in society have influenced their desire to bring about reforms for women?

3. Why might men (and fewer women) in some societies or periods of history have been the leaders in bringing about reforms for women?

4. How do you explain the fact that Japanese male reformers like Mori Arinori and Fukuzawa Yukichi supported education for women but excluded allowing the vote and other women's rights?

Mori Arinori, member of the Meiji Six and critic of the Japanese marriage system.

5. In what specific ways might these men have seen it to be in their own best interest to support changes for women? Why do many men today feel that increasing women's status and opportunities brings benefits to them?

6. Ueki Emori is considered a trailblazer among modern thinkers as the only Japanese male reformer to advocate equal rights for women — including the right to vote.[12] His *conduct* toward women was not consistent with what he wrote about their equal rights. He was known as a "womanizer" who led a life of debauchery. What do you think might explain his strong support for women's rights while in his personal life he used women as sex objects?

[12]Kuninobu, Junko Wada, "The Development of Feminism in Modern Japan," *Feminist Issues*, Vol. 4, No. 2 (Fall, 1984), p. 7.

CHAPTER 8

MINORITY WOMEN IN JAPAN THE AINU, THE BURAKUMIN, AND THE KOREANS

The Ainu, The Burakumin, and The Koreans

According to pre-historical Japanese myths, the female god Izanami gave birth to the islands of Japan, with the imperial family tracing its origins to the female sun god Amaterasu. The Japanese people descended from a number of clans, but their legends seem to suggest they had a common ancestry. Although the Japanese majority shares a similar heritage, three groups in Japan have been seen as outsiders to the Japanese culture. These groups are the Ainu, Burakumin, and Koreans. Each of these groups has been discriminated against in different ways. The roles of women within these minority groups have not been thoroughly investigated by scholars and only sketchily

recorded by historians, but perhaps a few issues can be discussed. These include suggesting the roles and status of women within these groups and what forms of discrimination they have suffered as part of a minority group.

In the early Chinese histories of Japan, the Ainu are mentioned as "hairy men." In one case some Ainu accompanied a Japanese envoy to the Chinese court. The Chinese chronicler reported that: "The Ainus also dwell on those islands [of Japan]. The beards of the Ainus were four feet long. They carried arrows at their necks, and without ever missing would shoot a gourd held on the head of a person standing several tens of steps away."[1] Archaeologist J. Edward Kidder describes the Ainu as "people with non-Japanese physical characteristics now residing in Hokkaidō. Probably an ancient people of Caucasoid origin. . . ."[2] In early times the Ainu controlled much of the northern part of the main island of Hōnshu, so early histories report frequent military campaigns against them. Over the years the Ainu were defeated and driven to the northernmost island called Hokkaidō. Until the 19th century this island was of little interest to the Japanese, as it was thought that rice could not be grown there, and the Ainu continued to be hostile.[3] Many Ainu were eventually assimilated into the majority Japanese culture. It is estimated that there are about 16,000 Ainu remaining in Japan, but many more have intermarried and so are of mixed Ainu and Japanese heritage.[4]

The Japanese, then, have generally looked at the Ainu as a hostile people to be conquered and absorbed or ignored. Travelers allowed into Japan after the period of isolation were sometimes more interested in this non-Japanese minority group and have described the customs of the Ainu women. Isabella Bird, an American traveling in Japan the 1890's, wrote that Ainu women were particularly hard-working, "never idle."[5] The list of their activities included cooking, root gathering, mat making, weaving with bark thread, and acting as the principal farmers. So proud were Ainu women of their agricultural abilities that a baby girl was often given a name relating to farming.[6] The primary duties of the men were as warriors and hunters but they sometimes aided the women in farm chores.

Bark-weaving was the skill for which the Ainu women were most noted. Their method involved stripping trees of their bark, twisting it into thread which is used both for weaving cloth on looms and sewing. Jessie Ackermann, an early 20th century British scholar, described the cloth made by the Ainu women: "The background is usually a dull, almost dirty, blue; and upon this irregular designs wander at large over the entire surface."[7] Although this description sounds uncomplimentary, tourists, even today, prize this bark cloth for its unique qualities and design.

In traditional Ainu society, some customs for women were quite different than those of Japanese women. One tradition involved their

[1]Ryusaku Tsunoda, tr., *Japan in the Chinese Dynastic Histories* (Columbia University Council for Research in the Social Sciences, 1951), p. 40.

[2]J. Edward Kidder, *Ancient Japan* (Oxford: Phaidon Press, 1977), p. 139.

[3]*Ibid.*, p. 11.

[4]George A. De Vos and William O. Wetherall, *Japan's Minorities: Burakumin, Koreans and Ainu* (Minority Rights Group, 1974), No. 3, p. 17.

[5]Isabella L. Bird, *Unbeaten Tracks in Japan* (New York: G. P. Putnam's Sons, n.d.), Vol. 2, p. 52.

[6]M. Inez Hilger, *Together with the Ainu: A Vanishing People* (Norman, OK: University of Oklahoma Press, 1971), p. 38-39.

[7]Jessie Ackermann, "The Ainu," in, T. Athol Joyce and N. W. Thomas, *Women of All Nations* (London: Cassell and Company, Limited, 1909), p. 518.

appearence. Until quite recently, Ainu women had the area around their lips tattooed as young girls. Jessie Ackermann compared this tattooing to Chinese foot-binding because it was done to young girls by their mothers or other women to enhance their chances for marriage. She stated that the tattooing started when a child was about two years old.

"The work, being very painful, is done a little at a time, and a period of two years is covered before it is complete, the result being a large diamond-shaped patch of dark blue completely surrounding the mouth and extending in points well towards the ears. . . . In olden times it was the custom to continue the work of decoration after marriage by tattooing a band across the forehead, rings on the fingers, and many circles about the arms." [8]

Ainu woman with tattoos on her face and arms — late 19th century. The practice of tattooing has been outlawed so only older Ainu women are now seen with this distinctive body decoration.

The following excerpt was written by the American traveler, Isabella Bird:

"[The Ainu women] are universally tattooed, not only with the broad band above and below the mouth, but with a band across the knuckles, succeeded by an elaborate pattern on the back of the hand, and a series of bracelets extending to the elbow. The process of disfigurement begins at the age of five, when some of the sufferers are yet unweaned. I saw the operation performed on a dear little bright girl this morning. A woman took a large knife with a sharp edge, and rapidly cut several horizontal lines on the upper lip, following closely the curve of the very pretty mouth, and before the slight bleeding had ceased carefully rubbed in some of the shiny soot which collects on the mat above the fire. In two or three days the scarred lip will be washed with the decoction of the bark of a tree to fix the pattern, and give it that blue look which makes many people mistake it for a daub of paint. A child who had this second process performed yesterday has her lip fearfully swollen and inflamed. The latest victim held her hands clasped tightly together while the cuts were inflicted, but never cried. The pattern on the lips is deepened and widened every year up to the time of marriage, and the circles on the arm are extended in a similar way." [9]

---

[8]*Ibid.*, p. 516, 518.

[9]Bird, *Unbeaten Tracks in Japan*, p. 79-80.

185

The Japanese government, as part of the Meiji reforms, first tried to outlaw the Ainu custom of tattooing girls in 1871 and again in 1899. The practice, however, had religious overtones, and even in the 1970's some elderly Ainu women were reported to have facial tattoos.

Other than comments by travelers about Ainu women's body decorations, there seems to have been a difference of opinion among observers of the status of Ainu women. The women worked very hard and did not seem to occupy important political positions directing Ainu affairs. Jessie Ackermann claimed that at birth "an Ainu girl is the most unwelcome creature ever thrust into being. She is but another burden-bearer among a peculiar people, doomed to a life of hardship and toil." [10] More recently an American, Inez Hilger, who studied the Ainu, commented on the fact that men and women ate together and that the house seemed to belong to the wife. An Ainu woman in the 1970's described the old custom:

"Unfailingly, formerly, the house and utensils of a married woman who 'died before her time' were burned to the ground at her death. The house was hers. She came to it as a bride, and she was considered to be the bride of that house. The spirit of it and of everything in it followed her spirit into that other world once the house had been burnt.

"Since Japanese law now forbids burning the house, one large enough for two or three persons to sit in it is constructed. The persons drink and eat in it and tell the spirit of the house to follow the spirit of the

woman they have just buried. This done, the miniature house is set on fire. There is an unshaken belief among the older Ainu, said Abe, that a deceased woman must be in possession of the spirit of her house, so she can welcome her husband to it after his death. It also gives her a place to live while she waits for him." [11]

When a man married more than one wife (somewhat rare among the Ainu), he would not, as did the Japanese at one time, bring them into his house. Instead, each wife had her own house.[12]

The women had a strong sense of their religion and prayed to a "Sun Mother." Ainu women were expected, by memorizing chants and songs, to preserve the history of the people. In both the 1890's and in the 1970's travelers found Ainu women singing songs as they wove their bark cloth. Some Ainu women can remember as many as 15 generations. As one Ainu man in the 1970's said:

"But then, it is well known that women have better memories for such things than men do. Maybe it is because women often pray when they are alone. One can then hear them mention their ancestors of

---

[10]Ackermann, "The Ainu," p. 516.

[11]Hilger, *Together with the Ainu*, p. 50.

[12]*Ibid.*, p. 162.

many generations." [13]

The women were also noted for their ceremonial dances. In recent years they seem to have given up the all-night marathon dances of former times that went on until only one woman was left standing.[14]

The Ainu have faced prejudice in Japanese society. An Ainu remembered the painful experiences of being discriminated against:

"For example, I have an Ainu name. My grandmother gave it to me when I was a baby, following an Ainu custom. When my children were born, we followed the Ainu custom and gave each an Ainu name. Japanese children knew from those names that my children were Ainu, and would designate them scornfully as Ainu. Discrimination against the Ainu by the Japanese was deep seated." [15]

The Japanese government has dealt with the Ainu in a way not unlike the United States government has with Native Americans. They placed the Ainu in areas set aside for them and legislated against some of their customs. The most obvious change for Ainu women brought about by the Japanese was the outlawing of tattooing. The Japanese government brought other changes for them through the education system. Many of the young people are currently moving away from Ainu settlements, and from farming to city jobs. A major problem for the Ainu is how to retain their old customs and still gain equal educational and employment opportunites. With limited resources,

one Ainu woman reported that, "I must admit that I gave my boys educational advantages that I did not give my girls." [16]

* * * * *

A larger minority group in Japan is the Burakumin (hamlet people) who make up about 2% of the population of Japan.[17] Particularly during the Tokugawa period, this group was considered to be the lowest class in Japanese society. They were not, like the Ainu, distinguished by different physical appearance from other Japanese but rather by their occupations. They provided the labor for what was considered the most menial and ritually polluting tasks such as the slaughtering of animals, tanning of hides, and the burying of the dead. Under Tokugawa law, these people were seen as "despised citizens" who could not marry into other classes and who were forced to live in segregated communities. To show the extent of the prejudice against them, a trial in Edo (Tōkyō) in 1859 decided a case in which a commoner had killed a Burakumin. The judge ruled that because the commoner had only killed one Burakumin — and the life of a commoner was worth seven — the commoner could not be put to death

---

[13]Quoted in, *Ibid.*, p. 46.

[14]*Ibid.*, p. 73.

[15]*Ibid.*, p. 198-199.

[16]*Ibid.*, p. 166.

[17]Edwin O. Reischauer, *The Japanese* (Cambridge: Harvard University Press, 1977), p. 36.

for murder.[18] Other restrictions identified the Burakumin; women were not allowed to wear sashes (obi) or have their windows face the streets.[19] Meiji reformers removed these official restrictions against the Burakumin, but deep prejudices remained.

Both women and men suffered discrimination through the years — socially, in employment, and in education. In years of famine Burakumin daughters — like other poor girl children — might be sold into prostitution or as geisha. A brother described the plight of his sister in the 1930's:

"'My older sister has practically no education. At the age when she should have been finishing the sixth grade she was sent out as a geisha. You might say that my parents should have found a job somewhere so that they would not have had to turn their daughter into a geisha. But discrimination was a fact of life. We were insulted as cow killers, dog killers, and called four-legged animals. No one would hire us. But girls could be sent out to work as geisha to help the family. Common sense tells us that this is contrary to morality, that it is a heartless thing to do. But we had no choice if we were to eat.' Because this family had to call on the young geisha for money time after time, she fell deeper and deeper in debt and was finally sold abroad to Korea." [20]

Even in better times, children were teased and tormented because they were Burakumin. These are two accounts from women, one born in 1913 and the other in 1934, both remembering harsh treatment:

"I cannot forget the discrimination I underwent in school. Often other children would tell me, 'Go away, you stink,' or they would say, 'That girl is from that village,' and would not include me in whatever they were doing. They would not let me join in when they were playing jump rope. They would block my way and sneer at me. Whenever something got lost, they would pick on buraku children saying, 'You must have taken it.' Once a teacher, who had just returned from the army, told us, 'It's you kids' fault,' when something disappeared. It made us so mad that we spent a week looking for the real culprit.

"Because I had to help with chores at home and also took care of my younger brothers and sisters, I had to cut school often. The more I missed school, the less I understood what was going on in class and got bored with my studies. So I would look out the window or do something mischievous. Then I would get scolded and be made to stand in the corridor. The pupils who were forced to stand in the corridor were mostly buraku children.

"There were lots of buraku children standing around in the playground. They were supposed to have

---

[18]Mikiso Hane, *Peasants, Rebels, and Outcastes* (New York: Pantheon, 1982), p. 142.

[19]*Ibid.*, p. 143.

[20]Quoted in, *Ibid.*, p. 153.

forgotten something and gone home to get what they had left at home. But, in fact, their families were too poor to bring whatever they were supposed to, such as money, and they were told by their parents to say, 'I forgot.' "

* * * * *

"When I was old enough to become aware of things, I realized that I was a poor child dressed in dirty rags. My father was a day laborer without regular employment; he had no job security. We grew up in the midst of poverty . . . My life was conditioned strongly by the fact that I was called 'buraku,' 'eta,' 'four-legged animal.' Schooling is ordinarily the most important and happiest time in a person's life. But my life was warped by elementary school. Elementary school! The mere mention of the word makes my skin crawl. I shall never forget my first day of school, for this is when I first experienced discrimination. After we heard the principal's talk in the assembly room, we started to leave, holding our classmate's hand. When I stuck out my hand to hold the hand of the girl next to me, she stubbornly refused to hold my hand. Not knowing why, I forcefully grabbed her hand. Then she began to cry. A female teacher came by and asked her why she was crying. . . . She responded that she did not want to hold my hand. The teacher asked her why. The girl said, 'Because this girl's hands are dirty.' The teacher looked at my hands and said, 'Her hands are clean, there's nothing on them.' Then the girl said, looking straight at me, 'My mother told me, "That child is smelly so you mustn't play with her."' " At that time I did not understand why she said that . . . I cannot forget the mother who taught her young child such things nor can I forget my confusion and bafflement as I quietly stared at the girl's face.

"After that, all the children of the class said I was smelly and dirty. There were several children from my buraku in my class, but they too started to avoid me. The teacher too began to treat me differently than other children. With each passing day the pain inside me got worse, and I began to hate going to school. Sometimes I lied, saying I was sick, and stayed home. So I was picked on by everybody. I would cry and cower in the corner. When I went home and complained to my mother, she would not listen to me.

"The first year of anger and anguish passed and I entered the second grade. Not realizing that I was to suffer even more than before, I looked forward to the second year. But I still had my old, dirty clothes, frostbitten hands and feet, and scared, skittish look and attitude. I suppose I was an eyesore for everyone." [21]

Prejudice against the Burakumin has lessened in Japan, but problems and discrimination remain. Since many marriages in Japan are still arranged by go-betweens, investigations are frequently made into the background of the proposed bride or bridegroom. Having lived in a Burakumin area is seen as an indication that a person

[21]Quoted in, *Ibid.*, p. 157-158.

might be an unsatisfactory marriage possibility. Some Burakumin people pass for non-Burakumins by covering up their backgrounds, but there is the danger of having their past revealed — with divorce and reported suicides as a likely result. To indicate how extensively mixed marriages between Burakumin and other Japanese have been avoided, 1967 statistics show that 90% of all Burakumin marriages are with other Burakumin.[22]

* * * * *

A third group to face discrimination in Japan are the Koreans. So deep has been the prejudice against Koreans that Western travelers in the 19th century were somewhat startled by having Japanese give them a hard time for being "Koreans." Since rural Japanese had not seen Westerners before, they assumed anyone strange looking must be a "Korean." Prejudice against Koreans did not go back to ancient times, since Korea had had a rich culture admired by the early Japanese. The 19th and 20th century invasions of Korea, and the rather brutal occupations of Korea by Japan, led the Japanese to see the Koreans as an inferior and conquered people. The Japanese forced Koreans to come to Japan as cheap laborers, particularly in Japanese mines. During World War II, Korean women were often used as prostitutes by Japanese soldiers.[23]

About 350,000 Koreans have applied for permanent residency in Japan today. Like the Burakumin, these Koreans have suffered severe educational and social discrimination. One Japanese woman recalled how, in the 1930's, she was shocked to find

one of her American teachers actually going to work with a Korean church. "I was shocked. We considered them inferior to us. A Japanese would never think of mixing with Koreans or visiting their neighborhoods."[24] Like the Burakumin, the Koreans have been discouraged from intermarrying with Japanese and have had to take jobs with the lowest status. For women, there has sometimes been the added sexual exploitation.

Ainu, Burakumin and Korean women might have less status than men in their own communities and yet suffer the same discrimination from the Japanese. There is much evidence "that minority women are the lowest of the low — first experiencing discrimination as minority members and then as women."[25]

There may be customs within minority groups that give these women added strengths. But the general discrimination toward these three groups is well documented and minority women must bear a double burden of prejudice against their sex and their group.

---

[22]*Ibid.*, p. 149.

[23]De Vos and Wetherall, *Japan's Minorities*, p. 16.

[24]Hiroko Nakamoto, *My Japan 1930-1951* (New York: McGraw Hill, 1970), p. 124.

[25]Susan Pharr, in written comments for this chapter to the authors.

Points to Consider

1. What specific things isolated the Ainu as a group and separated them from the majority Japanese? What things separated the Burakumin and Koreans as minority groups from the Japanese?

2. Which group do you think might suffer from the deepest prejudice? Explain your answer.

3. Jessie Ackermann's view of Ainu women was that they worked very hard, were painfully tattooed and, at birth, were not welcomed. She also wrote that:

   "When a woman marries she is not honored by bearing the name of the man of her choice, but is designated by her maiden name, or as the wife of So-and-so. If widowed, she takes the name of her son, if she has one, which is usually the case." [26]

   How does this observation perhaps reflect her own values as a British woman living in about 1900? How might the Ainu see this issue of changing names differently?

4. Minority women are thought by many to suffer from a "double burden." In what ways might women of these minority groups suffer more than men from prejudice?

---

[26]Jessie Ackermann, "The Ainu," p. 518.

CHAPTER 9

THE ''MODERN WOMAN''
1900-1930

A. Japanese Women as Industrial Workers

When the period of Japanese isolation ended in the 1860's, Westerners, long excluded, eagerly came to Japan to observe and record their travels. Many visitors commented on how hard Japanese women worked at numerous jobs, from farming to fishing. By the early 20th century, visitors noted that women made up a major part of the agricultural workers and, when statistics were analyzed, the *majority* of Japan's industrial workers.[1]

Visitors recorded seeing women loading coal into cargo ships in Japanese ports, working in mines and in the textile industry. About 80,000 women were reported working in coal-mining.[2] Their task was to pick up the coal from the men digging it, carry it in baskets on their backs, and deliver it to the cars that took it away. An American observer wrote that it was "a death-dealing kind of work" and quoted from a study done in the 1920's:

"The statistics of the number of still-born children and the appalling number of deaths of newly-born children in mining communities are an indication of the waste of life that is going on because of the employment of women at this dangerous work." [3]

---

[1]Allen K. Faust, *The New Japanese Womanhood* (New York: George H. Doran Company, 1926), p. 68.

[2]*Ibid.*, p. 69.

[3]*Ibid.*, p. 69.

The conditions in the mines were often terrible. An old woman who had been a miner later described her experiences:

"I was born in this mining community. The entire region along the Onga River [in Fukuoka] is mountainous, so most of the girls went into the mines to work. The mines were full of twelve and thirteen-year-old girls. My father died in the mines when I was ten. . . . I went into the mines to work when I was thirteen. They used to say that the god of the mines was a dog. When a dog barked loud, or when it barked in the direction of the mines, it meant trouble, they would tell me. . . . But I used to hide my puppy in my lunch basket and bring him into the mines with me. . . . The mines were a dangerous place. You were in constant danger of losing your life. A cave-in might occur at any moment. There were times when gas came out. Then a blue ball of fire would shoot through the mines. The sound was loud enough to burst your eardrums. Sometimes the beams and shafts would snap. The ground was rough, and you couldn't stand up straight and walk. The passages were narrow, too. Sometimes we had to crawl around, and water was always seeping in. The mine passages were steep .. and it was hot.

"The women's job was to transport the coal that had been mined. The coal was loaded into a 4-foot-square wooden box. The bottom of the box had metal runners. We had to pull this box with a sash over our shoulders. It was hard work. Where it was uphill, there were wooden logs to serve as rails to make it easier to

pull the box. Going downhill, when the angle of the slope was over thirty degrees, we would get on our hands and knees, grab the log railings firmly, hold back the box with our heads, and slowly crawl down backward. With a lamp in our mouths and with our heads holding back the box full of coal, we would feel our way down, inch by inch, with the tip of our straw sandals. If you slipped, it wouldn't be only you who got hurt, because there were others ahead of you. Some of the women had babies on their backs while hauling coal. Since water was dripping all the time, it was slippery. [After they hauled the coal to the coal cart, they had to push a cart full of empty boxes back to where the digging was taking place.] We were really slaves. Lots of people died when the boxes fell off the cart. That was the scariest part of our work. Once a friend of mine was coming down the slope with her daughter. We were going up. All of a sudden the boxes began to tumble down and her daughter was killed. . . . That friend had been a very religious person. She said, 'I was a devout believer, but my daughter died. It does no good to have faith! . . . '

"It was really hard to get a loaded coal box moving. We'd push it with our heads and our rears. After struggling hard and pushing the box for hundreds of yards, we were paid 8.5 sen. . . . With both my husband and me working, we made 30 to 40 sen a day. One sho [.48 U.S. gallons] of rice cost 12 to 13 sen then. We used to work twelve or thirteen hours [at a time]. Sometimes they would arbitrarily deduct one box from our work. . . . But we had to

accept that. If we uttered a single word of complaint we would be beaten within an inch of death. There used to be a saying that went, 'Complain and you'll get a club on your back. Your towel will be dyed with blood.'... "My first husband was killed by a runaway coal cart [in 1923]...

"I raised my children while working in the mines. It was really rough going into the mines then. I would get up at two in the morning and quietly prepare breakfast.... I would then wake my child up when it was still dark. The child would rub his eyes and complain. I would yell at him and take him to the nursery. ...They used to take care of him for 8 sen a day. I would leave him there, wondering if I would ever see him again.... "Will today be the day he is going to lose his parents?" I would wonder. So I was able to see my children only at night." [4]

Japan made it illegal for women to work in mines in 1928 but later allowed married women to work in them. In 1938, with the beginning of World War II in the Pacific, Japan's military needs sent women back to the mines.

Besides being mine workers, women made up the majority of textile workers. The importance of the textile industry, one economist has written, can hardly be overemphasized when considering Japan's modern economic growth. The cotton textile industry was the first big breakthrough for Japan into international markets.[5] Profits from the textiles helped the Japanese to accumulate the necessary capital

for further modernization. As historian Sharon Sievers has said, "Without the work of Japan's women, the apparent miracle of Japan's economic growth might not have been possible." [6]

But the workers who produced the textiles were primarily women who did not benefit a great deal from this "economic miracle." The following charts show the percentage of women involved in the major textile producing countries:

[4]Mikiso Hane, *Peasants, Rebels, and Outcastes* (New York: Pantheon Books, 1982), p. 233-235.

Communication among Competitors in the Japanese Cotton-Spinning Industry'' in, Hugh Patrick, ed., *Japanese Industrialization and Its Social Consequences* (Berkeley: University of California Press, 1976), p. 97.

[6]Sharon L. Sievers, *Flowers in Salt* (Stanford: Stanford University Press, 1983), p. 56-57.

Proportion of Women among Factory Workers (in percent)

Japan		France		United States	
1909	62.0	1866	42.7	1870	24.0
1920	53.0	1881	38.3	1880	28.8
1930	52.6	1901	31.5	1900	32.6
		1921	31.6	1920	24.2

Belgium		India		Italy	
1890	24.6	1911	17.4	1901	37.4
1900	23.9	1921	17.5	1911	46.2
1920	25.0				
1930	20.9				

Females as a Percentage of the Cotton Textile Labor Force (in percent)

Japan		United States		United Kingdom	
1909	83.0	1830	66.0	1835	55.1
1914	83.3	1850	63.0	1847	58.7
1920	80.0	1890	54.5	1867	61.3
1925	80.6	1910	48.3	1878	62.7
1930	80.6	1919	42.4	1895	62.3

India		France	
1884	22.5	1886	53.0
1894	25.9	1896	50.0
1909	22.1	1906	45.5
1924	21.6		
1934	18.9		

Other statistics suggest that the working conditions of these women textile workers were particularly harsh — the average worker held her job for less than two years, and the rate of workers who contracted tuberculosis was 25 percent. At the turn of the century, it is estimated that "one out of four or five of the twelve to fifteen-year-old children in the woolen mills died before her three-year term was up."[8]

The extremely high death rates were caused by both the impoverished backgrounds of the girls who worked in the mills and the harsh working conditions under which they toiled. The earliest female factory workers, however, were not necessarily from poor families. When a silk blight hit Europe in the 1860's, European investors worked with the Japanese to set up new silk-weaving plants in Japan. French and Italian workers were brought over to train Japanese women in the making of silk. One of these Italian women, Rosa Cavalleri, later described her experiences as follows:

"And so those [Japanese] girls had gone [to the factory] and their mothers were getting three lire a day for all the time they were gone. And nothing could happen to them, because that terrible strict boss,

[7]Saxonhouse, "Country Girls and Communication among Competitors in the Japanese Cotton-Spinning Industry," p. 99, 100.

[8]Robertson Scott, as quoted in "The Citizen-Subjects," in, *Fortune*, Vol. 14, No. 3 (1936), p. 82.

Japanese spinning mill workers — c. 1890.

Pietro, had gone with them. When those girls came home they told me that they were like prisoners with that Pietro. He pulled the shades on the train to the boat so they couldn't see where they were going. And in Japan they were locked up in the same building with the mill — they couldn't even go outside to take in some fresh air. In the mill they were dressed up nice in white embroidered aprons and stood behind the Japanese women and showed them with their hands how to reel the silk. And the Japanese women learned good how to make the silk, but they couldn't learn to sit down on stools. They were used to sitting on the floor with their legs folded under, so they kept folding them under on the stools too. The Italian girls would take their feet and put them down on the bars, but as soon as they weren't looking, the Japanese had their legs under them again. They couldn't learn to sit down! Me, I never could sit on my legs like that — I get the cramps." [9]

---

[9]Marie Hall Ets, *Rosa: The Life of an Italian Immigrant* (Minneapolis: University of Minnesota Press, 1970), p. 120-121.

In order to show that these early industries were not run by "blood sucking foreigners," upper-class families were asked by the government to send their daughters to work in textile factories. They were to set an example as loyal workers for the country's economic needs. Eiko Wada, who was one of the first to volunteer, wrote later about her long hours:

"Eiko related that she was able to endure the long hours, sweltering heat from the steam in the factory, and the humiliating treatment only because of her conviction that she must quickly learn the necessary skills in order to be of service to her country. While the French male supervisor was paid the equivalent of $600 a month and the French female technicians from $56 to $80 a month, the Japanese girls received from $1 to $1.75 for the same period." [10]

After this early patriotic period in which some women factory workers were from the upper classes, the workers were generally recruited from the poor villages. Recruiters came to each village and offered families a set amount for a working contract for their daughters. The recruiters would then take the young women back to the factories. These young women lived in dormitories and were restricted in their freedom to come and go. What little pay they received was sent back home to pay off the work contract. These examples, however, do not suggest how brutal this system could be.

Just getting from their villages to the factory might be a serious problem.

Nomugi Pass became known as a terrible place for young women trying to make their way through the mountains to the silk mills. The following are descriptions of the journey as the women later remembered it:

"Nomugi Pass is where many factory girls fell down into the ravine. When someone slipped and fell down, we would untie our sashes, tie them together to make a rope, and lower it down to the person in the ravine. . . . I can't tell you how many girls died in that ravine. . . . We used to tie ourselves to the girls ahead of us so as not to get left behind. Each step of the way we prayed for our lives.

"They walked as much as 35 ri (about 85 miles), climbing up and down mountain passes for four to five days, before they arrived at their destination. At the end of the year, when the pass was covered with several feet of snow they would retrace their steps to go home to Hida. One woman remembered the trip this way:

"The wish to make my parents happy with the money I earned with my tears during the year . . . made me cross Nomugi Pass at the end of the year full of joyous expectations. I used to walk 85 miles over the pass in my straw sandals to come home.

---

[10] Quoted in, Sheila Matsumoto, "Women in Factories" in *Women in Changing Japan*, Joyce Lebra, Joy Paulson and Elizabeth Powers, eds. (Stanford: Stanford University Press, 1976), p. 52.

We didn't have mittens in those days, so we tucked our hands in our sleeves, linked ourselves together with cords, and crossed the pass.

"Now, I have forgotten all the hardships of those days," another woman remarked. "All I remember are the pleasant things. But sometimes I dream about crossing Nomugi Pass or about being punished at Suwa, and I start crying and wake up with a start." [11]

Besides the physical hardships of the journey, some young women were at the mercy of the male recruiters in charge of seeing that they got to the mills. There were frequent rapes. Young women, already "sold" by their families, had little chance to protest. The sexual attacks and harassment continued in the mills after their arrival.[12]

The mills in the 1890's demanded long hours from its workers. The following was a typical work schedule as it might have been presented to the families of the young women:

Typical Work Schedule of Spinning Industry Workers (circa 1897)

Time period	Duration in minutes	Activity
Day shift		
6:10- 6:15 a.m.	5	enter factory
6:15- 6:20	5	oil machines and perform other preparatory works
6:20- 7:45	85	regular work
7:45- 8:00	15	breakfast
8:00-12:00 noon	240	regular work
12:00-12:15 p.m.	15	lunch
12:15- 6:00	345	regular work
6:00- 6:05	5	cleaning
6:05	—	exit
Night shift		
5:55- 6:00 p.m.	5	enter factory
6:00- 6:05	5	oil machines and perform other preparatory works
6:05-12:00 mid.	355	regular work
12:00-12:15 a.m.	15	supper
12:15- 6:15	300	regular work
6:15- 6:20	5	cleaning
6:20	—	exit [13]

[11]Quoted in, Hane, *Peasants, Rebels, and Outcastes*, p. 179.

[12]Sievers, *Flowers in Salt*, p. 210-211.

[13]Kazuo Kusano, "Industrialization and the Status of Women in Japan," unpublished Ph.D. dissertation, University of Washington, 1973, p. 117.

Women frequently worked longer than 12-hour days, sometimes as long as 17 or 18 hours. A woman described what factory life was like:

"From morning, while it was still dark, we worked in the lamplit factory till ten at night. After work, we hardly had the strength to stand on our feet. When we worked late into the night, they occasionally gave us a yam. We then had to do our washing, fix our hair, and so on. By then it would be eleven o'clock. There was no heat even in the winter, and so we had to sleep huddled together. Several of the girls ran back to Hida. I was told that girls who went to work before my time had a harder time. We were not paid the first year. In the second year I got 35 yen, and the following year, 50 yen. I felt that it was not a place for a weak-willed person like me. If we didn't do the job right we were scolded, and, if we did better than others, the others resented it. The life of a woman is really awful." [14]

Because of the crowded dormitories, difficult, dangerous work, and moist, close air of the textile plants, infectious disease rates were high. One saying of the time was, "A dagger is not needed to kill a girl worker. Just choke her to death with the texture and fineness of the fiber." [15]

Later plant conditions improved, but even in the 1930's the young women still lived in dormitories where their freedom of movement was restricted. The following was representative of their daily schedule, Monday through Saturday:

4:00 - 5:00:	Waking gong. Clean room. Eat breakfast.
5:00 - 10:30:	Work in the plant.
10:30 - 11:00:	Lunch.
11:00 - 2:00:	Work in the plant.
2:00 - 3:30:	Free time.
3:30 - 4:30:	Classes.
4:30 - 6:00:	Dinner.
6:00 - 9:00:	Classes.
9:00 - 4:00:	All sleep.

Sundays off. [16]

With such horrible conditions in these factories, why did young women put up with them? Some found that no matter how difficult the work in the factories, at least there was food, and in famine years factory work meant survival. Some did not stay, managing to run away despite a police chase. If caught, women who attempted escape were brought back to the factory and severely punished for breaking their work contracts. Other women committed suicide to escape their fate. One young worker, beaten by the foreman, threw herself into one of the large waterwheels in the Tenryū River.

---

[14]Quoted in, Hane, *Peasants, Rebels, and Outcastes*, p. 182.

[15]*Ibid.*, p. 184.

[16]Helen Mears, *Year of the Wild Boar* (Philadelphia: J. B. Lippincott Company, 1942), p. 276-279.

Women coaling a steamship at Nagasaki, 1904.

She left a note for her parents, "I am sorry that I have not yet been able to repay the debt owed the company. Please forgive me for being a disloyal daughter, but my body is no longer of any use. Good-bye."[17] No records were kept of the number, but suicides seem to have been frequent.

Some women tried to organize themselves into unions and to strike for better conditions. Women workers brought about Japan's first strike at the Amamiya silk mills in 1886. The women managed to prevent the company from adding an additional 30

[17]Quoted in, Hane, *Peasants, Rebels, and Outcastes*, p. 188-189.

minutes to their workday.[18] Other strikes followed, but women were unsuccessful in building strong unions, because of rapid turnover.

Other women simply endured the bad conditions as part of a fate they had been trained to accept. They felt they owed their families their sacrifice of work, whether it paid for the new plot of land, the old gambling debts of the father, the brother's education, or meant food for the survival of family members. One woman said:

"I don't know how many times I thought I would rather jump into Lake Suwa and drown. Even so, when I went home with a year's earnings and handed the money to my mother, she clasped it in her hands and said, 'With this, we can manage through the end of the year.' And my father, who was ill, sat up in his bed and bowed to me over and over. 'Sue,' he said, 'it must have been difficult. Thank you. Thank you.' Then we put the money in a wooden box, and put the box up on the altar and prayed. . . . Whenever I thought of my mother's face then, I could endure any hardship." [19]

Women workers in early industrial Japan did more than provide for their individual family's survival. Their toil provided Japan with products on which to build an industrial future. All countries experiencing rapid industrialization seem to have expected the lower classes to contribute heavily to production while working long hours under dangerous conditions. In the late 19th and early 20th centuries there were women who toiled in unsanitary mills in the United States and Britain. The high percentage of female workers in Japanese textile factories, however, means that the story of Japan's process of industrialization is part of women's history as well as that of economic history.

Points to Consider

1. In what ways was the labor of women in Japan's industrialization process of critical importance? In what ways did the women benefit from their labor? In what ways did they benefit little from the "economic miracle" of Japan's rapid industrialization?

2. Looking over the excerpts in this selection, list specific things that seem to have been the harshest for women working in coal mines and women working in textile factories.

3. Why might women rather than men be hired to work in textile factories?

4. In what specific ways might women be more vulnerable or open to abusive treatment by factory owners and operators than men?

5. In what four ways did women who worked under harsh conditions in the textile factories attempt to deal with — or change — their situation? Were they successful? How or how not?

---

[18]Sievers, *Flowers in Salt*, p. 81-82.

[19]Quoted in, *Ibid.*, p. 55.

B.   The Moga or Modern Girl A Group Exercise

In the 1920's, during the Taishō period of Japanese history, there appeared in Japanese cities — "mobo" ('modern boys') and "moga" ('modern girls'). These young people wanted to be thought of as "modern" and up-to-date by adopting Western customs. This movement of youth to become "modern" was found primarily in cities and among the middle and upper classes.[1] The following is a list of quotations, descriptions, or data from the Taishō period.

- For each item, suggest a traditional Japanese cultural value that might have been challenged by the adoption of Western culture or styles.

- For each, also suggest whether your group would see the challenge as:

  A.   Superficial — with only surface differences.

  B.   Moderate — might shake up the established custom or affect the particular value but the crucial aspects of the value or custom would remain.

  C.   Severe — changing to this Western custom would bring an almost totally new system of cultural values.

As one source of traditional Japanese values you may want to review the Imperial Rescript on Education (Chapter 7-A) that was part of the Japanese educational system. Another

---

[1]Mikiso Hane, *Peasants, Rebels, and Outcastes* (New York: Pantheon Books, 1982), p. 34.

"Modern Girls" or "Moga" with short skirts, bobbed hair, and Western style clothes walk with young woman in traditional kimono — 1920's.

source for Japanese traditional values as they apply to women might be found in the chapters on "good wife, wise mother" and filial piety (Chapter 7-D).

* * * * *

1. In 1928 Hitomi Kinue was the first Japanese woman to go to the Olympic games. She received second place in the 100 meter race and an ovation in the press when she returned to Japan. (Sources follow the exercise.)

2. Sunata Komako and her husband Tokunaga Bunroku produced a film in Japan showing a Japanese wife pulling a heavy cart on which were riding her husband and a geisha who was entertaining him.

3. Margaret Sanger, an American

leader of the birth control movement, was invited to Japan to speak. The Japanese government forbade her to lecture, but Baroness Ishimoto Shizue invited her to appear at several social occasions.

4. A young woman described her dilemma about whether or not to wear Western clothes:

"Foreign dress is worn by school teachers and their older pupils, by bus conductors, office girls, theater ushers, nurses, elevator girls and department store lunch servers, but in each case this is recognized as a uniform, and is little noticed by the masses. Young women, however, who wear stylish foreign dress and hat do attract attention, even when their actions are most circumspect. This is a disadvantage. A mild one, perhaps, but no girl likes to be gazed at with even silent disapproval. I think few Westerners appreciate this gentle cowardice, but it is almost universal in Japan . . .

"One afternoon when I went to see Oji Sama [uncle], in a Japanese dress, he said kindly that I was growing more graceful day by day. Now Oji Sama, [uncle] although he is rather progressive in thought, is very old fashioned in his love for old customs; so I laughed and told him that it was my dress that won that compliment from him, but that he needn't worry, for I was

never going to wear foreign dress on his rude old street again.

"To his surprised questioning I told him that when I went away the last time I came to see him, the coolies mending the street had all stopped work to stare at me as I passed; and one had said to another, 'Moga! — new woman!' and laughed.

"Oji Sama looked at me with a queer little smile on his face, and his eyes twinkled.

" 'Wearing unusual dress for use and for adornment are two different things, Chiyo San,' he said. 'Those coolies working on the street would have taken no notice of a plain foreign dress on a busy woman. It would be accepted as a sort of uniform. Now your dress, although modest . . . was evidently too frilly for a dress made only for use, and some over-patriotic workman showed his disapproval. But that remark was mild. Just let a girl go by in a fly-away dress with bare arms and pink silk hose and bobbed hair, and it will arouse a species of resentment in every workman in sight. Why resentment, I don't know — but it's a fact!' "

5. Soprano Miura Tamaki appeared at the Imperial Theater in Tōkyō and was the first Japanese woman to appear abroad as Butterfly in Puccini's opera ''Madame Butterfly.''

6. The severe earthquake of 1923 led Tōkyō women's groups to

Soprano Miura Tamaki, internationally known for her portrayal of Madame Butterfly, autographed pictures for fans in New York City in 1924.

band together to open shelters, provide food and clothing, and generally organize relief. The Tōkyō Federation of Women's Societies was created to deal with the problems that followed the earthquake.

7. In 1921 Yajima Kaji, age 89, went to Washington, D.C. as part of the international disarmament movement of the 1920's. She presented President Harding with a petition bearing 10,000 signatures of Japanese women supporting peaceful disarmament.

8. In 1921 Hani Motoko and her husband founded the Jiyu Gakuen (Freedom School) in which girls were forbidden to take notes in class so that they could take part in class discussions.

9. A president of a college in Japan wrote:

"A few years ago in the larger cities quite a craze for dancing sprang up. The conservatives were horror-stricken when they saw some of their young women fox-trotting around with men. A sort of miniature insurrection broke out against these performances considered so outrageous. On several occasions ruffians with drawn swords entered the hotels where dancing was going on and forced the Japanese women to leave the place. Soon afterwards police regulations were drawn up which forbid any dancing after ten o'clock at night."

10. Woodcuts of the Taishō period [1912-1925] are compared to past historical times by a recent historian as follows:

"Edo [Tokugawa period] artists in the woodcut admired slender beauty, certainly, but it is an abstract, fleshless sort of beauty, very far from this wasted flesh. The . . . girl [in Taishō illustrations] may look ill, but she smiles sometimes, although wanly. The Edo [1603-1867] beauty did not smile, and the Meiji [1868-1912] beauty did but rarely. All manner of smiles flash across Taishō paintings and posters, and give a sense that Western things have been absorbed and become part of the organism as they had not earlier been."

Sources

1. Yoko Matsuoka, *Daughter of the Pacific* (New York: Harper & Brothers, 1952), p. 26-27.

2. Allen K. Faust, *The New Japanese Womanhood* (New York: George H. Doran Company, 1926), p. 96.

3. Mary R. Beard, *The Force of Women in Japanese History* (Washington, DC: Public Affairs Press, 1953), p. 167-168.

See also Baroness Ishimoto Shizue, *Facing Two Ways* (New York: Farrar & Rinehart, 1935).

4. Chiyono Sugimoto Kiyooka, *Chiyo's Return* (Garden City: Doubleday, Doran & Company, 1936), p. 250-254.

5. Edward Seidensticker, *Low City, High City* (New York: Alfred A. Knopf, 1983), p. 274.

6. Michi Kawai and Ochimi Kubushiro, *Japanese Women Speak* (Boston: The Central Committee on the United Study of Foreign Missions, 1934), p. 127-128.

7. *Ibid.*, p. 176-177.

8. Noriko Shimada, Hiroko Takamura, Masako Iino, and Hisako Ito, "Ume Tsuda and Motoko Hani: Echoes of American Cultural Feminism in Japan," in Carol V. R. George, ed., *"Remember The Ladies": New Perspectives on Women in American History* (Syracuse: Syracuse University Press, 1975), p. 175-176.

9. Faust, *The New Japanese Womanhood*, p. 132-133.

10. Seidensticker, *Low City, High City*, p. 259.

C.   The Japanese Women's Movement—"The Third Wave"

In the late 1970's, an 82-year-old woman was interviewed. She was then a member of the Japanese Diet or Parliament. Ichikawa Fusae was asked how she saw herself compared to the "women libbers" of the day.[1] Ichikawa Fusae's answer was, "I myself am one of the old libbers."[2] By that comment she meant that the quest for the vote and other rights for Japanese women dated back to the Meiji period (1868-1912.) But by the late Taishō period in the 1920's it seemed as if suffrage was about to be achieved for Japanese women. However, by 1931 the hopeful drive for women's suffrage began fading away in defeat. The Taishō was, then, a "period of hope" that dimmed quickly.[3]

There were several reasons to be hopeful about women's suffrage in the 1920's. During World War I (1914-1918) women throughout the world had generally proved themselves to be strong supporters, both economically and patriotically, of their governments. In countries like The Soviet Union, The United States, Great Britain, and Germany, women received suffrage rights as the result of their political

---

[1]"Women's lib" was the abbreviation for the "women's liberation movement" of the 1960-1970's, more generally referred to now as the "women's movement."

[2]Haruko K. Watanabe and Yoko Nuita, "Japanese Women Pioneers," *Frontiers*, Vol. 3, No. 3 (1978), p. 61.

[3]Fusae Ichikawa, as quoted in, Dee Ann Vavich, "The Japanese Woman's Movement: Fusae Ichikawa — A Pioneer in Woman's Suffrage," *Monumenta Nipponica*, 22, #3-4, 1967, p. 418.

Ichikawa Fusae, campaigned for women's rights in the 1920's, was silenced by the military government in the 1930's, and elected to the Diet after World War II.

participation of women in political parties.

One of the first targets for reform was the Peace Preservation Law of 1887 which prevented women from attending political meetings. Hiratsuka Raichō and Ichikawa Fusae, with others, formed a New Women's Association. Hiratsuka Raichō explained:

"The time has come for women to unite for the sake of all women to fulfil our natural obligations, and attain our natural rights. . . . we must cooperate with the men, and participate in the actual movement of postwar social reconstruction. If women do not stand fast at this time, the future will be no different — women will again be excluded from society which will remain the monopoly of men. If this occurs, it will be a great catastrophe for the world, for mankind." [4]

actions and wartime participation. Japanese suffrage leaders met with American women leaders like Carrie Chapman Catt and Alice Paul and took part in an international congress for women's rights. These activities by Japanese women seem to suggest that the worldwide pressure for voting rights for women in the early 20th century might have an effect on Japan.

Within Japan itself a growing coalition of women worked for the vote. The earthquake of 1923 had mobilized women's groups and made networks of women more visible. Such diverse groups as the Women's Christian Temperance Union and the socialists supported women's rights, although they differed on what those rights might bring. One reason women's religious and charitable groups were important for women working for their rights was that the Japanese government had forbidden the

After a campaign of petitions, they got the Peace Preservation Law revised in 1922. Japanese women were thus allowed to attend political meetings but still could not join political parties.[5] Ichikawa Fusae and others then organized the Women's Suffrage Union to work for women's rights — the vote, more educational opportunities, and equality in family rights.

---

[4]Dorothy Robins-Mowry, *The Hidden Sun: Women of Modern Japan* (Boulder, CO: Westview Press, 1983), p. 66.

[5]Susan J. Pharr, *Political Women in Japan* (Berkeley: University of California Press, 1981), p. 19.

The women who worked for women's rights did not have an easy time of it. Ichikawa Fusae and Hiratsuka Raichō were arrested for attending a YMCA meeting. Kondo Magara, a socialist, would borrow a baby to wear on her back when she handed out leaflets advocating women's rights — otherwise she risked arrest.[6] Ichikawa Fusae was attacked on stage when she tried to speak. Insults were common. In 1928 the home minister (secretary of state) told the women reformers, "Go back to your homes and wash your babies' clothes! This is the job given to you and there is the place in which you are entitled to sit!" [7]

Two years later, however, the new government ministers were more sympathetic to women's right to vote. A bill was passed in 1930 that allowed women to join political parties and vote in local elections. It looked as if the women might also get the right to vote in national elections. Prime Minister Inukai Tsuyoshi had promised suffrage leaders that he would give them his support.

Events in Japan, however, prevented suffrage from happening. Prime Minister Inukai Tsuyoshi was assassinated, the Manchurian Incident occurred,[8] and the Japanese economy declined as the world slid into the Great Depression. All of these events contributed to the rise of a militaristic government in Japan that saw activist women as critics of its policies. The suffrage act was not passed, and the activities of suffrage leaders were closely watched by the military in the 1930's. Like the "first" and "second" waves of Meiji feminists, the "third wave" of women reformers of the 1920's was defeated. Yet this suffrage

movement had gained some support from women's groups and male politicians. Japanese women received the right to vote during the Allied occupation of Japan after World War II. This achievement marked the end of a long suffrage campaign by Japanese women. The Japanese women's movement had had international ties but the right to vote was not an alien gift given to Japanese women by the occupying Allied forces.

Points to Consider

1. One "lever" that women leaders used in the cause of women's suffrage, particularly in the Western world, was the contribution women made to their governments during World War I. During and after the war, women gained attention by acting in non-traditional roles. Historian William Chafe wrote that in the United States by 1917:

". . . At the height of the fighting in France, thousands of women in Bridgeport, Connecticut,

---

[6]Robins-Mowry, *The Hidden Sun*, p. 67-69.

[7]Quoted in, Vavich, "The Japanese Woman's Movement," p. 418.

[8]In 1931, using the excuse of a bomb that was set off at a Japanese railway near Mukden, China, Japan occupied Manchuria — the northeastern part of China and set up the puppet state of Manchukuo.

Springfield, Massachusetts, and other cities across the country swarmed into factories to take up the work of men at the front. The number of women employed in iron and steel trebled. Over 100,000 women entered munitions factories. Countless others served as streetcar conductors, elevator operators, furnace stokers, and bricklayer helpers. Female lawyers were appointed to the government's legal advisory committees, and female doctors for the first time gained access to the U.S. Public Health Service. The Women's Bureau — established in large part as a result of the war — required four pages to list all the jobs in which women substituted for men during the fighting." [9]

Chafe, however, argues that these improvements in the status of female workers in the United States were "misconceptions."

"In 1919 the Central Federated Union of New York declared that "the same patriotism which induced women to enter industry during the war should induce them to vacate their positions after the war." [10]

By the 1920's the participation of American women in the work force had actually declined from 1910 (from 20.9 % to 20.4 %).[11]

Unlike American and European women, Japanese women did not fill many non-traditional roles during World War I as Japan's part in the war was not large. But in some ways the earthquake of 1923 gave Japanese women the opportunity to carry out non-traditional work in much the same way as did Western women during World War I.

How did Japanese women react to the problems caused by the earthquake?

In what ways were the opportunities for non-traditional activities after the earthquake similar to those for Western women during World War I? In what ways do they seem to have been different?

List reasons why women in both the Western world and Japan might have needed these "levers" (of war or natural disasters) to claim their political, economic, and other rights?

2. In the case of both Japanese and Western women the optimistic forecasts of women leaders that these events would cause women to gain economic equality of opportunity did not occur. Japanese women only attained limited suffrage — and for Western women the right to vote did not translate into political power.

---

[9]William H. Chafe, *The American Woman* (New York: Oxford University Press, 1972), p. 51.

[10]*Ibid.*, p. 53.

[11]*Ibid.*, p. 53.

Why do you think women felt that filling non-traditional roles during times of national crises would help achieve political and economic equality?

Why do you think that women did not achieve more permanent economic and political opportunities from these events which forced them into non-traditional, highly visible roles?

3. In a recent book, political scientist Susan Pharr described Ichikawa Fusae as she appeared in the 1920's as, "A tall woman who smoked and wore her hair short, she was an object of ridicule in the Japanese press for her manner as well as her convictions. But her single-minded commitment to suffrage over other issues helped to hold together a movement that was by that time heavily factionalized [divided]." [12]

Considering Japanese culture at the beginning of the century, why did Ichikawa Fusae's appearance make her an object of ridicule in the press?

In what specific ways might her appearance and behavior have hurt her cause of gaining women the vote? In what ways might it have helped it?

Why do you think she might have continued to smoke and wear short hair even when it meant the press ridiculed her?

4. What events brought the "third wave" of the Japanese women's movement to an end? When did Japanese women gain the right to vote?

5. What do the authors mean when they say, "This achievement [of the right to vote] marked the end of a long suffrage campaign by Japanese women. The Japanese women's movement had had international ties but the right to vote was not an alien gift given to Japanese women by the occupying Allied forces."

---

[12]Susan J. Pharr, Political Women in Japan, p. 19-20.

CHAPTER 10

JAPANESE WOMEN
FROM A MILITARY WORLD
TO AN ERA OF LIBERATION
1930-1952

A.   Back to
Good Wife / Wise Mother

The 1930's are considered the dark valley of Japanese women's history. During the 1930's the military, and in particular the army, expanded its power and finally ruled Japan. A policy of overseas expansion was also undertaken by the military controlled government. Although the Japanese navy was somewhat skeptical of the policy, with the support of the army the Japanese military expanded into Manchuria China in 1931 and later into Southeast Asia. The army, however, focused on the idea of creating a "Great Co-prosperity Sphere for Asians" that would increase Japan's power. As the Japanese army became more involved in foreign expansion, it also became more concerned about

any opposition at home to their policy of expansion. Various groups, like the socialists and peace activists, had their rights severely limited during this era. But women were increasingly seen as a group that had to be brought into line with military needs.

If women's actions were to be fitted to military aims, women's opposition to war needed to be silenced. Various individual women in different periods had opposed Japanese military ventures. Yosano Akiko, in the early 1900's, wrote a poem attacking Japan's involvement in the Russo-Japanese War. She wrote of the uselessness of her brother going to war:

...ner; no, you must not

...e damn fortress at Port Arthur
fall
Or let it stand, what difference can it
make
To merchant folk who are not called
to cramp
Their lives in patterns cut for
samurai?
"O no, my brother, no: you must not
die.
Can it be true that, while the
Emperor
Remains himself immune from risks
of war,
He urges others on to kill their kind
And, calling death in battle glorious,
Sends them to die the deaths of
savage beasts?
If, as it is, the Emperor's heart is
noble,
How could such thoughts find
lodgement in his mind?
"O youngest brother, not in
senseless war
Can you, nay, may you, throw your
life away." [1]

During the 1920's Japanese women
had collected signatures on petitions
supporting a conference on naval
disarmament held in Washington, D.C.
in 1923. In 1931 a number of women
spoke out against the Japanese
military takeover of Manchuria, China.
The Women's Suffrage Party criticized
Japanese military imperialism and
domestic policies, as did various
Christian women's groups.

The following selection is from a
speech by Mrs. Sakamoto, one of
several speeches given on
International Prayer Day in 1933:

"I am probably the only person
present here who has actually seen
fighting and suffering in the fighting
area. That is the reason the
Japanese in general do not hate war
with China, because we have never
shed blood on Japanese soil. We
don't know what it means. We
should realize our debt to China for
our culture, but instead we have
gone to China to fight! This is what
the men have done, but we women
must redeem it. God lives and works,
and if we educate the young aright,
a different Japan will develop."

["These addresses were followed by
much praying. Following the meeting
a cable was sent addressed to the
women of China and to the women
of America, and also a protest was
made to the Radio Company for its
militaristic broadcasts."] [2]

In 1931-1933 the Women's Peace
Association wrote letters to the
women of China. The following is one
of these letters:

"Dear Friends:

"We, the members of the Women's
Peace Association in Japan, are
burdened with agonizing grief over
the present rupture between your

---

[1]Quoted in, Atsumi Ikuko and Graeme Wilson,
"The Poetry of Yosano Akiko," *Japan Quarterly*,
Vol. 21, No. 2 (April-June 1974), p. 184.

[2]Quoted in, Michi Kawai and Ochimi Kubushiro,
Japanese Women Speak (Boston: The Central
Committee on the United Study of Foreign
Missions, 1934), p. 174-175.

country and ours. Some of you may feel that we women here are indifferent in regard to this matter. Allow us to say, though, that it is quite the contrary to the fact. We are greatly concerned about this grievous state of affairs, and we earnestly desire to maintain the most friendly relationship between us, as we are responsible in maintaining peace over a large section of the Orient...

"In so far as there is any truth in the reports of the unfortunate events which have occurred in your country through the insults of our people, we are ready to ask your forgiveness, and we trust that you are willing to take the same attitude toward us. When one is carried away by excitement, even the beautiful spirit of patriotism is so often marred by fanatic action, and we deeply deplore these things, because we sincerely want your friendship and cooperation in the work for peace." [3]

This opposition to Japanese actions against China was increasingly silenced by the Japanese military government during the decade of the 1930's. Newspapers and suffrage leaders were banned from expressing anti-government opinions, and Christians were condemned as "foreign" and disloyal. People who tried to speak out against the military were silenced in a variety of ways — assassination being one method. In a series of these assassination attempts in the mid-1930's, women of the families of the targeted male leaders became involved as well:

- Viscount Saito, a gentle 80-year-old man, was shot repeatedly, and his wife was shot in the hand when she tried to defend his body.

- Count Makino, another older man, had his guards killed, but his granddaughter Kazuko helped him to climb onto a ledge, then spread her kimono in front of him. The soldiers did not shoot.

- Baron Suzuki Kantaro was attacked with daggers by assassins, but his wife grabbed the dagger before the final blow and saved his life.

- When assassins attacked General Watanabe, his wife lay down with her husband in her arms so that the gun that killed him had to be forced under her body. [4]

Opposing the war became increasingly dangerous for men and women.

It was not only women who spoke out for peace who were seen as a threat by the government. Women who spoke out for women's rights were also seen as opposing the plans of the military regime. As part of a new emphasis on "samurai" military values, women were to be subservient to the needs of the military state. The military justified its overseas expansion partly on the grounds of a need for more room for the increasing Japanese population. Some Japanese proposed birth control as a method of

[3] Quoted in, *Ibid.*, p. 180-181.

[4] Joseph C. Grew, *Ten Years in Japan* (New York: Simon and Schuster, 1944), p. 171-176.

limiting the population, thereby eliminating the need for conquest. Baroness Ishimoto Shizue was one of the leaders in expressing this view that limitation, not imperialism, was the answer to Japan's population problem. She opened a birth control clinic in Tōkyō in 1934 despite, as she later wrote, the opposition of "a government concerned with an abundant supply of soldiers."[5] The Japanese military took the position that Japan would actually need *more* people in order to have a strong army abroad. A new motto, "Lets Have Children," was advocated for women, and birth control clinics, such as the one opened in 1934, were discouraged. By the early 1940's Tōjō Katsuko, the wife of the prime minister, was quoted as saying that "having babies is fun." Birth control was made illegal, and government subsidies were promised to couples with large families.[6]

For women who opposed these views, there was the terror of arrest. Baroness Ishimoto was arrested in 1937 for advocating birth control as well as for her opposition to the military. Her son Arata was greatly disturbed by the shame of having his mother arrested, but then began to change his mind:

"Spiritual agony overcame me. How is she being treated? When will she come home? Isn't it hard to be kept in jail in such a cold climate? I had known that there is no heat in the jail at the police headquarters. What is the truth of this case? I was terribly confused. At least it seemed to me there was no remedy to be applied at once. Yet as time passed, my astonishment and indignation

subsided by degrees and it seemed to me even shameful to be astonished by such an event, a persecution which all the social pioneers have to suffer and endure, a trial which the real social battler must undergo to win the final brilliant triumph. This idea gradually consoled me — the idea that my mother's mission was the supreme consideration and that the persecutors imprisoning her were only making her career more glorious."[7]

Because of international protests, Baroness Ishimoto was later released. With government arrest possible under the vague Peace Preservation Law, there was little women could do to oppose government policies. As Ishimoto Shizue said later, "All I could do was to keep silence. That was all I could do. That was my silent resistance."[8]

Not only were women's suffrage and social reform movements stopped during the 1930's, but the military government's propaganda used Confucian ideals of ranking or hierarchy plus loyalty and duty to

---

[5]Baroness Shizue Ishimoto, *Facing Two Ways* (New York: Farrar & Rinehart, 1935), p. 373.

[6]Thomas R. H. Havens, "Women and War in Japan, 1937-45," *The American Historical Review*, Vol. 80, No. 4 (October 1975), p. 928.

[7]Quoted in, Mary R. Beard, *The Force of Women in Japanese History* (Washington, DC: Public Affairs Press, 1953), p. 171.

[8]Quoted in, Dorothy Robins-Mowry, *The Hidden Sun: Women of Modern Japan* (Boulder, CO: Westview Press, 1983), p. 76.

support its policies. According to their interpretation of the Confucian system, the Chinese were seen as inferior and should obey the culturally superior Japanese. The lowly soldier should give complete obedience to the emperor. A wife should obey and give unquestioning loyalty to her husband. In the early 1940's the ministry of education issued the following instructions to Japanese women:

"We must admonish Japanese women to reject individualistic ideas and encourage them to cultivate and improve such virtues inherently belonging to them as submissiveness, gentleness, chasteness, perseverance, and service."* [9]

As a part of this return to old Tokugawa-samurai values, the traditional role of wife and mother was emphasized. A British woman described what she was told about marriage in the 1930's:

"A young, beautiful and highly talented girl of society whom I knew was going to be married, a suitable and advantageous marriage having been arranged. In the course of conversation with some of the girl's near relations, I said that I hoped she would be happy. The ladies, who knew Europe and America well, replied with a smile, 'You know, that is not the way we look at it: we do not aim at her individual happiness. It is her duty to marry and become the mother of children, and in fulfilling this duty she will find happiness.' Which is true enough. I should imagine that all women thus dedicated must adore their children; their babies are in fact adored. The

husband may be lovable, may not be; the babies certainly are.

"All the gifts of intellect and artistry, all the vivid interest in the changing world of Japan, all this must be utterly subordinated to the strict discipline of life in the home. If the girl goes to live in the household of her husband's parents in the old-fashioned way, she starts her married life under auspices that we in England would avoid for our own daughters. Liberty, that lovely precious thing, is hers no longer.

"Where the family is 'old-style' in its customs and behavior, she will not be able to leave the house without the permission of her mother-in-law. When the scented spring air tempts her energies, she cannot open the door and go for a walk: she may not any more run down to the shops for small purchases, but must wait until it is convenient for someone to go with her: she does not invite her former girl-friends, because the process of doing so would be so laborious and upsetting to the quiet regime of her new home that it would not be worth the trouble. She must spend long hours sitting with her mother-in-law, whose years of retirement will probably have stultified in her any aspirations she may once have had to knowing what was going on outside her four walls. If the young husband is able to control his destiny to a certain

---

[9]Quoted in, Kazuo Kusano, ''Industrialization and the Status of Women in Japan,'' unpublished Ph.D. dissertation, University of Washington, 1973, p. 173.

The Japanese military government disapproved of Western style entertainment such as this 1935 musical theater company.

extent, he and his wife will be able to go to the cinema together in the evenings and make themselves happy in their own way. But during the hours that he is away at work his wife belongs to her mother-in-law." [10]

The subordination of the wife to the family was shown in an incident from the 1930's which created a scandal in the press. Upon returning to Japan, a prominent Japanese man reported

that he was glad to be back, particularly because he was happy to be reunited with his wife. He was

---

[10]Katharine Sansom, *Living in Tokyo* (New York: Harcourt, Brace & Company, 1937), p. 46-47.

forcefully criticized for not speaking of his parents or his duty to Japan but for mentioning his wife who was not on his level.[11]

Women were encouraged to return to Japanese-style dress. One Japanese writer of the time found this a satisfactory state of affairs:

"Not ten Japanese women in a hundred, not five, not even two, wear European dress, although this is much cheaper and perhaps more convenient than the native kimono. At the most one in a hundred wears European dress, and this only in the large towns. We are not particularly proud of the 'modern girls' in European dress, who are somewhat contemptuously called 'compact girls' by the populace, in reference to the 'compact powder' which the girls publicly dab on their faces upon every available occasion." [12]

One woman described how her mother continued to dress in Western clothes even though her father's superiors applied pressure:

"Mother's habit of wearing Western dresses apparently displeased His Excellency, for he told Father it was a disgrace and that Mother should be wearing kimonos. However, Mother never yielded to this fancy, and Father stuck by his stubborn wife. Perhaps this was an expression of their protest against a ruthless and rigid society. When I realize how inconsequential this sort of resistance was, in proportion to the risk involved — for it could have resulted in Father's discharge — I become acutely aware of the immense power which the rulers

This woman is wearing the traditional dress the military government directed for Japanese women in the 1930's.

exercised under such a social system." [13]

[11]Ruth Benedict, *The Chrysanthemum and The Sword* (Cambridge: The Riverside Press, 1946), p. 208.

[12]Komakichi Nohara, *The True Face of Japan* (London: Jarrolds Publishers, 1936), p. 18-19.

[13]Yoko Matsuoka, *Daughter of the Pacific* (New York: Harper & Brothers, 1952), p. 45.

Even wearing Western clothes might be seen by the military government as being an anti-Japanese statement and so an act of disloyalty.

The 1930's saw the closing down of reforms started in the Taishō Period. Women went back to work in the mines. The famines of the 1930's brought increased prostitution — and the government looked the other way, ignoring the fact that prostitution was illegal. The suffrage movement was doomed to failure, and women activists were silenced. Schools stressed the submissiveness of women as a social ideal. The military government, however, soon found itself needing women to be more than "good wives/wise mothers." In the 1930's, before World War II, no one could predict how women would be needed. But it soon became clear.

Points to Consider

1. What specific things might have led some Japanese women to refer to the late 1930's as "the dark valley" of women's history for Japan?

2. In what ways did individual women and women's groups oppose a number of the military government's policies in the early 1930's?

3. Review neo-Confucian ideals for women as they appeared during the Tokugawa period (see: Chapter 5-B).

   List the neo-Confucian values that the military government restored in the 1930's.

Why do you think that the military put so much stress on neo-Confucian values? Why do you think they were particularly interested in having women return to these Tokugawa period values and customs?

4. What risks were there for women who defied the "dress code" of the military government or spoke out against government policies?

5. During the Nazi military rule in Germany which came to power in the 1930's, the ideal for women came to be — "kinder, kuche, und kirche" (children, kitchen and church). What do you think the Nazis meant by this slogan? In what ways is it similar to the ideals for women expressed by the Japanese military government in the same time period?

6. Why do you think the Japanese government would come to need women as more than just "good wives/wise mothers" in the 1940's?

B.   Peasant Women in the 1930's A Group Exercise

Divide the class into groups of four or five students. Appoint a recorder for each group.

1. Review the roles and duties expected of Japanese women by the military rule before and during World War II (Part A.)

2. Read the ten excerpts which are descriptions of life in a rural, Japanese village in the 1930's (Part B.)

3. Write a paragraph in your group that compares or contrasts each excerpt in Part B with the official expectations for Japanese women in the 1930's and 1940's in Chapter 10A.

4. After the groups have completed their paragraphs compare answers in class discussion.

Part A: Review of Japanese Women's Expected Duties, 1930-1945

*   *Instruction Manual for Wartime Family Education* (distributed by the Japanese Ministry of Education in 1942 during World War II):

"We must admonish Japanese women to reject individualistic ideas and encourage them to cultivate and improve such virtues inherently belonging to them as submissiveness, gentleness, chasteness, perseverance, and service."

*   The government in the 1930's emphasized the superiority of males over females.

*   The utmost importance was placed

225

Peasant women work winnowing rice — 1930's.

on family lineage — traced through the father. Women who did not have children, particulary sons, were despised.

- Women who worked outside the home were treated with contempt (even though they were eventually needed in the munitions factories during the war.)[1]

(Also review Chapter 10-A for a discussion of the expected behavior of women in Japan in the 1930's continuing into the war years.)

Part B: Japanese Village Life — Excerpts, 1930's

Two American anthropologists, John and Ella Embree, went to the small, rural village of Suye Mura [Sue Mura] in the 1930's to study a Japanese community. The following short excerpts are some descriptions of the lives of women in Suye Mura from their diaries.[2]

1.   "Matsumoto Shima claims that Toride has been cutting wood and gathering bamboo shoots on her land, so she told his young son to stay off it. His father arrived this morning in a rage and to the amusement of the villagers, who assembled at

---

[1]Kazuo Kusano, "Industrialization and the Status of Women in Japan," unpublished Ph.D. dissertation, University of Washington, 1973, p. 173.

[2]Excerpts from, Robert J. Smith and Ella Lury Wiswell, *The Women of Suye Mura* (Chicago: The University of Chicago Press, 1982), p. 3, 8, 47-48, 75, 94, 95, 151, 188, 268, 45. Ella Lury Embree and John Embree were the only anthropologists to study in Japan during the 1930's. They left Japan in 1936. John Embree was killed in an accident in 1950. In 1965 Ella Lury Embree Wiswell suggested to Robert Smith that her journal and some of John's unpublished notes might be worth publishing. This book was the result of their collaboration.

once, proceeded to say what he thought. When Shima grew too impertinent, he made a gesture as if to strike her in the face. She yelled, 'If you hit me, I'll hit back,' and picked up a *geta* [wooden clog] with which she did strike him. [To strike another with a piece of footgear is a grievous insult.] They called each other *baka* [literally, fool, but the most insulting word in ordinary discourse] a couple of times. He said that he would go to the village office about this, and she said that she will write to her older brother, which she did after he left. 'He takes advantage of women,' she grumbled. After a long argument, he started off, turning around now and then to tell her that she had no right calling him such things, that she was a liar, that he will go to the village office, and that he will beat her up if she says that again. When he turned away from her, he would smile, then make a fierce face again and add a few more imprecations. She followed him verbally all the way down the street with her protests."

2. "Taking flower-arranging bothered her a bit because the other women laughed at it and often talked about the expense involved. 'What? Twenty-five sen for these wild flowers?' they would exclaim. 'Why, you can pick them free right here in the woods!' The hamlet women teased her so much that at one time she refused to carry her flowers through the village on her way from school [where the

Early 20th century Japanese women tea pickers. They have been asked to "look pleasant" for the photograph but tea pickers were considered to have very difficult lives.

lessons were given] and would leave them at my house so that she could come back and pick them up later in the evening. Eventually, using the hot weather and her pregnancy as excuses, she stopped coming to the lessons altogether."

3. "About noontime I heard some drumming from the Kitadake shrine, so went to investigate. A group of five women, all but one from Suye, were eating, drinking and making merry. They said they were beating the drum and dancing, 'to please the god.' (Actually they said it is a goddess of crops who also gives children if prayed to.) The non-Suye woman, a brazen wench from Menda, sat before the shrine with her hands up in imitation of the mudra [symbolic hand gestures] of a deity, and the others made as if rubbing their rosary beads and praying

227

before her amid general laughter. Even my jaded senses got something of a jolt."

4. "Yesterday Mrs. Sato gave a farewell party for Mrs. Soeshima who will soon be leaving the village to move into town. Almost all the hamlet women came. No men were present. The dancing was exuberant, especially that done by the guest of honor. She wore *Otafuku* mask-like make-up [Otafuku is a comic mask of a jolly country girl] and stuffed a cushion under her kimono to make her look pregnant. She was impersonating a geisha who is disgusted with her fate. . . Each woman brought eleven sen and a small measure of rice. The guest of honor got special food, and the party went on until after midnight. The women were not very drunk, but just as with the school dance programs, there was no thought of stopping."

5. "Horizuka Suzue is a girl from Hamanoue, about sixteen years old. She is a maid at Makino's and complains about the work. She says that it is much too hard and that a factory job would be much easier, and you can make friends in such a place. Here she cooks three meals a day, cleans the house, and is required to do a great deal of work in the fields. Today I met her as she was carrying rice bran to the mulberry fields up near the cemetery. The baskets were so heavy that I could hardly lift one on my shoulder. She said that she will make five trips."

6. "At the house in Hirayama, the daughter-in-law never stopped working, her strong muscular legs bare almost to the buttocks, constantly in motion. She had dried some rice which was spread out on large heavy mats in the sun. She collected it into heaps, and then spread it again with a rake to dry some more. Later, when it was ready, she put it all in a can, which she carried into the shed. The only time she asked one of the younger girls to help her was when she took in the heavy mats. Then she threshed some rice by hand and winnowed it. In between these tasks, she would play with the baby for a few minutes or give it a suck at her breast. She let the baby come to her and pretend to help her, fussing around with the rake and getting in the way. At the end of the long day she helped roast the tea-leaves, first washing the ceramic container and mixing some fresh clay with her feet to spread over some cracks in it, and chopping wood for fire."

7. "Remarriage is quite common here. A woman in Oade was married once to a man in Hitoyoshi, but left him because she did not like her mother-in-law. Then she married a man in Hamanoue and didn't like her husband — it is said that she would not sleep with him — and finally married a man in Oade by whom she has had six children." Of this case Ella Wiswell wrote, "Today I met Mrs. Maeno. She told me that one of their six children died. Before marrying Maeno, she said with a smile,

she had two husbands. The first marriage lasted only six months because she could not stand her mother-in-law's constant criticism, so she left. Her second marriage lasted only a month. She disliked the man and made her bed separately. This third marriage was contracted sight unseen. It is working out fine. Maeno knew about her history but took a chance, she said, and she had decided to start out on a new venture without ever laying eyes on him.''

8. "While John was away, the young men were hanging around late [at the widow Matsumoto's house]. When I went to look, however, I could see no one nor did I see any signs of activity at the widow Matsumoto's. I think that what is significant is not whether anyone actually goes to see her, but that it is a recognized pattern that widows entertain men. Even Mrs. Tanimoto says it must be nice to be a widow, 'For then you can have any number of lovers.' ''

9. "The women said that witchcraft is practiced only by women and passes from mother to daughter or daughter-in-law. The old lady Tanno, they say, has already passed hers on to her niece, who is known for such activity. They remembered that old lady Nagata was a bad witch. She had seventy-seven dog-spirits, and when she died a goodly number of them survived and passed on to her daughter-in-law.''

10. "Early September is a slack season on the farms and women drop in on one another all the time. Mrs. Shimoda was at Mrs. Sato's and Mrs. Maeno at Mrs. Nawahara and Mrs. Takayama went over to see old lady Tanno. At Kawabe's there was a woman from Shoya who was just being served tea. She had bicycled over to discuss something about raising chickens. Mrs. Ouchi was there, too, and later a child was sent to fetch Mrs. Maeno who was not far away gathering persimmons. There was much chatter and laughter. Mrs. Tomokawa was passing by some distance down the street, and they called to her to come join them. She went on to her house and shortly reappeared with some dumplings, which were enjoyed by all.''

C. Japanese Women and World War II

Some Japanese women opposed the policies of the military government during the 1930's. A number of outspoken critics and peace activists were silenced by threats and arrests. There were Japanese women, however, who did not oppose the military government of Japan.

The women of Japan had demonstrated their loyalty in various ways during modern times. Some had been nurses in the China-Japan War of the 1890's as well as in the Russo-Japanese War of 1905. The Japanese surgeon-general, Baron Ishiguro Tadanori, wrote about the first field nurses:

"This employment of female nurses met with loud opposition ... because of antiquated notions regarding the relative status of men and women in Japan. But I stoutly maintained my original position, and employed the Red Cross Hospital nurses in the military hospitals of Hiroshima and elsewhere. The result amply justified my course of action, for all these nurses proved an unqualified success. ...

"At the close of the war ... a number of lady head-nurses were decorated with the Order of the Crown, which order had been specially created some years previously, to decorate women for distinguished service." [1]

---

[1] Chimnabai II and S. M. Mitra, *The Position of Women in Indian Life* (London: Longmans, Green & Co., 1911), p. 345-346.

Japanese women in school uniforms training as militia during World War II.

While a limited number of women were wartime nurses, many Japanese women proved their concern for soldiers in the Russo-Japanese War and World War I by sending soldiers "comfort bags" of towels, rice, toothpaste, and other small items. One man wrote that as a soldier in Korea he had "received a safety razor in one of these bags . . . and [it] was an extremely valuable item."[2] Red Cross workers had rolled bandages, organized bazaars for hospital relief, and supported the war effort in both the Russo-Japanese War and World War I. World War II was to prove a greater test of Japanese women's loyalty and courage. Not only were they required to do more war work, but the war itself came home to them.

In the 1930's the Japanese government stressed women's roles as wives and mothers, but by the 1940's Japanese women were needed in the war effort. During the early months of the war, women's activities were mainly directed toward propagandizing the cause of the war. Various voluntary patriotic women's societies were eventually formed into the Great Japan Women's Association. This organization was run by men and controlled by the government. At first this society made "comfort kits" and rolled bandages, just as had been done in previous wars. One of the activities encouraged was the "1000 stitches." A Japanese fighter ace from

---

[2]Kimura Ki, ed., *Japanese Literature; Manners and Customs in the Meiji-Taisho Era* (Tokyo: Obunsha, 1957), p. 258.

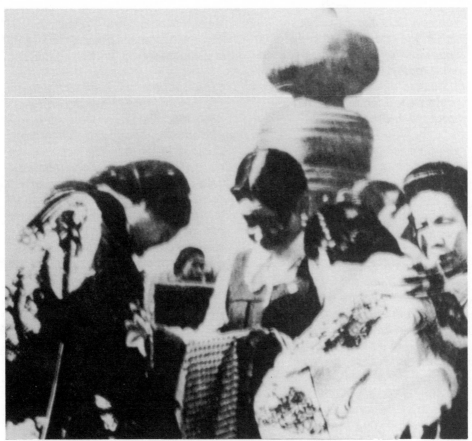

Women gathering the 1000 stitches for sashes to send with soldiers for good luck.

World War II later described a letter he got with the band of cloth he received — and his reaction to these gifts:

"That evening I found several letters from home, and a small package from Fujiko. She had sent me a cotton band to wrap about my stomach, with one thousand red stitches; this was Japan's traditional talisman against enemy bullets.

"Fujiko wrote, 'Today we were told that our fatherland launched a great war against the United States and Great Britain. We can only pray for our ultimate victory and for your good fortune in battle.'

"'Hatsuyo-san and I have stood at a street corner several hours a day for the last several days, and have begged 998 women who passed to give us each a stitch for this band. So it has the individual stitches of one thousand women. We wish you will wear it on your body, and we pray that it may protect you from the bullets of the enemy guns. . . .'

"Actually, few Japanese airmen held faith in the charm. But I knew what it meant for Fujiko and my cousin to stand for long hours on the streets in the cold air of winter. Of course I would wear it, and I wrapped it about my midsection." [3]

Other activities included cutting out luxuries. A foreign observer noticed a change in Japanese women:

"It is really amazing and astonishing how the timid and humble Japanese woman, who for countless generations has quietly and modestly fulfilled her duty in the home, suddenly, with all her forces, is sharing the additional burden of her country. We see the happenings of things incredible, we thought, in Japan. For instance, since August 1, 1940, we see patrols of women on the streets of Tōkyō handing out cards to all persons seen dressed luxuriously, calling their attention to the right recognition of the present situation of the country, the cards bearing such slogans as: 'Let us refrain from luxurious dress,' 'Let us abolish rings. These public-spirited women are stationed at Hibiya, Yūrakucho, Ginza, Nihonbashi, Ueno, Shinjuku, Ikebukuro, all places well known, as crowded centers, to any visitor to Tōkyō whether for only one week or more." [4]

Women also gave up permanent waves and cosmetics. The government encouraged them to wear mompe, a kind of trouser.

After the Doolittle air raid on Tōkyō in 1942, it became apparent that the war was going to come to the mainland of Japan. Although the raid itself did not inflict much damage, it changed Japanese attitudes about the war. As one Japanese woman wrote later:

"The Doolittle raid radically changed the casual attitude toward anti-air raid drills. The ladies were no longer shy about appearing in their mompe. Besides these ill-fitting trousers, we were asked to wear shoes instead of geta or zori, as Japanese footwear comes off too easily. Most women wore sneakers. A long-sleeved blouse, a pair of gloves, something to cover one's head, and a piece of white triangular cotton cloth (which would be needed in case of injury) completed the 'anti-air raid costume.'. . .

"Every Sunday morning around nine o'clock, the leader of the neighborhood Association, who served for a month in a system of rotation, would shout through his megaphone: 'Boku-enshu!' — 'Anti-air raid rehearsal!' From every house properly attired men and women would come out — each with an empty bucket — and line up in the middle of the street. The leader would then decide which house was supposed to be on fire. Swiftly the men and women would form two lines between the nearest house with a well and the house on fire. Someone would pump the well with

---

[3]Saburo Sakai, *Samurai!* (New York: E. P. Dutton and Company, Inc., 1957), p. 81.

[4]H. van Straelen, *The Japanese Woman Looking Forward* (Tokyo: Kyo Bun Kwan, 1940), p. 165-166.

all his might; the one standing next to him would start passing buckets of water, which at the end of the line would be splashed on the 'burning' house. Empty buckets were returned to the well by the second line of people. This would go on for about fifteen minutes, until the leader decided the fire was properly squelched." [5]

As more and more men left for distant battlefields, women were assigned as fire marshalls in government districts. When the heavy American bombing raids began, the fire fighting abilities of the women fire marshalls was severely tested. Women also dug trenches for bomb shelters and organized search and rescue teams for those who had been bombed.

These activities of women were acceptable because they were seen as a natural part of the "household" duties of women during wartime. As the war went on the Japanese government slowly shifted its view to include other wartime activities for women. One woman later wrote rather bitterly about this shift:

"About this time, all unmarried girls who were not working outside of their homes were recruited to work in factories. It was no longer patriotic to marry young and bear many children. The old slogans disappeared from sight, and women were exhorted now to produce 'more airplanes.' Kwoko commented cynically, 'It would take twenty years before a human being could be useful as a soldier. Apparently the Government decided they couldn't wait that long. And pregnant women are not very useful in factories.'" [6]

The conditions in the wartime factories of Japan were harsh. The young women worked on little food and little sleep. Night air raids began to be a continual threat, as one woman described it:

"When the sirens sounded, we pulled on our mompe, the work slacks or coveralls we wore in the factory, and sat silent in the darkness, waiting for the all clear. Then we would tumble back into bed. But it seemed that before we could fall asleep, the sirens would start again and we would have to get up.

"The rules were that we had to be up when the sirens sounded and that we could not go back to bed until the all clear was heard. However, there were times when we were too tired to obey the rules. We did not care whether there were planes above us or not. All we children wanted was to sleep.

"But there was no sleep.

"I had my thirteenth birthday while working in the factory." [7]

Although as time went on more young women were drafted into war work, perhaps because of the attitude of the military, Japan did not use women workers in World War II as much as

---

[5]Yoko Matsuoka, *Daughter of the Pacific* (New York: Harper & Brothers, 1952), p. 172-173.

[6]*Ibid.*, p. 178-179.

[7]Hiroko Nakamoto, *My Japan 1930-1951* (New York: McGraw-Hill Book Company, 1970), p. 52.

Japanese women like these worked in munitions plants but fewer Japanese women were used in war industries than in the United States and other allied nations. The ideal woman, according to the Japanese military government, was a to be a "good wife/wise mother" who focused on her family's needs.

the Soviet Union and Great Britain.[8] Not until 1943 did Prime Minister Tōjō change his position, "We are able to do our duties only because we have wives and mothers at home."[9]

There may have been fewer women in factories in Japan doing war work than in the Soviet Union or Great Britain, but much of the daily survival of the country was carried on by women. Women raised crops, scrounged for food, nursed at the hospitals, raised and educated children, and cleared away wreckage. Some women, their houses burned out, carried family

belongings on their backs:

"Nearly half of the crowds were women — brown, wrinkled women, and chubby-cheeked little girls all hauling loads bigger than themselves. And indeed, anyone

---

[8]Thomas R. H. Havens, "Women and War in Japan, 1937-45," in, *The American Historical Review*, Vol. 80, No. 4 (October 1975), p. 918.

[9]Time-Life Books, *Japan at War* (Alexandria, VA: Time-Life Books, Inc., 1980), p. 114.

having anything to carry on his back, felt sincerely happy, for countless burnt-out refugees, stripped of all earthly possessions, lay like discarded rags in the corners of the station hall." [10]

An American woman, married to a Japanese diplomat, spent World War II in Japan and experienced air raids and wartime struggles. Her view of the Japanese women was as follows:

"Many of the women had to work late at night, every night, to catch up with their housework. In addition to that, most single women above a certain age were mobilized for war work and industry, leaving a heavy burden on the housewives at home. The women of Japan carried on magnificently. They did not receive enough credit and recognition for their tireless cooperation in a war that had overtaken them without their playing any part in its making. They carried out orders humbly and obediently, without protesting that they had no choice in the matter." [11]

The women had much to endure. As one Japanese pilot put it, there was no longer any great difference between the battlefront and the home front.[12] The Japanese at home faced two of the worst devastations ever inflicted in military history. One of these was the Tōkyō fire bomb raids. It is estimated that over 200,000 people died in these raids. The irony was, as one woman described it, that the American bombers looked so beautiful as they came in over the city:

"In the eastern sky loomed a flight, another flight and yet another of B-29's. Keeping a 10,000 meter height and trailing white streamers of exhaust gas, they sailed in perfect formation through the blue-gold sky. To a purely aesthetic eye they looked like shawls of pearly fish riding through the seas of the universe. . . A pious American Japanese lady had once remarked that they looked exactly like angels, more like angels than any of the painted angels of the great masters. . . So, completely apart from traditional religious associations, the ethereal beauty of the mighty bombers was Destiny itself to the people trembling below them." [13]

The devastation from the beautiful planes was terrible. The March 10, 1945, raids included incendiary bombs. A Japanese politician during the postwar era described his view of the city the morning after the raid:

"The next morning, I stood on the cliffs of Susaki and gazed down at the thousands of corpses of citizens who had lost their lives in the burning hell of the night before. The majority of the dead were women. Some still had children strapped to their backs. Others had one child on

---

[10]Sumie Seo Mishima, *The Broader Way* (New York: The John Day Company, 1953), p. 30.

[11]Gwen Terasaki, *Bridge to the Sun* (Chapel Hill: University of North Carolina Press, 1957), p. 108.

[12]Sakai, *Samurai!*, p. 148.

[13]Mishima, *The Broader Way*, p. 31.

their back and two dead children tucked beneath both arms. I saw with my own eyes the noble picture of the mother love of these women, who, despite the shower of incendiaries and the crashing detonation of ear-splitting bombs, had sought to protect the lives of their young. All over the place I saw the burned corpses of mothers and children — floating like debris in ponds and on the sea, on scorched earth and on smoking piles of devastation. As I walked through the streets, I saw the smoke rising from numerous pyres of dead being cremated and smelt the stench of burning flesh. From the depths of my heart, I cried out against the cruelties of war and its sins." [14]*

However devastating the Tōkyō raids, worse was to come. Atomic bomb attacks at Hiroshima and Nagasaki followed in August of 1945. The initial casualty rates of these two attacks were no greater than the Tōkyō fire bomb raids, but the effect on the people of Hiroshima and Nagasaki has been longer lasting. There is no way to summarize the suffering of Hiroshima and Nagasaki. The survivors tell us of the terrible wounds, the frantic searches for loved ones, the slow deaths, and the complete destruction of their cities. A family was considered fortunate if it had lost only two of its members.[15] The story of one woman's experience may suggest something of Hiroshima's destruction:

"Whenever I see strong sunshine, I remember the day very clearly, the day I will never forget as long as I live. That day, in one quick second, my world was destroyed. The day

was August 6, 1945.

"It was 8:15 in the morning, and I was on my way to work. I was walking. The night before, as usual, there had been alerts all night. I was groggy from lack of sleep. The all clear had sounded just as I left home. Now all seemed calm and quiet. I did not hear any sounds of airplanes overhead.

"Suddenly from nowhere, came a blinding flash. It was as if someone had taken a flashbulb picture a few inches from my eyes. There was no pain then. Only a stinging sensation, as if I had been slapped hard in the face.

"I tried to open my eyes. But I could not. Then I lost consciousness.

"I do not know how I got there or how long it was before I awoke. But when I opened my eyes, I was lying inside a shattered house. I was dazed and in shock, and all I knew was that I wanted to go home. I pulled myself up and started stumbling down the street. The air was heavy with a sickening odor. It was a smell different from anything I had ever known before.

"Now I saw dead bodies all about me. The buildings were in ruins, and from the ruins I could hear people crying for help. But I could not help

---

[14]Yoshio Kodama, *I Was Defeated* (Japan: Radiopress, 1959), p. 155-156.

[15]Michihiko Hachiya, *Hiroshima Diary: The Journal of a Japanese Physician* (Chapel Hill: University of North Carolina, 1957), p. 29.

them. Some people were trying, as I was, to walk, to get away, to find their homes. I passed a streetcar that was stalled. It was filled with dead people.

"I stumbled on. But now a great fire came rolling toward us, and I knew it was impossible to get home.

"I passed a woman on the street. She looked at me, then turned away with a gasp of horror. I wondered why. I felt as if one side of my face was detached, did not belong to me. I was afraid to touch it with my hand.

"There was a river nearby, and the people who could walk began walking toward the river — burned people with clothes in shreds or no clothes at all, men and women covered with blood, crying children. I followed them.

"My relief bag was gone. It contained identification papers and other records we were required to carry. Now I felt sure that I would never find my family or see my home again.

"All the time, as these and many other terrible thoughts filled my head, I stumbled on with the others toward the river.

"When I reached the river, I saw that the wooden bridge which I crossed each day on my way to the factory was on fire. I stopped. And for the first time I looked at my body. My arms, my legs and ankles were burned. And I realized that the left side of my face must be burned too. These were strange burns. Not pink, but yellow. The flesh was hanging loose. I went down to the water's edge and tried to pat the skin back

with salt water from the river, as I saw others doing.

"But we could not stay by the river. The fire was coming closer, and the heat was more intense. Everyone started moving again, away from the fire, moving silently, painfully.

"There were no streets left, only the wreckage of buildings.

"I crawled through ruins and climbed piles of debris, falling, getting up, trying to hurry from the fire. Once, climbing over a fallen roof, I recognized the shattered building below me as Hiroshima's Higher Industrial School. So, for a moment, I knew where I was. Then soon again, I was lost in chaos.

"It hurt to walk on my burned feet. It was impossible to move anywhere without stepping on nails, splintered wood, broken glass.

"I found myself on a wide street. I saw a number of burned people standing around a policeman. He had a small bottle of iodine, and with some cotton he was dabbing it on the badly burned back of a man. I stared, too dazed to realize how futile and pathetic it was.

"I did not know where I was going, but I walked on. I saw now that my clothes were mostly burned off me. I came to a little shop that was open. A blouse hung on a hanger in the doorway. I touched it wistfully. Then I remembered. I could not have it. My bag with my ration card had been lost.

"An old woman came up to me and explained that she was the owner of the shop. She looked at the blouse, *then at me.*

"She opened her relief bag and took out a blouse and slacks of her own. In her shop I put on the clothes she gave me.

"I folded up my burned clothes and took them with me. I had some strange idea that I could use them to cover my head in case of a bombing. In our relief bags we were required to carry a hood for that purpose.

"For some reason, I put the burned clothes up to my face. The smell was so terrible, for a minute I thought I was going to faint.

"The old woman looked at me with pity. Instead of letting me go on, she took me to a small clinic nearby.

"There she left me, first putting a few coins in my hand, saying, 'Take this and find a streetcar to take you home.'

"She did not know what had actually happened in Hiroshima. There were no streetcars, there was no home. Most of the city was in ruins, and the fires that were to envelop it by midafternoon were already well under way." [16]

Even when wounded victims found hospital aid, it turned out that the immediate effects from radiation were only the beginning of its harm on those exposed. Pregnant women suffered miscarriages or their babies were born dead. The radiation effects are described as they happened to one Hiroshima woman, an actress noted for her beauty:

"A report on the last days of the actress Midori Naka runs as follows: 'On 16th August she entered the hospital of Tokyo University. Almost nothing remained of that facial beauty and elegance of deportment which had made her famous. In the days that followed, her black hair began to fall out, and her white corpuscle count sank to between 300 and 400 (normal count: 8,000 approx.). In the hospital everything possible was done to save this marvelous woman. She was given one blood transfusion after another. At the beginning her temperature was 37.8 centigrade and her pulse eighty. But by 21st August her temperature had risen to forty-one, and on 23rd August purple patches, each as big as a pigeon's egg, appeared upon her body, to the number of twelve or thirteen. On the following day her pulse had risen to 158. Midori maintained that she felt better that morning, but a few hours later she was dead. Only a few tiny hairs still adhered to her skull. When she was lifted off the bed, even those fell out, and floated slowly to the ground. . . .' "* [17]

Thousands died in August 1945, but many continued to die, even to the present day, from leukemia and other effects of radiation and the bomb. For many of the survivors visible scars have marred their chances for a normal life and marriage. The surviving women have also been seen

---

[16]Nakamoto, *My Japan 1930-1951*, p. 56-60.

[17]Quoted in, Robert Jungk, *Children of the Ashes* (New York: Harcourt, Brace & World, Inc., 1959), p. 34-35.

as poor marriage choices because of the high risk of birth defects or cancer in their children. There have been psychological scars as well. The sense of guilt for not having saved loved ones — or not having died themselves. The sudden loss of family made some envy those who still had loved ones. As one woman said, "When I see other mothers I feel so lonely."[18] One man said about Nagasaki, "We carry deep in our hearts, every one of us, stubborn unhealing wounds."[19]

To ease the pain of "unhealing wounds," survivors have been encouraged to draw pictures of their experiences after the atom bomb attacks. One survivor described her drawing of corpses:

"Here a woman had perished, still clutching her child. . . A group of students, probably from the city girls' school, lay on the ground. Some women who looked like their mothers were staring at the girls. . . . I weeped as I gazed at the horror, and vowed some day to tell others what I had experienced." [20]

Another woman described the scene in the courtyard outside her office building immediately after the blast at Hiroshima:

"I saw a scorched woman holding her baby — both were dead — but the mother was still standing up; clutched to her breast was the baby she had been shielding. Even now I cannot forget that awful scene." [21]

A recurring theme of survivors' remembrances is that of mothers trying to protect their children from the atomic blasts. The overwhelming

Mother and child, survivors of the atomic holocaust.

majority of the victims of the atomic attacks were women and children. Although there were military

[18]Quoted in, Arata Osada, *Children of the A Bomb* (New York: G. P. Putnams, 1959).

[19]Takashi Nagai, *We of Nagasaki* (New York: Duell, Sloan and Pearce, 1958), p. 189.

[20]From, "Hiroshima Remembered," PBS Special Program. Fortieth Anniversary of the Dropping of the Atom Bomb. August 1985.

[21]*Ibid.*

installations near Hiroshima and Nagasaki, the purpose of the attacks was to frighten the Japanese into surrendering, not to destroy strategic military targets. Most men were off fighting so women, children, and the elderly were the major victims.

Another theme told over and over again by the survivors was of lost children and the desperate searches for loved ones which took place among the dead and dying. Again, most were women who were separated from their children. Sometimes it was many years before survivors found family members. Many never knew what had happened to their children, friends, or kin. Sometimes it was a mother who did not return. Thirty years after the attack, a woman finally found the children of her friend and could tell them about their mother's last days.

Mrs. Fugi and Mrs. Nikawa were neighbors and friends. They were together when the bomb fell. "The children were at home, sick, but their mother never came home," Mrs. Fugi explained, "Mrs. Nikawa lost her sight [after the atomic blast], then her ability to move about. I kept her photograph with me ever since. . ." Mrs. Fugi lived alone after the war. In spite of severe injuries, her only wish was to find the children of her friend and tell them about their mother. Once her wish was fulfilled she and the adult son and daughter went to the place where their mother died in Mrs. Fugi's arms. "There was nothing I could do. Please, don't think I abandoned your mother," she told the sister and brother, "even in her suffering she kept asking for her children."[22]

Dropping the atomic bombs on Japan

ended the Second World War, although it did not end the suffering of the Japanese survivors of the war. Up until the last days of the war, people were told that it was still possible for Japan to defeat the Allies. Women were being trained to use bamboo spears against invading American forces. Suicide pilots and the sailors of the battleship Yamato prepared for battle and death and wrote last letters to mothers, daughters, and wives. The Vice Admiral Ito Seiichi wrote as follows:

"To my wife Chitose, I am proud and highly honored to have received an order to do battle. I will fight with my entire soul trying to give thanks to the emperor for this opportunity, even though it may amount only to one ten-thousandth of the love he has given Japan.

"I must take this opportunity to say that the life we have shared was full of happiness. But the time has now come for me, as a naval officer, to prepare to meet my end. I have no doubts at all about asking you, whom I believe in and love, to take over everything after I go. I am truly happy that I can ask this of you.

"I know that you will have difficult and lonely times but to make it easier for you, understand that I believe in what I am doing and that in my last moments I shall be happy.

"From the deepest part of my heart I am praying for your happiness. My

[22]*Ibid.*

242

dearest Chitose." [23]

If Japanese women survived, they might be among the 1,900,000 Japanese widows left from the war.[24] It would be up to them to support themselves and their surviving children.

During World War II the women of Japan had acted as was expected by their government. They had been good wives and protective mothers; fire fighters and nurses; laborers and munitions workers; coal miners and farmers. If the Japanese military failed in World War II, the women had not.

Points to Consider

1. When the United States became involved in the Spanish-American War in 1898, the army had no women nurses. Since many were needed, women nurses were recruited and given army training at Chickamauga, Georgia. A nurse from Minnesota, Theresa Ericksen, was asked to join the Minnesota Thirteenth Voluntary Regiment in the Philippine Islands after her training. The commander of the American troops in the Philippines, General Elwell S. Otis, was opposed to women nurses and "snorted and fumed" at Theresa's arrival. Theresa Ericksen's excellent service changed his mind about women as army nurses, and General Otis refused permission for her to return home with her regiment the following year.[25]

Looking back to the excerpt from the Japanese surgeon-general, Baron Ishiguro Tadanori, and at the above paragraph, why do you think that women nurses were opposed by the military in the United States during the Spanish-American War (1898) and by the Japanese in the Russo-Japanese War (1904-1905)? Why were they finally allowed to serve in both wars?

Before you answer these questions, consider each of the following factors:

a) Clara Barton worked as a nurse during the American Civil War (1861-1865). She was appointed superintendent of nurses for the northern army in 1865 and later organized the American Red Cross. There is a monument in Washington D.C. to the Roman Catholic nuns who served as battlefield nurses during the Civil War.

b) The four cardinal or fundamental virtues to be upheld by American and European 19th century, Victorian women were: "Piety" (religiousness),

---

[23]Russell Spurr, *A Glorious Way to Die* (New York: Newmarket Press, 1981), p. 170.

[24]Kasuo Kusano, "Industrialization and the Status of Women in Japan," unpublished Ph.D. dissertation, University of Washington, 1973, p. 140.

[25]Unpublished papers of Theresa Ericksen, Archives, Minnesota Historical Society, St. Paul, Minnesota.

"Purity," "Submissiveness," and "Domesticity."[26] Although these virtues were changing by the end of the century, they remained ideals for most women.

c) The ideal Japanese woman of the Tokugawa Period (1603-1867) had been the "good wife/wise mother." Although this ideal was modified during the Meiji Period after the end of Japanese isolation in the 1860's, the ideal adult woman was still expected to stay close to home, put family needs before her own, and focus on domestic concerns.

d) Between 1898 and 1905 two wars took place — in Cuba and the Philippine Islands (Spanish-American) and China (Russo-Japanese).

2. List specific things Japanese women did during World War II (1940-1945) to show their patriotism and support for their country and Japan's fighting men.

3. How did the military government change its view of the proper place and roles for women during World War II?

Why do you think that some women were bitter about this change?

4. Hibakusha is the Japanese name for direct or generational (the children of direct) victims of the atomic attacks and radiation. Hibakusha:

- are largely female.

- have triple the national

average unemployment rate.

- have a life expectancy of 66 years compared to Japanese non-victims of 78.9 female; 73.4 male.

- suffer from high incidence of miscarriage, birth defects in their offspring, and their children have high rates of cancer, retardation, tumors, and other diseases.

- who were disfigured by the atomic blasts were abandoned by their husbands by the thousands after World War II.

- have difficulty finding spouses willing to marry them — especially the women victims.

- receive a special cash allowance and free medical care from the Japanese government after they have been officially designated as Hibakusha.

- are often ostracized. The word *hibakusha* is sometimes used as a term of derision.[27]

Considering the above information as well as what you have read in this selection, what things seem to you to be the most difficult

---

[26]Barbara Welter, "The Cult of True Womanhood: 1820-1860," American Quarterly, Vol. 18 (Summer 1966), p. 151-166.

[27]Information on the hibakusha is taken from, Robin Morgan, ed., *Sisterhood is Global* (Garden City, NY: Anchor Press/Doubleday, 1984), p. 376-381.

about being a surviving victim of the atomic attacks? Why?

Give several specific reasons why, as a group, women survivors have been more affected than men by the atomic blasts:

- at the time:

- with later results:

    It seems particularly cruel to blame the victim for the results of the atomic attacks. How do you explain the fact that the term hibakusha is sometimes used as a term of derision? That hibakusha are sometimes ostracized?

5. The Mushroom Club, a Japanese organization of mothers and their children who were atomic bomb survivors was formed after World War II. These women and their children work for world peace and to alleviate the suffering of atomic survivors. Why do you think that Japanese women have been extremely active in peace movements? Why might these hibakusha mothers want an organization of their own?

D. Japanese Women and the Allied Occupation

After the surrender in August of 1945, American troops began to enter the main islands of Japan. Japanese women had been told to take measures against attack by American soldiers. Some families kept their daughters hidden for weeks.[1] Others had cyanide tablets or daggers ready in case of rape. The first mainland meeting of United States airborne troops and Japanese women seems to have been at Atsugi Airfield. A chapter of the Japanese Women's Christian Temperance Union set up a refreshment tent there. English-speaking women, dressed in black dresses with white ribbons which was the uniform of the Union, invited the airmen to tea.[2] The occupation was not always this courteous and civil, but it did not live up to the worst fears of either the Japanese or the Americans who had expected continued violence.

Japan's occupation was carried out by those countries which had been allies in World War II, but the United States played the leading role. The government of the United States set several goals to be accomplished by the occupation of Japan. The primary one was to prevent another military takeover of the government of Japan. To make sure this did not happen, several measures were undertaken that aimed at making Japan more

---

[1]Hiroko Nakamoto, *My Japan 1930-1951* (New York: McGraw-Hill Book Company, 1970), p. 80.

[2]Charles W. Iglehart, *A Century of Protestant in Japan* (Rutland, VT: Charles E. Tuttle Company, 1959), p. 269.

democratic. Landholdings were broken up to curb the power of the large landholders. Titles such as baron and baroness were outlawed. Minority groups like the Ainu and Burakumin were given civil rights. Education was made universal, and privileges were removed that favored members of elite groups in admittance to colleges. The American plans for reforms in Japan also included giving women more rights. Women were to be given the right to vote and to a co-educational public school education. The system of family law — marriage, divorce, child custody — was to be changed to give women more equality. Part of these reforms reflected the American belief in the concept of equal political rights for women, but part also reflected a belief that the votes of Japanese women would help to keep the old military establishment in check.

Japanese women, as can be seen from their lack of progress under the military regime in the 1930's, received little in the way of civil rights from the military. The attitude toward women on the part of the Japanese soldiers had often been an arrogant one. In a number of biographies of Japanese women, they mentioned how startled they were to find American soldiers more courteous than Japanese soldiers.[3] American soldiers who stood up on buses to let women with babies sit down, opened doors to let women through first, or offered rides to women struggling with bundles went against the Japanese military government's treatment of women. American soldiers offered an alternative model for the treatment of women by men.

United States occupation troops included female as well as male soldiers. Members of the WACs (United States Women's Army Corps) such as Lt. Ethel Weed were assigned to meet with Japanese women leaders like Ishimoto Shizue and Ichikawa Fusae and other members of the former suffrage groups and international organizations to make plans that would encourage women's rights. With the backing of these Japanese women leaders and the strong support of General Douglas MacArthur, the United States commander of the occupation troops, the right for women to vote was put into the new Japanese Constitution adopted after the war. Even further, the new Japanese constitution included an ERA — a section guaranteeing women equality as a constitutional right.

Paper legislation, however, would neither get women to run for office nor get them out to vote. Lt. Weed, other WACs, and Red Cross workers joined with Japanese women leaders to carry the concept of voting to the countryside. American and Japanese women met in small groups to discuss what was meant by democracy. As one Japanese woman said, "The hardest thing for us to realize now is, not what we should want with our newly won rights — but the fact that suddenly we are permitted to want at

---

[3]Sumie Seo Mishima, *The Broader Way* (New York: The John Day Company, 1953), p. 65.

Japanese women vote for the first time — in a bathhouse.

all.''[4] The drive to get women to vote and be candidates for election was a successful one. Thirty-nine women were elected to the House of Representatives, and 67 percent of all women eligible voted.[5] Fears that women would take orders on how to vote from the men in their families seemed to have been unfounded. A reporter asked an older woman how she decided on how to vote:

"[The reporter] stopped a tiny, bent old lady in dark kimono and somber obi. 'Did you vote?' he asked. 'Mochiron — of course,' she answered. 'How did you vote?' 'It is a secret ballot,' she replied and peered up at him with bright shrewd eyes, glad, I am sure, to give back the information that the nation's radio for two or three months had been dinning into her ears from 6 a.m. to 12 p.m.

"I laughed. He laughed and patted her on the back. 'You're all right,' he said. 'But tell me this. How did you make your decision?' His interpreter went off into paragraphs of explanation during which I caught the words 'husband' and 'eldest son' and I knew that he was asking the old lady who had told her how to vote.

---

[4]Lucy Herndon Crockett, *Popcorn on the Ginza* (New York: William Sloane Associates, Inc., 1949), p. 150.

[5]Dorothy Robins-Mowry, *The Hidden Sun: Women of Modern Japan* (Boulder, CO: Westview Press, 1983), p. 95.

"She appreciated the point and paused a moment as if to savor it. 'Well,' she finally said, 'I listened to my husband. I listened to my eldest son. I listened to the ward officials. I went to the meetings and I listened. And then I thought it all over and voted the way I thought was best. It is a secret ballot.' That disposed of the matter." [6]

Besides voting, there were other changes that were meant to benefit women:

- Arranged marriages could not be forced on women or men.

- Equal divorce conditions were imposed.

- Equal inheritance rights were given.

- Women could be legal guardians of their property and children.

- Equal pay for equal work was a principle in the law.

- Co-education from elementary school through the university was instituted.

Japanese males were not necessarily happy with these changes. Some professors claimed that women in colleges were destroying higher education.[7] One Japanese man expressed the resentment of women adopting Western styles and the competition of American soldiers that others may have felt:

"The defeat of war has brought discredit upon the male sex. The cries of Liberty! Freedom! and Women's Suffrage! have caused to fly away even those womanly virtues which were the last refuge of the male sex. It is only natural for girls to prefer kind and stylish GI's to Japanese men who have become shabby dirty. Speaking frankly, men are all sick and tired of life." [8]

One Tōkyō suburban newspaper tried to damage the reputation of the women elected to the Diet (Parliament) by printing a story that 30 of them were former prostitutes. A WAC officer happened to see the article and forced an apology from the editor. The newspaper also ran truthful biographies of the women to show that he had made up the story.[9]

The occupation had other problems besides the resistance to reforms for women by Japanese men. American soldiers and Japanese women were frequently involved with each other, sometimes in relationships of mutual affection and sometimes in exploitive situations. Particularly poignant was the plight of racially mixed children, especially if black and Japanese, who were generally rejected by both Japanese and American societies. Also, although the United States policy was to encourage co-education in Japan, the textbooks produced for the

---

[6]*Ibid.*, p. 95.

[7]Tamie Kamiyama, "Ideology and Patterns in Women's Education in Japan," unpublished Ph.D. dissertation, St. Louis University, 1977, p. 232.

[8]Robins-Mowry, *The Hidden Sun*, p. 103.

[9]John LaCerda, *The Conqueror Comes to Tea* (New Brunswick: Rutgers University Press, 1946), p. 142.

occupation under United States supervision turned out to be sexist. Elizabeth Vining, American tutor to the Japanese crown prince, was quite disgusted with the results. She wrote:

"The former practice of issuing entirely different texts for boys and girls, emphasizing the superiority of the one and the subservience of the other, had been discontinued, but distinctions still lingered on. In the English text which my boys were using I found this page: 'What are these boys doing? They are sailing a boat. They are driving a motor car. They are carrying a big box.' All were activities to give a boy an impression of power and importance as compared with the girls on the page, who were mending their stockings, sweeping the street, feeding the rabbit — not the horse or the dog, but the timid and lowly rabbit!" [10]

Further, in the 1950's the United States went through a period of encouraging American women to give up their wartime employment and go "back to the home" devoting their time to husbands and children. The American model given to Japanese women during the occupation was one that focused on home, larger families, and housewifely virtues. Ichikawa Fusae, one of the leading suffrage advocates, was purged (prevented from political activity) in this period for supposedly supporting the former military regime. Japanese war brides were frequently accepted by their new families in the United States, but some women had problems adjusting to their new country and some men treated their Japanese wives poorly.

Los Angeles county, for example, saw an estimated 2,000 "war brides" abandoned by their husbands.[11] The Japanese culture also went through change. Older Japanese might agree with the woman who said to an American, "Your occupation was kind . . . You gave us, especially us women, much that was good. But you also plucked up our roots."[12]

Historian Mikiso Hane has suggested that some of those "roots," especially regarding minority peoples, peasants, workers, and women needed changing.[13] Others view the Allied occupation as a joint venture in which both sides, despite much bumbling, turned out fairly well:

". . .For those who lived through that time, Japanese and American, the memory of the experience remains amusing and sad, prideful and embarrassing. In a sense the experience was too strong, too heady. It fostered in both peoples an attitude and a relation to each other which was not, in the long, run, healthy, but which took a long time

---

[10]Elizabeth Gray Vining, *Windows for the Crown Prince* (Philadelphia: J. B. Lippincott Company, 1952), p. 92.

[11]Jack Seward, *The Japanese* (New York: William Morrow & Company, Inc. 1972), p. 121.

[12]Quoted in, Sara Harris, *House of the 10,000 Pleasures* (New York: E. P. Dutton & Co., Inc., 1962), p. 174.

[13]See: Mikiso Hane, *Peasants, Rebels, and Outcastes* (New York: Pantheon Books, 1982).

to die. History will probably record that, on balance, those years reflect credit on both players in the game." [14]

For Japanese women, the end of the Allied occupation saw them with voting and legal rights which, if enforced, could bring about real equality. These rights had not just come as a gift from the occupying forces. They were rights Japanese women had worked to achieve for many years before the war. They were also rights that they knew they gained partly because of the services and loyalty they had given to Japan during World War II. The Allied occupation could not have imposed voting and legal rights unless Japanese women already knew that they deserved to have and use them.

The task of group one is to figure out the *advantages* for Japanese women that a major goal of the Allied occupation was achieving the vote and other civil rights for women.

The task of group two is to figure out the *disadvantages* for Japanese women that a major goal of the Allied occupation was achieving the vote and other civil rights for women.

Group one may hypothesize (make educated guesses) about the advantages (or group two about the disadvantages) but for each hypothesis reasons should be given.

In the class debate, each group might present one advantage/disadvantage and allow for the opposition to respond. Then the opposition could present one of their points.

After the debate, the discussion could be opened to the class.

A Student Debate

Two student groups (or two individuals) should volunteer or be appointed to read this selection and to take part in the debate.

After meeting in two groups and comparing ideas about this selection, the following topics should be discussed with a recorder taking down the group's ideas. The conclusions of each group will then be presented to the class.

---

[14]Frank Gibney, *Japan: The Fragile Superpower* (New York: W. W. Norton & Company, Inc., 1975), p. 69.

CHAPTER 11

WOMEN IN CONTEMPORARY JAPAN 1952 TO THE PRESENT

A. Life Stages and Japanese Women

The status of women in the history of Japan, as in many cultures, depended on a variety of factors such as:

- the time in which a woman lived.

- the class into which she was born.

- her individual talents.

An additional and important factor determining the status of women in Japanese culture has been their stage of life. In general, older women have had more power and respect than younger women. Within each stage many factors might increase or decrease the status of individual women. A woman who married the eldest son might have more status within the family she married into than one who married a younger son. A young bride's stature rose when she gave birth to children — especially boys. A woman who was considered outstanding (rippa) was particularly admired for her thrift, hard work, and high housekeeping standards.

Throughout most of Japanese history, boy children were favored. Brightly colored, paper kite-banners in the shape of carp, a symbol of fertility, were flown from a pole in front of the family home to announce the birth of a son. Girl babies were not similarly announced. In traditional families, having a boy as the first child was considered most fortunate but "as proof of the mother's fertility, even a girl baby is welcome."[1] The eldest son

---

[1]Richard K. Beardsley, John W. Hall, and Robert E. Ward, *Village Japan* (Chicago: The University of Chicago Press, 1959), p. 290.

Child nursemaids — early 20th century.

(chōnan) is given special care and privileges while the eldest daughter (chōjō) does not enjoy more privileges than her sisters. If, however, there are no sons, the chōjō is treated like a chōnan. The most indulged and spoiled child is usually the last born — whether a boy or a girl.[2]

Although boy children may be preferred, the birth of a girl has usually been seen as a happy family event. Place in the birth order and the number of girls and boys in the family may determine how a child is treated. One young woman reported that as the only daughter among sons she grew up very wagamama — self-centered and unruly.[3]

Traditionally, education for women — from childhood to adulthood — was intended as preparation for marriage and motherhood. Girls did domestic

_____

[2]Takie Sugiyama Lebra, *Japanese Women: Constraint and Fulfillment* (Honolulu: University of Hawaii Press, 1984), p. 40-41.

[3]*Ibid.*, p. 41.

work and took care of younger brothers and sisters. Boys were not expected to do housework. One 60-year-old woman was asked recently if her brother had worked in the kitchen. She exclaimed, "Heaven's no! If he did, we women would have been criticized as slobs."[4] Some little girls from poorer families were sent off to work as maids in wealthier homes. Before World War II middle and upper-class girls attended sex segregated high schools which taught them proper manners, sewing, and cooking, as well as academic subjects. They might also go to small private schools (juku) to learn cooking, sewing, flower arranging, how do conduct the tea ceremony, playing the shamisen, classical dancing, and calligraphy.[5]

Until recently, however, the real testing period for a Japanese woman might come after her marriage and center on her relationship with her mother-in-law. Her marriage (probably an arranged one) usually involved her move into or nearby the home of her husband. Her first obligation was to give respect and service to her parents-in-law, and next, to her husband. The young bride was often treated miserably, and it was the mother-in-law who doled out the severe treatment. In a recent book, anthropologist Takie Sugiyama Lebra pointed out that older Japanese women she interviewed often described themselves as victims of difficult family situations as young married women. Surprisingly many of them also expressed gratitude for the hardships which they suffered as brides. They saw this harsh treatment as a good lesson for married life and later thanked their mothers-in-law for the severe training. They took a dim

view of women who had an easier life by not living with their parents-in-law.[6]

The following 20th century examples describe a number of experiences of young brides and relationships with their mothers-in-law. After reading over these excerpts, complete the points to consider that follow.

* * * * *

Ishimoto Shizue, who became a leading Japanese feminist, was married to the Baron Ishimoto Keikichi in 1914. She later wrote that upon marriage she "was formally being given to Baron Ishimoto's *family*."[7] This excerpt from her autobiography described her wedding night at her new home — that of her husband's family. Her experiences were probably representative of those of many upper-class brides in the early 20th century.

Ishimoto Shizue

"My FIRST bridal night was cut short by my maid Ō-ko who waked me at five in the morning. It was dark and cold. I had to dress before my mother-in-law left her bed, and she had a habit of retiring late and of waking up early. It was the duty of a bride to please first her mother-in-law and serve her husband next. My mother-in-law did not treat me like a young girl as my parents did. She

---

[4]*Ibid.*, p. 48.

[5]*Ibid.*, p. 59.

[6]*Ibid.*, p. 297.

[7]Ishimoto Shizue, *Facing Two Ways* (New York: Farrar and Rinehart, 1935), p. 110.

257

looked on me as a full-grown woman. Perhaps this was natural since my husband was much older than I and I must correspond with his age. Besides, I had to behave with an elder sisterly dignity toward my brothers-in-law some of whom were several years older than I.

"I took my first breakfast in the midst of the entire family. My mother-in-law and my husband sat on silk cushions, but I, with the rest of the family, sat directly on the mat without a cushion. I had three sets (one consisting of five pieces) of cushions for the guests and three pairs for my own use in my trousseau, yet I had to sit on the cold mat, shivering, to show my humble attitude toward my elders. After the meal, my mother-in-law admitted that I was still too young to take on my shoulders the whole responsibility for the house, but she would show me the ways of the Ishimoto family and I must learn them as quickly as possible. She did not lay down any definite rules or principles. She wanted me to learn by observation. She did not fail to remark, however, that I had to serve my husband with respect as he was the head of the family since the death of his father. I must wait on him when he dressed and bow to him when he went out and again bow him in at the entrance hall when he returned. Of course the same formalities were to be observed toward my mother-in-law herself." [8]

* * * * *

Anthropologist Takie Sugiyama Lebra interviewed older women about their experiences as young brides married in the pre-World War II period:[9]

Ayano

"First, the bride was expected to supply labor. A good yome [bride] was supposed to be a hard worker. Many mothers-in-law [were examples] by being compulsive workers themselves and by demanding that the daughters-in-law work with them. 'Our grandma [mother-in-law] was an extraordinarily hard worker,' said Ayano. While hanging the laundry, for example, if any part of an article of clothing was found to be worn, she never failed to patch it right away while it was still wet and then she hung it again. Every night before going to bed, she took pains to sweep the rooms, clean the fireplace, and put everything in perfect order so that there would be no problem in an emergency, such as an earthquake. She was never found sitting around doing nothing; as soon as she sat down after doing the dishes to listen to the radio, she started sewing. Everything in the chests of drawers was spotless and ironed. This mother-in-law Ayano admires as rippa, outstanding, but also admitted that it was painful to live up to her expectations as a daughter-in-law since the same standard of diligence was applied to her. When she and her husband were

---

[8]Ibid., p. 134-135.

[9]Ayano and Harue were in their mid-50's when these interviews were conducted in 1976-1980. Although it is not clear how old the last two women are, they appear to have been married in the pre-war or war period.

about to relax after a day's work, the mother-in-law was standing with a needle and thread signaling that the two women were to sew together. 'For my mother-in-law, playing, joking, or eating cake was all wasteful nonsense.' "

* * * * *

Harue

"Harue was also subjected to nightly sewing (yōnabe) with her mother-in-law and sister-in-law. At ten o'clock she wished to retire but the in-laws hinted that it was still too early. The mother-in-law instructed her that, in order to get ahead of other people, one should get up one hour earlier and go to bed one hour later than others. When carrying firewood too the mother-in-law used to say, some would carry a few pieces, but some would load themselves with as much as possible. The difference would show up soon. This mother-in-law was also described as rippa, and once again the admirer felt as if she were strangled."

* * * * *

The Fisherman's Wife

"A fisherman's wife was the sole domestic worker and sewed all the kimonos and futon bedding for everybody in the ten-member household, her mother-in-law being a disgruntled but lazy recipient of her services. When she visited her natal [birth] home after six months of marriage, her mother stroked her cheeks, saying in tears: 'Your face has changed, you look like a man.' "

* * * * *

The Patient Daughter-in-Law

"What was most unbearable even to a patient daughter-in-law was the overt or covert restriction on the amount of food she could have.

'I don't know if I should tell all this. I was always the last to eat a meal. When I was going to have a second bowl of rice, my husband's sister asked her mother [pointing to the rice container]: 'Grandma, is this enough for lunch?' Grandma said: 'Men go out to work, therefore they must eat a lot. Children, too, need a lot because they are growing up. But women are just playing in the house, they don't have to eat.'

"The daughter-in-law withdrew her rice bowl. Apparently all this was not witnessed by her husband — in an interview he stressed how harmonious the relationship between his mother and wife had been."

* * * * *

Hiroe

"A similar deprivation was experienced by Hiroe. When she distributed the fish onto individual plates, her mother-in-law complained that Hiroe served herself more than others. As a young nursing mother right after childbirth, she was hungry all the time. Awake and unable to wait longer, she got up before dawn to eat the leftovers from the previous supper, which enraged her mother-in-law." [10]

---

[10]Lebra, *Japanese Women — Constraint and Fulfillment*, p. 142-144.

Journalist Jane Condon interviewed a woman farmer, Muramatsu Haruko. Born in 1908, Muramatsu Haruko is representative of the pre-World War II and World War II periods. She told of the hard work on the farm and harsh treatment by her mother-in-law:

Muramatsu Haruko

"My husband and I always went to the fields together in the dark around 4:00 or 5:00 A.M. We worked for a while before breakfast . . . with the other employees (three peasants and ten daily workers). We took a break for breakfast, then we went back to work. It was hard work. But I was happy to be outside, working with my husband.

"The hardest part of each day came when I returned home around 5:00 P.M. to help my mother-in-law in the kitchen. . . . I would say, 'I'm home,' but she never answered. She just looked away.

"Of course, every night there was always more work to be done in the house. . . . Oh, how we cleaned. I can still remember my mother-in-law waving her duster in the air. We had to wipe and wipe and wipe. Everything had to shine for her. My husband's brother's wife lived in the same house, but since she was the daughter of a relative, my mother-in-law was kind to her.

"We ate dinner around six, cleaned up the kitchen, and did all the cutting and chopping necessary for tomorrow's breakfast. We usually spent about an hour cleaning the rooms and the walls. Then there was the washing, mending, and sewing to be done for my own family of five

children. . . . *I used ashes to wash the clothes. She let us have no light, no candles to work by. Being the lowliest member of the family, I was always the last to take my bath. And I had to clean the bathtub afterward. By this time, it was 10:30 or 11:00, and we had to be up again at 3:00 or 3:30 in the morning, so I washed in the dark and got up in the dark. I was so tired that sometimes I fell asleep while weeding in the fields.*

"Even on snowy days, my mother-in-law opened the sliding wooden door with a bang at 3:00 A.M. so that if the noise didn't wake us up, the snow, which flew in, did. I couldn't sleep, I had to get up — even though it was dark outside. Oh, how she nagged and nagged. But that's past, and I don't want to talk about it anymore." [11]

* * * * *

Another woman, Tanabe Ayako, interviewed by Jane Condon described her married life during World War II:

Tanabe Ayako

"At first I was just the daughter-in-law in the family. I had to say 'Hai, hai' [Yes, yes] to everything my mother-in-law said until my son was born. My son never met his father because my husband had been sent to the front a month before the baby

---

[11]Jane Condon, *A Half Step Behind — Japanese Women of the 80's* (New York: Dodd, Mead and Company, 1985), p. 228-229.

was born. In those days almost all men were sent to the front. It was considered a shame for a man to stay at home at such a critical time for the nation. At least, he died an honorable death, in action, on Tinian Island. He didn't die from an illness or in prison. How did I feel? Well, there were a lot of war widows in my neighborhood. War is just part of the passage of time. People can't do anything about it. Things just turned out that way. And since I was living with his parents and three sisters, I didn't feel particularly lonely." [12]

* * * * *

Historian Gail Bernstein, described how family relationships are changing in rural Japan since World War II:

"An indication of the new social status of the young farm woman is her [acquiring], earlier rather than later in her marriage, the 'rice scoop' — the power of the purse and the privilege of cooking the meals, dishing out the food, supervising the children's upbringing, and taking charge of the household. Stories told in village Japan describe women ... who deferred to a mother-in-law in all household matters until the older woman's death. As late as the 1960's it was not unusual for a woman to wait until she was 40 and had been married for 20 years before she was allowed to cook for her husband and raise her children in her own way. Rural women say that today such cases are the exception.

"[Showing] the change in the daughter-in-law's status, a new word has appeared in her vocabulary — hatsugen-ken, the right of expression. 'I have the right to

express myself,' one woman said. 'I can now argue with my mother-in-law or my husband.' Under the old family system and prewar Confucian ideology, women hesitated to speak freely out of deference [respect] to their in-laws, in whose house they lived. And 'right' was not a legitimate term. Since the Second World War, however, the new value system taught in the schools — which recognizes the concept of democratic rights — along with social and economic changes in the position of farm women, have helped establish hatsugen-ken as a common term of reference." [13]*

* * * * *

Some contemporary Japanese women may choose to divorce when a mother-in-law is too interfering. There is a trend, particularly in urban Japan, toward nuclear (husband, wife, children) families rather than extended ones with several generations living together or nearby. Mothers-in-law have less say than in pre-war times. Still, 65 percent of Japan's old people live with one of their children — frequently the eldest son. [14] Overwhelmingly it is the women — daughters-in-law or daughters — who care for the elderly. One young

---

[12]*Ibid.*, p. 22.

[13]Gail Bernstein, *Haruko's World — A Japanese Farm Woman and Her Community* (Stanford: Stanford University Press, 1983), p. 162.

[14]Condon. *A Half Step Behind*, p. 95.

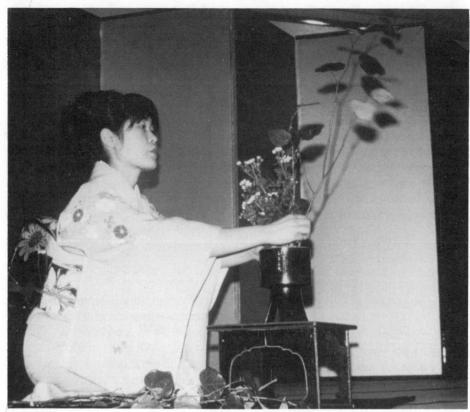

Woman arranging flowers — an art frequently learned by young women in Japan.

woman described the way in which her husband's attachment to his mother was a major factor in the break-up of her marriage.

"My husband is a very conservative person. He's the first son and the only son. A lot of women these days don't want to marry the first son because of all the family responsibilities he has, like organizing family gatherings . . . Although the law says all children are supposed to take care of the parents in their old age, custom still dictates that the first son (that is, the first son's wife) take care of them when they are old and sick.

"My husband's mother came over to our house every day — to make sure I was taking proper care of him, I guess. And my husband was always talking about how good a cook his mother was. He said things like, 'But my mother cooks curry rice this way.' . . . His biggest complaint was about my working outside the home. He didn't want me to. 'My mother never did,' he said." [15]

---

[15]*Ibid.*, p. 47.

262

Most Japanese women do continue to see caring for elderly in-laws as their duty. Sometimes a daughter-in-law will finally become the authority figure in her own home as her mother-in-law becomes elderly and dependent upon her. This happened to Ayano when she was 41 years old:

"In our [home], Grandpa [father-in-law] and Grandma [mother-in-law] tightly held sovereignty for a long time. My husband, their only child, knew too well what hardship they had gone through in raising him to resist their authority. Then, Grandma got injured and was forced to stay in bed. A strange thing [happened]. I wonder if words have a force of a living thing. Until that time Grandma called me Aya-chan and I called her Mother. When bedridden, she began to call me Oka-chan [Mommy] and I naturally felt like calling her Granny. It was then, I believe, that I became a true mistress of the house [shufu]." [16]

* * * * *

Takie Sugiyama Lebra pointed out that relationships between mother-in-law and daughter-in-law are changing in contemporary Japan:

"Some of the in-law's demands are no longer tolerated by a young daughter-in-law and will fail in securing support from his/her son. Suzuko, after she moved to live with her parents-in-law, learned that her husband's monthly salary was to be taken by the mother-in-law as had always been the case, and that she was to receive an allowance only. She thought this outrageous, and through negotiations between the
two pairs of nakōdo [go-betweens] it was decided, against strong resistance from the in-laws, that the young couple should live apart from the old couple. 'Ichirosan had to choose between his parents and me, and decided in my favor.' " [17]

As the above excerpts show, there has been a change in family relations in Japan during the 20th century. The idea that the daughter-in-law is to give her mother-in-law absolute respect and obedience is lessening. But the idea that aged parents are to be respected and that a mother-in-law can demand attention and dispense advice to her daughter-in-law continues to influence Japanese society. With a rapidly growing elderly population and younger women increasingly working outside their homes, it is difficult to predict how relationships between mothers-in-law and daughters-in-law may evolve in the future.

---

[16]Lebra, *Japanese Women — Constraint and Fulfillment*, p. 254.

[17]*Ibid.*, p. 148.

Points to Consider

1. Looking back over the excerpts, what things do you think would be the most difficult about each of these women's situations?

   Ishimoto Shizue

   Ayano

   Harue

   The Fisherman's Wife

   Patient Daughter-in-law

   Hiroe

   Muramatsu Haruko

2. Ishimoto Shizue wrote "I owe my mother-in-law much, as she gave me a thorough training in our traditional art decoration. . ."[18] Ayano also expressed appreciation for her mother-in-law's training after she too became a mother-in-law:

   "The in-law relationship is stronger than blood parenthood. Many aspects of Grandma [mother-in-law] are living with me. Uneducated, but she knew many proverbs . . . 'Hard at night, then easy in the morning [yoi no shinku asa no raku].' Finish the work at night, says the lesson, however painful, so that you will have an easy time next morning. I repeated these proverbs to my daughter-in-law, and have found them living on in her. 'Mother,' she says, 'as you told me, I finish up everything at night. Indeed, it's easy in the morning. Yoi no shinku asa no raku, isn't it?' So I say to her,

Grandmother Kurokawa Suzu, in a photograph taken in the 1960's.

   'How nice! Now that all these have been transmitted to you, Grandma has finally come to bloom.' " [19]

   List all the reasons that you can think of for these severe, hardworking mothers-in-law to later be forgiven and even admired by their daughters-in-law.

---

[18]Ishimoto Shizue, *Facing Two Ways*, p. 136.

[19]Lebra, *Japanese Women — Constraint and Fulfillment*, p. 266.

Historian Gail Bernstein has compared the training of young brides by their mothers-in-law to basic training in the armed services. What goals of the training of these brides and soldiers are similar? What outcomes of the training might also be similar?

3. The Japanese have an expression yome-ibiri (bride hazing). From the excerpts above, what do you think this means in terms of most young Japanese brides, particularly those who move near (or into) their husband's home?

Hazing is customarily associated in the United States with the harsh treatment of freshmen by upperclassmen at military schools like West Point or in college fraternities. What do you think are the purposes of hazing in military schools and clubs? What similarities do you find to yome-ibiri? How might this relate to Gail Bernstein's idea that the training of brides by mothers-in-law can be compared to basic training?

B. The Complementary Marriage System

The term "complementary" marriage has been used to describe one type of marriage system in Japan. What are seen as appropriate roles for women and men within marriage varies greatly from culture to culture. In some cultures, polygyny may be the accepted marriage form, where it is expected that married women focus most of their attention on their children rather than on husbands. In others the ideal marriage is one in which the wife and husband are companions for life — and behave like "best friends." In Japan's complementary marriage system the husband and wife are expected to fill roles that complement or balance each other but are different. These complementary roles aim at fulfilling the functions of family support, but the marriage is not necessarily one of companionship involving shared activities and feelings.[1] Not all Japanese marriages are complementary ones. Many are love matches in which companionship is emphasized. There seems to be an increasing number of love marriages,[2] but a complementary marriage system remains a part of Japanese culture.

Here are major elements that make up a complementary marriage as it has operated in Japan:

---

[1]Sumiko Furuya Iwao, "The Feminine Perspective" in, Kenneth A. Grossberg, ed., *Japan Today* (Philadelphia: Institute for the Study of Human Issues, 1981), p. 22.

[2]Takie Sugiyama Lebra, *Japanese Women: Constraint and Fulfillment* (Honolulu: University of Hawaii Press, 1984), p. 114.

- The marriage is an arranged one.

- The husband works long hours away from home.

- The children are overwhelmingly the mother's responsibility. Children are seen as a mother's possession and sometimes even as a part of herself.[3]

- The wife is in charge of the family income and pays all household expenses.

- The spending of large amounts of time together by the wife and husband is not thought necessary for a good marriage.

- The wife does not work outside the home. If she has any outside activities they are community ones.

Although not all Japanese marriages illustrate these qualities — particularly those of younger couples — these elements are typical of many Japanese marriages in the 1960-80's.

When Japanese describe arranged marriages of the complementary marriage system, they no longer mean the traditional arranged marriage common in the past to many cultures including Japan. These traditional arranged marriages involved two families deciding upon their children's marriage, with the bride and groom having no say in the matter. Currently, what is meant by an arranged marriage in Japan is when a matchmaker, an employer, a friend, or member of the family sets up a meeting between the prospective bride and groom. It is more serious than an American blind date, as the couple intends to marry unless they have serious doubts about each other

after the first meeting. It is estimated that even today approximately 40 percent or more of marriages are arranged by a go-between (nakōdo).[4] Sometimes background descriptions are available on prospective partners, telling their education and social level, so that what is seen as a proper match might be made. Matchmakers may arrange a miai or first meetings for their customers — a young man and woman. Some attend these meetings with relatives, but blind dates, where the young woman and man meet, are more usual now.[5]

If the two young people seem reasonably satisfied and interested in each other, they may marry. The pressures to marry are high in Japanese culture, and a person who chooses to remain single is seen as very unusual. A Roman Catholic priest relates that he continually gets invitations addressed to "Father and Mrs." because being unmarried seems inconceivable to his Japanese hosts.[6] As Ichikawa Fusae has said, "Marriage is still the goal that is held

---

[3]Machiko Tomita, "Motherhood in Japan: Room for Additional Roles?" *Global Education Center Newsletter*, College of Education, University of Minnesota, Vol. 2, No. 3 (January/February 1986), p. 3.

[4]Robert C. Christopher, *The Japanese Mind* (New York: Linden Press/Simon & Schuster, 1983), p. 63.

[5]Lebra, *Japanese Women: Constraint and Fulfillment*, p. 104.

[6]Christopher, *The Japanese Mind*, p. 63.

before girls."[7] Ninety five percent of all Japanese women are married by age 35, and by age 60, 98.5 percent of all women are, or have been, married.[8]

Once married, the life of a typical urban Japanese couple probably would have these characteristics: The man works long hours at his job. After office hours he will also socialize with people with whom he works, so the dividing line between office and social life becomes blurred. Social activities would not take place in individual homes (which are often small apartments, located far from work), but in bars where groups of men from work meet. Thus, a man may be gone from home from 7:00 a.m. to 11:00 p.m. and be home for any length of time only on weekends, often only on Sundays. The husband who has such a schedule is not seen as a "workaholic" who neglects his family, as he might be in the United States, but as an admirably ambitious person. Among some Japanese women there is a saying that "a good husband is healthy and absent."[9] The statement implies that the husband is working hard and moving up the "escalator" to career success.

Such a schedule leaves little time for companionship between a wife and husband. For partners who would like to spend more time together, the long separations make for difficult times. As one woman said:

"I would like to spend more time with him. When I was younger I always complained about his schedule, but now not so much. It's bad to be in low spirits. . . My husband likes to be very busy and his job is very difficult." [10]

The period between the woman marrying and the coming of the first child has been described as one of "almost unbearable loneliness."[11] A newspaper survey in the 1970's showed that the average Japanese husband and wife talk for two and one-half minutes a day.[12] Even vacations may be spent apart. Japanese men made up 81.7 percent of the Japanese tourists going to Thailand in 1976.[13] Women may go without their husbands on shorter vacations with their P.T.A. (Parent Teacher Association) groups or networks of old school friends.

With the husband gone so much, the wife assumes the major household activities. Japanese men generally hand over their paychecks to their wives, so women decide how the family money should be spent. There

---

[7]Edward R. Beauchamp, "The Social Role of Japanese Women: Continuity and Change" in, *International Journal of Women's Studies*, Vol. 2, No. 3 (May/June 1979), p. 251.

[8]Suzanne H. Vogel, "Professional Housewife: The Career of Urban Middle Class Japanese Women" in, *Japan Interpreter*, Vol. 12, No. 1 (Winter 1978), p. 17.

[9]Christopher, *The Japanese Mind*, p. 67.

[10]Quoted in, Sonya Blank Salamon, "In the Intimate Arena: Japanese Women and Their Families," unpublished Ph.D. dissertation, University of California (Berkeley), 1965, p. 66.

[11]Anne Cooper, "Japanese Women," *Women's Studies*, p. 41.

[12]James Trager, *Letters from Sachiko* (New York: Atheneum, 1982), p. 82.

[13]Ruang Pamornsai and Marie Fua, "Thai Women: A Long March to Liberation," *Feminist Japan* (February 1978), p. 40.

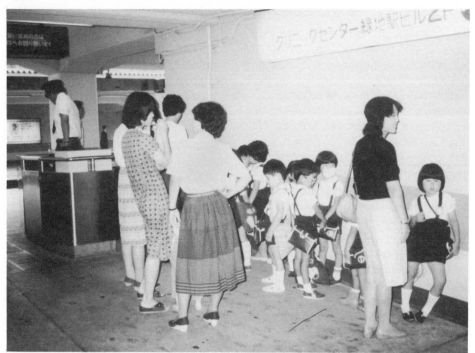

Mothers bring kindergarteners to the train station where they are met by their teacher.

is some debate on whether or not this illustrates a kind of "matriarchy" or women's control over family finances. Some say that this does give Japanese women power, as most major family purchases are decided by women. Others point out that men decide the amount that is allocated for their own personal allowances, and these funds are spent primarily for entertainment purposes. Therefore, men actually spend their money for their own pleasure while women have the responsibility of making sure that necessary expenses are met.

Beyond the family finances, it is generally assumed that the wife is in charge of the children. She has been expected to supervise the children closely and is "nailed in the house,"

as one source put it.[14] Particularly in the highly competitive Japanese educational system, the mother's duties include supervision of her children's education. The term "education mama" (kyōiku mama) has been used to describe the concerned, demanding mother who tries to find the best schools for her children, make sure they do their homework, and involve themselves in school activities to assure their child has the best conditions for an education. Going to top schools means getting

---

[14]Salamon, "In the Intimate Arena," p. 96.

top jobs for young men. A Japanese mother's success in life is sometimes seen as being tested by her children's ability to get into good schools.[15] This leads to a rather mixed relationship between mothers and children, particularly sons. On the one hand, the mother is very supportive and does all she can to help her children to succeed. It has been suggested that the Suzuki method of learning the violin, in which parent and child learn together, is a method "typical" of Japan — that suits the common urban family relations.[16] With the father away so much, the child gets most of her/his mother's attention and concern. On the other hand, this may create tensions between the parent and child. In an international survey, children of various countries were asked the question, "Is your mother nice to you?" Japan was the only country in which mothers were seen as less nice than fathers. In comparison to other countries, 63.9 percent of Japanese children thought their mothers were nice to them in comparison to 98.3 percent of American children.[17] The results of this survey probably suggest the heavy role of Japanese women in being disciplinarians and the motivators of their children.

As part of a mother's responsibilities to her children, the one community organization most women belong to during their children's education period is the P.T.A. Women go to meetings and self-improvement classes, raise money for schools, and help to supervise school field trips and other activities. For some, this may be one of their few social outlets and graduation of their children may mean a loss of social support for women. They may feel they are now useless to the community.

Middle-class, urban Japanese women usually have few outside activities as volunteers or in community organizations. Most women do, however, keep strong ties to their old school friends. In keeping a record of calls of a group of urban Tōkyō women, a researcher found that most talked to an old school friend at least once a day, and some made as many as 24 calls a day.[18] These female networks often become a major support system for these urban wives, and they may rely upon these friends in times of trouble more than on their husbands.[19] Sometimes these networks of friends do not provide enough support, as is indicated by the fact that Japanese women have one of the highest suicide rates in the world.[20] For most, however, networks of female friends and relatives maintained by telephone provide adult companionship that may be lacking in marriage.

The complementary marriage system

[15]Christie W. Kiefer, "The Psychological Interdependence of Family, School, and Bureaucracy in Japan," *American Anthropoligist*, Vol. 72 (February 1970), p. 68.

[16]Vogel, "Professional Housewife," p. 27.

[17]Sato Kinko, "Is Your Mother Nice to You?" in, *Japan Echo*, Vol. 9 (1982), p. 33.

[18]Salamon, "In the Intimate Arena," p. 93.

[19]Vogel, "Professional Housewife," p. 22.

[20]Nan Weiner, "Employment of Women in Japan," Working Paper Series, The Ohio State University, March 1982, p. 5.

of Japan does not aim at husband-wife companionship but at balancing the responsibilities of women and men in the family. Even though many marriages are rather distant ones, another characteristic of complementary Japanese marriages is their relatively low divorce rates. The reasons for this low divorce rate may partly be the result of the lack of alimony and child support available for divorced women and the lack of employment opportunities for older women. Another reason is that children from single parent families are looked upon as "handicapped," and employers have been known not to want to hire young adults from single parent families.[21] Remarriage for divorced women is still considered difficult. Yet another reason for the lack of divorce may be that marriage is seen a family institution and there are no expectations of close companionship between wife and husband.

There are indications that Japanese marriage is changing, that younger couples wish to spend more time together and share more. Marriage has changed since the days when parents completely determined their children's choice of partners, when families lived in joint households, and when the mother-in-law would have real control over the household. It is yet to be seen what further changes will occur.

Points to Consider

1. Write two paragraphs in which you compare and contrast the Japanese complementary marriage system to the

companionship marriage system, the ideal in the United States.

2. Considering the ideas you gave in your paragraphs, how do you explain the following statistics?

United States:

Divorce rate per 1000 population (1980): 5.2.

Birth rate per 1000 population (1982 estimated): 16.

Percentage of women in the workplace: 43 percent.

Percentage of women attending four-year colleges or universities (1982): 53 percent.

Women's wages (1983): 64.7 percent of those of men.*

Japan:

Divorce rate per 1000 population (1979): 1.17.

(Although statistics were not available, the divorce rate has risen since 1979).

Birth rate per 1000 population (1977-78): 15.

Percentage of women in the workplace (1981): 38.7 percent.

(Estimated at over 40 percent in 1986).

Percentage of women attending four-year colleges or universities (1980): 22 percent.

Women's wages (1983): 53 percent of those of men.*

[22]

[21]Nancy Andrew, Catherine Broderick, Chizuko Ikegami, Yayori Matsui, "Change in Japan: What Are We Up Against?" in, *Feminist Japan*, No. 4 (February 1978), p. 53.

*Full-time workers only — men and women.

Housewives meet for conversation after seeing their husbands off to work. Women use bicycles as a major form of transportation.

Thinking over your answers to questions 1 and 2, what additional information would you like to have that might explain aspects of Japanese society such as their low divorce rate, complementary marriage system, and modest birth rate?

3. Why might younger, urban couples be more inclined toward "love" marriages in recent years?

4. Considering the heavy social emphasis on marriage and children and other factors, why do you think many couples still choose to have a go-between and are comfortable with a complementary marriage?

5. On January 29, 1985 a Japanese born housewife, Fumiko Kimura,

along with her two children ages four and six months, tried to commit suicide by walking into the Pacific ocean near Los Angeles, California. She was in suicidal despair over her husband's purported infidelity. Passersby pulled the unconscious woman and her children from the ocean, however, the children could not be revived and died. The mother lived and was charged with two counts of murder with special circumstances and two counts of child endangering. If convicted she could have been sentenced to the death penalty.

Her lawyer argued that it was "absurd" to say Kimura *drowned* her children, because of the tradition of Hahako shinju, meaning mother and children suicide, a not uncommon Japanese tradition. Japanese educator, Dr. Machiko Tomita, explained Hahako shinju:

"The Japanese society admits that a mother believes most surviving children would not be loved and taken care of as they would have been by the mother; therefore, if she chooses to die, the part of herself that exists in her children would better die with her." [23]

---

[22]Statistics from, Robin Morgan, ed., *Sisterhood is Global* (Garden City, NY: Anchor Press/ Doubleday, 1984).

[23]Machiko Tomita, "Motherhood in Japan: Room for Additional Roles?," p. 3.

The charges were finally reduced to voluntary manslaughter as part of a plea bargain — but the cultural considerations that Kimura was doing the right thing as a mother were ruled out. Kimura could be sentenced up to 13 years in state prison.[24]

What things mentioned in the last selection might explain the custom of Hahako shinju?

Do you feel the Los Angeles courts should have taken into account "cultural considerations" in deciding the case? Why or why not?

---

[24]"Mother Accepts Lesser Charges in Drownings," *Washington Post*, October 19, 1985.

C.   The Dual Track Employment System

"Japan's economic boom was really the result of men working long hours and women working part time at low pay," said Shibayama Emiko, the author of books on women workers in Japan.[1] This quotation points to the condition of workers where different "tracks" or plans for workers are applied to men when compared with women.

The Japanese employment track that is generally recognized and discussed in the media in the United States is the masculine one. Japan has become known for an employment system in which a person joins a company and stays with it until retirement. Loyalty of employees to a company is therefore strong and the company tries to keep its employees even through hard economic times. As was seen in the previous section, the social life of employees often takes place with other company personnel after work. This track or employment pattern is one that is generally applied to Japanese men only. This pattern of lifetime employment tends to work against Japanese women workers. Women in middle management or corporation leadership positions are few. There are more Japanese women executives in New York than in Tōkyō.[2]

To explain the job discrimination — the double track — in Japan is not

---

[1]Quoted in, Terry Trucco, "In Japan, Problems of Working Women," New York Times, June 19, 1983, p. 12Y.

[2]Atsuko Chiba, "Japanese returning home from abroad find social exile," Minneapolis Tribune, March 6, 1983, p. 13A.

easy. Legally, the constitution of Japan says that there should be "no discrimination in economic relations because of sex" (Article 14.17). Even though discrimination is illegal, it does occur. For example, doors of many companies are closed to women who have gone through the educational system and graduated from college. In trying to compete for jobs after college, they find many barriers to employment. A survey of large Japanese companies showed that 400 of 1,734 companies surveyed refused even to interview female graduates of four-year colleges. These included SONY, Citizen Watch Co., and Bridgestone Tire Co.[3] The reasons companies give for neither interviewing nor hiring women college graduates are that women will merely quit work when they marry and the company will lose the cost of training them. They also claim that lower level jobs for which women are hired require no special training and would bore a college graduate. The fact that many companies aim to employ people for life, then, works against women who may need to go in and out of the work force as they marry, have children, and perhaps return to work later. Unless women are going into professions such as teaching or medicine, a four-year college degree may actually lessen their chances for employment.

Businesses prefer to hire women who have graduated from two-year junior colleges. They are hired as "office ladies" or "office flowers" (shokuba-no-hana). The term "office lady" generally describes a clerical office job with few opportunities for advancement. The following is a description of one such woman's job:

"Every morning she leaves home at 7:30 and rides a 300-percent overcrowded train for nearly one hour to work. By the time she reaches the office, she is tired. After changing to an office uniform in the locker room, she swabs the desks of her office with other girls and sharpens pencils for others before the male workers show up. As they arrive and sit down at their desks, Yukiko serves tea to them. Before long, she is asked to Xerox papers, a humdrum job that takes two hours. Then she is told to make fair copies of papers. After lunch with her colleagues, she is told by her manager to deliver papers to affiliated companies. She returns to the office at 3:00, tea time. She finishes filling out and filing slips and washes teacups. This is how her average day's office work goes, and she has already continued this routine work for nearly five years." [4]

Women clerical workers are given booklets to help them become proper "office flowers." The instructions include advice to smile continuously, offer to work overtime, and not to refuse to date a prospective marriage partner suggested by her boss.[5]

[3]Trucco, "In Japan," p. 12Y.

[4]Bamba Tomoko, "The 'Office Ladies' Paradise: Inside and Out," *Japan Quarterly*, Vol. 26, No. 2 (April-June 1979), p. 243.

[5]Robin Morgan, ed., *Sisterhood is Global* (Garden City, NY: Anchor Press/Doubleday, 1984), p. 377.

A secretary serving tea.

Men with similar educations will be promoted to better jobs, but the "office lady" will have no chance for advancement or change. After a few years, the woman may be so bored that she will quit her job. At this point the vicious circle sets in. As one Japanese woman explained it, "Employers at large companies won't give women good work to do, then complain that women do not work as well as men. When women quit because they are bored, they say that women won't stay on the job."[6]

Actually, the fact that women get bored and quit these clerical jobs is a way of subsidizing the company. Women workers who have received pay increases because of longevity quit and are replaced by new women workers at lower pay. Some

[6]Trucco, "In Japan," p. 12Y.

companies have had a policy of forcing women to quit their jobs at age 30 because, theoretically, they were too "old." A president of a Japanese broadcasting company said, "A woman who wants to work after she reaches 30 cannot be so good." [7] The president went on to say, "I fired my female employees because they weren't beautiful anymore." [8] Young, pretty "girls" are seen as "office flowers" to brighten up their surroundings. This excuse given for firing a woman because of her age often masks the real issue of the advantages to the company of a system that replaces clerical workers with more longevity with lower paid new female workers.

Japanese women have tried, with mixed success, to fight job discrimination. In a major case against the Nissan Motor Co., Nakamoto Miyo claimed discrimination because she was forced to retire at age 50. Men worked until 55 and therefore received a better pension. Nissan's case was built on the argument that a woman of 50 was physically the equivalent of a man of 70 and that women were not "breadwinners." The judge in the case, however, decided against the company and said their discrimination violated the Japanese constitution which guarantees equal rights for women. The court rulings have generally favored women in lawsuits against employers when charges of discrimination have been brought.

Newspaper want ad columns continue to advertise jobs that are headlined "male only." This too would seem to violate Japan's constitution. Some business men continue to feel that women cannot handle executive

positions and frequently give the following reasons for their opinions:

- The primary duty of a woman is to her family, and she cannot raise children and work long hours.

- Women cannot comfortably attend the geisha parties or bars where employees are expected to socialize and carry on informal work.

- Respectable women cannot travel unattended on business trips, especially to foreign countries.

- Protective laws say that women are not supposed to work after 10 p.m., so their usefulness is limited in some jobs.

- The business community is overwhelmingly male, and women do not fit in.[9]

- Japanese men do not wish to work under women's control.

The few women who have made it as professionals or in business admit that the strain of a career and taking care of a household *is* hard. "I'm working my head off," reporter Shimomura Mitsuko commented.[10]

In order to have time to maintain the household and work, many Japanese

---

[7]Taiji Kawate, as quoted in "Thirty and Out in Japan," *Newsweek*, November 27, 1972, p. 87.

[8]*Ibid.*, p. 88.

[9]Takeuchi Hiroshi, "Working Women in Business Corporations," *Japan Quarterly*, Vol. 29, No. 3 (July-September 1982), p. 320.

[10]Dorothy Robins-Mowry, *The Hidden Sun: Women of Modern Japan* (Boulder, CO: Westview Press, 1983), p. 174.

women have part-time jobs. These "part-time" jobs often require almost the same number of hours as full-time ones but pay less in fringe benefits and bonuses. The following chart suggests the difference in benefits for full or part-time workers:

Table 1. Labor Indexes for Females and Males (1981)

	Females	Males
Working population (million)	22.1	35.0
Ratio of working population to 15-and-over population (%)	47.7	79.8
Nonagricultural employees (million)	13.8	26.3
Ratio of nonagricultural employees to 15-and-over population (%)	29.8	59.9
Ratio of married nonagricultural employees (%)	55.7	68.0
Ratio of married temporary workers (%)	70.0	45.2
Ratio of part-time nonagricultural employees (%)	19.2	4.8

Source: *Rado ryoku chosa* (Survey on the Labor Force). Statistics Bureau, Prime Minister's Office, 1981.
Note: Part-time work is defined as that totaling less than 35 hours per week.

Income of Female Workers (June 1980)

	Part-timers	Full-timers
Years of continuous employment	3.3	6.1
Working days per month (a)	23	22.9
Working hours per day (b)	6	7.9
Hourly wage (c)	*Y492	Y646
Annual bonus (d)	Y72,800	Y364,800
Annual income	Y888,000	Y1,767,000
Ratio of part-time to full-time income (%)	50.3	100.0

*Y = yen (in 1986 165 yen = approx. $1.00). [11]

Thus, part-time workers can be paid at lower rates for their labor and may be more easily laid off in a recession.

Recently, there have been signs that the "dual track" system may be modifying somewhat. Many Japanese limit the size of their families to one or two children; Japanese women are currently among the most long-lived in the world with a life expectancy of 79 years. These demographic factors would suggest that more married women will be reentering the labor force after their children are raised or in school. In previous years that was difficult when 30 was thought to be too old for a woman to hold a job. Current statistics show that married women are increasingly a part of the labor force — and many will want to continue working after 30.

[11]Eiko Shinotsuka, "Women in the Labor Force," *Economic Eye*, September 1982, p. 24.

Women Employees by Marital Status

(non-agriculture)   (10,000 persons)

	1962		1982	
	Number	Percent distribution	Number	Percent distribution
Total	802	100.0%	1,408	100.0%
Single	443	55.2	443	31.5
Married	262	32.7	828	58.8
Widowed and divorced	96	12.0	136	9.7

Source: "Annual Report on the Labour Force Survey." Statistics Bureau, Prime Minister Office. [12]

There have also been some changes in the sorts of jobs available for women as the chart below shows:

Employed Women in Selected Occupation

Selected occupation	Number (Persons)			As percent of total employed		
	1960	1975	1980	1960	1975	1980
Technicians	2,400	14,600	24,100	0.7%	1.8%	2.4%
Teachers	277,970	464,100	570,700	34.6	40.5	43.1
Physicians	9,610	13,000	17,100	9.6	9.6	11.6
Pharmacists	13,940	35,700	39,500	39.5	51.4	54.6
Nurses	194,260	385,400	528,300	98.3	97.3	97.7
Artists	6,990	38,100	44,000	15.0	24.5	25.8
Scientists	2,280	3,900	4,300	7.0	5.1	6.4
Judges, Prosecutors, Lawyers	120	400	500	1.2	2.5	3.1
Kindergartner	24,350	73,800	93,600	84.2	94.6	95.0
Nursery nurses	45,000	171,800	234,400	100.0	100.0	99.6
Social workers	5,150	40,200	63,900	34.2	58.9	60.1
Managerial workers (non-governmental)	29,330	98,800	155,400	5.4	8.8	11.7
Clerks	978,910	2,612,300	3,240,700	32.5	44.2	47.8
Stenographers, Typists	66,990	76,600	79,700	95.9	97.2	96.5
Operatives (electric machinery)	159,460	383,000	526,100	40.8	43.8	50.7
Operatives (yarn, thread and fabric mills)	868,530	531,600	410,300	75.3	66.0	63.7
Service workers (except household)	1,252,790	1,960,700	2,244,600	68.7	64.3	64.8
Household workers	308,200	105,800	97,400	99.1	97.5	98.1
Civil servants in managerial posts	600	1,100	2,600	0.8	0.9	1.7
Telephone operatives	118,400	125,900	95,400	94.9	97.1	99.1
Farmers	7,114,640	3,361,700	2,608,800	54.8	52.8	51.7
Accounting clerks	616,500	1,639,900	1,573,100	48.5	65.4	69.9
Saleswomen and sales clerks	1,276,970	1,991,500	2,178,200	56.1	53.4	60.6
Garment and related textile fabrics workers	605,590	959,100	992,800	71.7	79.9	82.4

Source: "Population Census." Statistics Bureau, Prime Minister's Office. [13]

[12]Women's and Young Workers' Bureau, Ministry of Labour, Japan, *The Status of Women in Japan*, 1983, p. 14.

[13]*Ibid.*, p. 17.

"Elevator Girls" are stationed in department stores to greet customers.

Notice, however, that "women's" jobs (ones with large percentages of women) are concentrated in many of the lowest paid categories.

Despite changes, the dual track system of employment still exists. It continues, even though the Japanese constitution outlaws discrimination, partly because of traditional views as to the proper roles for Japanese women. A currently assigned Japanese social science textbook reads, for example, "families where wives work . . . do not function properly." [14] Unions do not represent part-time workers, who are largely female, because part-time workers are seen as only "temporary." American firms hire the "cream of the crop" of Japanese women executives because many Japanese companies will not even interview women. One woman, a

[14]Nan Weiner, "Employment of Women in Japan," Working Paper Series, The Ohio State University, March 1982, p. 4.

graduate of the prestigious Tōkyō University, was turned down for even low paying editorial jobs by two large publishing firms. Her bitter remark was, "Japan is an escalator society, and women just never get on the escalator." [15]

In 1985, the Japanese parliament approved an Equal Opportunity Employment Law. Although it carries few provisions for its enforcement, the law prohibits discrimination against women in the workplace, and includes a number of measures that may lead to improvements in the situation affecting working women.

Points to Consider

A Group Exercise

Divide the class into small groups of four to six students. Each group should appoint a recorder. After deciding on group answers to the following problems, answers may be compared in class discussion. (These 'Points to Consider' may be done by individual students and then answers compared in class discusssion.)

In groups or as individuals answer the following items:

1. List specific ways in which women in Japan have been discriminated against in employment.

2. The Japanese constitution specifically declares that women may not be discriminated against because of their sex. Yet, discrimination continues even though it is against the law. For each category below, give examples of how you think each

might lead to job discrimination against women.

A. Japanese society's expectations for women and traditional ideas of proper roles for women.

B. It is considered "bad form" for Japanese to bring law suits. Disputes are not generally settled in the courts — (as is common in 'litigation happy' United States).

C. Japanese protective laws give women days off during menstrual periods, forbid women working overtime, and prevent women from lifting heavy weights or doing dangerous work.

D. Limited day care (and social pressure) may require women to stay home while their children are young and reenter the job market when children are older.

E. Socializing with one's friends from work rather than with mutual married friends.

3. It may seem surprising that the job of "office lady" is often sought after by young women as a desirable one. In a survey conducted by a Japanese bank, 60 percent of the young women

---

[15]Quoted in Susan J. Pharr, "The Japanese Woman: Evolving Views of Life and Role" in, Sylvia A. Chipp and Justin J. Green, eds., *Asian Women in Transition* (University Park: The Pennsylvania State University Press, 1980), p. 50.

who had been working for the bank for five years lived at home. They received an average wage of 92,000 yen a month, 41,000 was spent and 29,000 saved. Most live at home, spending their salaries on clothes and trips and other things, while saving a portion for the future. On the other hand, the average male salaried worker, aged 35, has two children, a condominium, and earns 200,000 yen a month. It is estimated that he can spend 30,000 yen pocket money.[16]

Why do some call the young unmarried women working in offices "unmarried aristocrats?"

Even though the job may be boring, why do you think these young women still see office work as desirable?

4. What conditions may force a change in Japan's dual track employment system?

---

[16]Bamba Tomoko, "The 'Office Ladies' Paradise," p. 242-243.

D.   Women in Diverse Roles

Traditionally, the ideal role for Japanese women was summarized in the saying that women should be "good wives/wise mothers." All Japanese women were to be married — it was almost unheard of to remain single for life. All Japanese women were to have children, and being barren or childless was considered a tragedy. Women worked outside their homes but, historically, most women workers were rural agricultural workers. In the 19th and 20th centuries women worked as miners and factory workers and, more recently, for businesses as "office ladies." Modern urban women workers have worked under the disadvantages of the dual track system. Some modern Japanese women have continued to work in traditional occupations and while others have different careers.

Women in contemporary Japan continue to be farmers. About 50 percent of the agricultural laborers are women. Their work requires strength and physical endurance. By their own description, their lives are often difficult ones because they are expected to take a major role in field work while single-handedly maintaining their households and attending to children. Many male farmers have found it increasingly difficult to find wives because women recognize this double burden. When one woman farmer found herself particularly overworked, she later said:

"I envied the wives of the salaried men, . . . Their chores consisted of merely cooking and washing. For farmers' wives, cooking, washing, and caring for children did not count as work. In the morning, my husband

Haruko, in face mask, hauling rice from a store room with the rice
husker.

*and I always worked in the paddies
together. If I was late coming out to
the field after my housework, he
would ask me, 'What were you doing
there?' "* [1]

Her day's work during the rice
transplanting season was described:

*"During the two-week rice-
transplanting season in late May,
Haruko's routine never varied. Rising
at three in the morning so as not to
fall behind in the day's work, she
would slip quietly out of the house
and walk to the seedbeds, where she*

*picked about a hundred seedlings
and tied them together. Then she
would walk home again to make
breakfast for herself and the children
before taking them to a nursery or to
the home of an older woman who
baby-sat. Returning to the paddies,
she would plant seedlings until*

---

[1]Quoted in Gail Lee Bernstein, *Haruko's World
— A Japanese Farm Woman and Her
Community* (Stanford: Stanford University Press,
1983), p. 48.

seven or eight o'clock at night, then walk to the pigsty and feed the pigs in pitch darkness." [2]

While some women farmers find satisfaction in agricultural work, the financial uncertainties and hard work have created a "bride famine" in some rural areas.[3]

According to some observers, women may be somewhat reluctant to stay in farming communities, partly because rural families tend to be the traditional extended ones, and mother-in-law and family restraints on young married women are more severe.[4] In rural fishing villages, on the other hand, the status of women has traditionally been higher than in farming communities. Women have had to be more independent as the men usually went to sea leaving women to make the day-to-day household decisions.[5] At the same time women in fishing villages worked hard gathering seaweed, caring for their households, and mending and caring for fishing nets. Women also harvested food from the sea. One observer described Ainu women from a fishing village collecting sea urchins in the Pacific Ocean. "Women in hip boots, their heads protected against the sun by white scarves, were picking up sea urchins from the floor of the shallow sea. When large waves moved in, they stood hip-deep in water, only to stoop again to continue their work when the waves had passed."[6] After a day of harvesting, the urchins need to be washed, cracked open with a knife, prepared for sale to exclusive "sushi" [7] shops in the cities.

Women have become the principal divers in certain areas. They may dive for seaweed or, in some areas of Japan like Hekura, they dive for "awabi," a kind of shellfish considered a delicacy. An Italian author in the 1960's interviewed some of the villagers and asked why it was that the women did the diving and not the men. This is the reply he received:

"Because women are much tougher, of course. If we men stay in the water for two hours, we're half dead of cold, but women are not, they are covered with fat, like seals. Also, they can hold their breath longer, and they're calmer. In the old days men used to dive too, but everybody knows that their work was less profitable, and so it would be today." [8]

The scarcity of the awabi meant that divers would have to go down as much as 60 feet. The following is a description of a woman's dive:

---

[2]*Ibid.*, p. 48.

[3]Gail Lee Bernstein, "Women in Rural Japan" in, *Women in Changing Japan*, Joyce Lebra, Joy Paulson, and Elizabeth Powers, ed. (Stanford: Stanford University Press, p. 45.

[4]George De Vos and Hiroshi Wagatsuma, "Value Attitudes Toward Role Behavior of Women in Two Japanese Villages," American Anthropologist, Vol. 63 (1961), p. 1226.

[5]*Ibid.*, p. 1205.

[6]M. Inez Hilger, *Together with the Ainu: A Vanishing People* (Norman, Oklahoma: University of Oklahoma Press, 1971), p. 21.

[7]Japanese delicacies of raw fish, seafood, spices, and rice, formed into small balls and eaten with sauces.

[8]Fosco Maraini, *The Island of The Fisherwomen* (New York: Harcourt, Brace & World, Inc., 1962), p. 67-68.

"Next to the boat two Ama girls lay on the surface like strange insects, looking down at the sea-bed. Then one of them made up her mind. Her head vanished for a moment above the silver ceiling (no doubt to take a deep breath) and then immediately reappeared; her body arched, and with a movement of her hips she began her rapid dive.

"When she reached bottom she started groping among the seaweed. The greeny blue or brownish Posidonia is familiar to everybody; it is the commonest seaweed on our coasts also. Here it was thick and abundant enough frequently almost to conceal the diver's body, leaving only her back visible. Then she took her metal tool in her right hand and placed it against the rock on the underside of a projection; this action caused her to turn right over, and for a moment she was face upwards. But now her breath was running short. She tugged, and was quickly pulled up. In her hands she had two fine awabi, and she held her legs together and her arms to her sides to offer a minimum of resistance. A silvery triangle of air bubbles came from her nostrils.

"When they reach the surface the Ama girls hold on to the side of the boat to rest for a moment and give a characteristic whistle (ama-bui). A dive lasts for forty-five or fifty seconds, sometimes for a whole minute. After about twenty dives, or an hour's work, the girls climb into the boat and rest for half an hour or so. If the sky is overcast, or if it is cold, a wood fire is lit in the brazier in the middle of the boat and the girls cover themselves with a crude embroidered kimono, forming a kind of cloak. At midday they either stay in the boat or go ashore for their lunch and take a longer rest in the sun. Then they go back to work until four or five o'clock. Such is the Ama girls' working day.

"Obviously it is very hard work. Diving now and again for the pleasure of underwater fishing is one thing; doing it day after day from June to September, often when the weather is bad or cold, is quite another." [9]

Despite the hard work, one woman sensed the beauty of the diving. When asked what it was like down below, she replied, ''Wonderful, absolutely wonderful.'' But she added, ''Sometimes it's a bit lonely, particularly if there is a shark swimming about.'' [10]

The Japanese tradition of women divers is seen in the cultured pearl industry of today. Women divers get the pearls from the Mikimoto pearl beds. There women dive in shallow beds to boxes containing oysters. They haul up the oysters which are then opened and sorted by color and size. Japan has one of the major pearl centers of the world.

Going from the depths of the sea to the heights, Japanese women have also been noted recently for their mountain climbing. In 1975 a team of 15 Japanese women attempted to climb Mount Everest, in Nepal/Tibet.

---

[9]*Ibid.*, p. 70-71.

[10]*Ibid.*, p. 92.

One of their group, Tabei Junko, reached the top and became the first woman to conquer the tallest mountain in the world. Hisano Eiko, the leader of the expedition was quoted as saying, "Men are stronger, it's true. But we women have lots of endurance." [11] Another woman, part of a Himalaya mountain-climbing team, was 65-year-old Kuwabara Chiyo who managed to keep up with younger climbers. She and another woman, a physician, also 65, seemed to be less affected by the high altitude than younger women. As part of Japan's "Respect for Elder People Day," Kuwabara was featured as a role model for older women.[12]

Climbing mountains is sometimes easier than climbing the ladder to the upper levels of the Japanese business community. Some women have done so. One of these women is Saisho Yuriko who founded the large advertising company Nippo Marketing and Advertising, Inc. Saisho Yuriko, like some other women of her World War II generation, found that the financial resources of her family were destroyed, leaving her the main economic support of her family. In her comments on, "How I Succeeded in Business in a Male-Dominated Society," she said, however, that a woman would need to work harder to succeed than most men. She would also have to be extremely persistent. She described how she got her first accounts:

"I would beat a path to the TV station every day without fail to go over the previous day's program performance, willingly accepting criticism and advice. The people at the station would laugh and remark

Saisho Yuriko, president of Nippo Advertising Company

'boy, not a day goes by without you showing up!' "[13]

In her advice on how women might gain executive-level positions, she also stressed the importance of having a mentor. Saisho Yuriko advises a woman as follows:

"She needs a good connection with a high-standing, socially influential person, directly or indirectly, who is willing to introduce her to whomever he wishes to contact. Without this procedure she will, in most cases, be rejected on the ground that they are

[11]Quoted in, Elizabeth Powers, "Women in Sports" in, *Women in Changing Japan*, Joyce Lebra, Joyce Paulson, and Elizabeth Powers, eds. (Stanford: Stanford University Press, 1976), p. 262.

[12]James Trager, *Letters from Sachiko* (New York: Atheneum, 1982), p. 118-121.

[13]Yuriko Saisho, *Women Executives in Japan* (Tokyo: Yuri International, Inc. , 1981), p. 21.

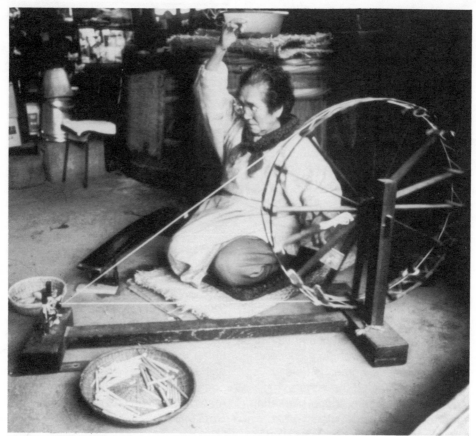

Yoshino Chiba is a living legacy of the ancient art of indigo dyeing technique, "Japan Blue." Home-grown hemp is spun into thread, woven on a hand-operated loom, and then dyed.

tightly scheduled. However, it is simply because she is a stranger. They must know of her social standing and how she may be able to effect them and their profits, not only from her directly, but from someone who is socially respectable and influential. This is done through a formal introduction." [14]

Some breakthroughs have been made for women in the business community. Women seem to have more

opportunities in smaller companies or in starting their own enterprises than in the large "escalator companies." More women professionals are becoming medical doctors and administrators. Women in these fields, however, often recognize that they pay a special price to be there. The

[14]*Ibid.*, p. 17-18.

290

female director of the Matsuda Sanitary Department, said that in order to be an administrator, "I had to work twice as hard as a man for the same job." [15]

In the arts, several Japanese women have achieved international reputations. One is Ono Yoko, who was married to the British singer-composer John Lennon, but who is also known for her own talents as a song writer. Aniyoshi Sawako has become a much admired novelist. Miyawaki Aiko is known for her world famous art design. Mori Hanae helped to establish Japan as a major center for fashion design with a New York show of her fashions in 1965. She is now head of a publishing and real estate company as well as being active in fashion design. Kawakubo Rei is considered a leader in fashion design today.

Younger artists are also making a name for themselves. Torikai Ushio is known for her skill at performing on traditional musical instruments like the shamisen. Torikai Ushio also composes music which uses traditional Japanese instruments with synthesizers and other modern innovations. In 1986 she performed in Minneapolis at a Japanese music festival which was part of a world famous exhibit of Japanese art.

Besides the arts, Japanese women serve in the Japanese Self-Defense Forces where they made up about 1.24 percent of the forces in 1979. While this percentage is not large, there has been an increasing number of women applying to serve in the military in the following areas:

Administration

Personnel Management

Languages

Archives

Counseling

Supply and Accounting

Aircraft Fuselage Maintenance

Aircraft Electronic Technique

Aircraft Weapons Maintenance

Aircraft Engine Maintenance

Communication

Electronic Techniques

Intelligence

Photography

Map Reading

Computers

Physical Exercise

Meteorology [16]

These assignments are generally away from combat situations. Japanese women are still not admitted to the Defense Academy for officer training for top military positions. They do, however, play a limited role in the military.

Japan, then, like many nations, has some women in more diverse occupations than might be expected from the social ideal that demands that Japanese women focus major attention on their families. Currently it seems that it takes something of an exceptional woman to break into many "non-traditional" fields. The women who have paid the costs to enter their chosen field and build a career often

---

[15]Quoted in, Gloria Marsha Shurman, "Japanese Women: History, Role Transformation and Cases of the Achievement of Eminence," unpublished Ph.D. dissertation, United States International University, 1978, p. 151.

[16]Karl L. Weigand, "Japan: Cautious Utilization" in, *Female Soldiers — Combatants or Noncombatants?*, Nancy Loring Goldman, ed. (Westport, Connecticut: Greenwood Press, 1982), p. 186.

seem to thrive on the satisfaction of doing what they feel is worthy and enjoyable.

Points to Consider

1. Among various cultures and in many historical time periods an ideal for women has been that they focus their major attention on family — caring for children and husbands. However, this cultural ideal — which saw women as not working outside the home and spending their energies on family — often was *not* the ideal for lower-class women but only of the upper classes.

    Why do you think this cultural ideal for women was not applied to economically lower-class women?

    In many cultures middle-class women were more strictly held to the ideal (secluded at home with few outside activities) than upper-class women. Why do you think that the upper classes might allow more freedom for women than the middle classes?

2. Why do you think that women as agricultural workers have been called "the invisible laborers?"

3. List reasons why there have been "bride famines" in some rural areas of Japan?

4. Contrast the situations of farm women, fisherwomen, and women divers. What things seem to be the most difficult about their occupations? Rewarding?

5. Thinking back on Chapter 9-B, The Dual Track Employment System, why do you think it was an exceptional woman who was able to start an advertising company as Saisho Yuriko did? What added motivation did she have that might have helped her overcome some of the barriers to success?

6. What kinds of positions do women hold in the Japanese Self-Defense Forces? Why might promotion for women to higher ranks in the Self-Defense Forces be difficult or impossible?

7. Why might climbing mountains be easier than climbing the ladder in government or business for a Japanese woman?

E. Women in Japanese Politics

A large percentage of women vote in Japan, but women are not elected in large numbers to the Japanese Parliament or Diet. For the most part, government leaders have been male, with only two women appointed as cabinet ministers, the first in 1960 as Minister of Health and Welfare.[1] The following are statistics on the voting rates and numbers of women elected to government positions in Japan between 1946 and 1980:

(House of Councilors Elections)

Election	Eligible Voters (millions)		Votes Cast (millions)		Voting Rates (%)		Women Elected (1)
	Male	Female	Male	Female	Male	Female	
1st (Apr. 20, 1946)	20	21	13	12	66.4	54.0	10
2nd (June 4, 1950)	21	23	16	15	78.2	66.7	9
3rd (Apr. 24, 1953)	22	25	15	14	67.8	58.9	9
4th (July 8, 1956)	24	26	16	15	66.9	57.7	5
5th (June 2, 1959)	26	28	16	15	62.6	55.2	8
6th (July 1, 1962)	27	29	19	19	70.1	66.5	8
7th (July 4, 1965)	29	31	19	21	68.0	66.1	9
8th (July 7, 1968)	32	34	22	24	68.9	69.0	5
9th (June 27, 1971)	34	37	20	22	59.1	59.3	8
10th (July 7, 1974)	36	39	27	29	72.7	73.6	8
11th (July 10, 1977)	38	40	26	28	67.7	69.3	8
12th (June 22, 1980)	39	42	29	31	73.7	75.3	9

Source: Election Bureau, Ministry of Home Affairs
Note: (1) 252 seats in total
Election for half of the members shall take place every three years.

[1]Robin Morgan, ed., *Sisterhood is Global* (Garden City, NY: Anchor Press/Doubleday, 1984), p. 376.

Eligible Voters, Votes Cast and Voting Rates by Sex and the Number of Successful Women Candidates
(General Elections of House of Representatives)

Election	Eligible Voters (millions)		Votes Cast (millions)		Voting Rates (%)		Women Elected (1)
	Male	Female	Male	Female	Male	Female	
22nd (Apr. 10, 1946)	16	21	13	14	78.5	67.0	39
23rd (Apr. 25, 1947)	20	21	15	13	74.9	61.6	15
24th (Jan. 23, 1949)	20	22	16	15	80.7	68.0	12
25th (Oct. 1, 1952)	22	24	18	18	80.5	72.8	9
26th (Apr. 19, 1953)	22	25	18	17	78.4	70.4	9
27th (Feb. 27, 1955)	24	26	19	19	80.0	72.1	8
28th (May 22, 1958)	25	27	20	20	79.8	74.4	11
29th (Nov. 20, 1960)	26	28	20	20	76.0	71.2	7
30th (Nov. 21, 1963)	28	30	20	21	72.4	70.0	7
31st (Jan. 29, 1967)	30	33	23	24	74.8	73.3	7
32nd (Dec. 27, 1969)	33	36	23	25	67.9	69.1	8
33rd (Dec. 10, 1972)	36	38	25	28	71.0	72.5	7
34th (Dec. 5, 1976)	38	40	27	30	72.8	74.1	7
35th (Oct. 7, 1979)	39	41	26	28	67.4	68.6	11
36th (June 22, 1980)	39	42	28	31	73.7	75.4	9

Source: Election Bureau, Ministry of Home Affairs
Note: (1) 466 seats in total, up to 26th General Election
　　　　467 in total, up to 30th
　　　　486 in total, 31st, 32nd
　　　　491 in total, 33rd
　　　　511 in total, 34th, 35th, 36th[2]

As can be seen from the chart, the percentage of women voting is remarkably high — in 1980, 75.4 percent of eligible women voted.

While women vote in large numbers, they do not vote as a block or group — their votes are spread throughout the range of political parties.[3] A few have joined the extreme left wing party called the Red Army, like Shigenobu Fusako, involved in plotting the terrorist attack on Tel Aviv, Israel in 1972.[4] Others, like the socialist, Tanaka Sumiko, have worked peacefully for better medical services for women. Kawanobe Shizu of the Liberal Democratic Party worked in the area of reform social issues. One exceptional woman, Ichikawa Fusae,

the long-time feminist discussed earlier, was even elected to the Diet without the backing of a political party because of her impressive record of

[2]From, Women's and Young Workers' Bureau, Ministry of Labour, Japan, The Status of Women in Japan, 1983, p. 3-4.

[3]There are five major political parties in Japan: Liberal Democratic Party, Japan Socialist Party, Komei Party, Democratic Socialist Party, and Japan Communist Party as well as minor parties.

[4]Eileen Carlberg, "Women in the Political System" in, Joyce Lebra, Joy Paulson and Elizabeth Powers, eds., Women in Changing Japan (Stanford, CA: Stanford University Press, 1976), p. 241.

independence.

In September 1986 a woman, Doi Takako, was elected chair of the Japanese Socialist Party. Doi Takako has been a member of Parliament since 1969. She is considered to be a political moderate and a specialist on foreign affairs. If the Socialist Party received a majority of the seats in Parliament Doi Takako would become Prime Minister of Japan. This is unlikely, however, since the Socialist Party won a record *low* of 86 seats in the lower house of the Japanese Parliament in the July 1986 election. Perhaps this poor showing encouraged the members of the Socialist Party to elect a woman — quite a radical move in Japan where few women are elected to political office.[5]

Despite the variations in the political parties that they support, one characteristic of Japanese women in politics is that they have generally become involved in issues that reflected their concern over family welfare. The peace issue and anti-nuclear feeling have united women of many political groups. At times they came together to demonstrate for their common concerns. Susan Pharr, an American political scientist, described a bus ride to a demonstration in which she took part:

"On a crisp day in early October of 1971 I turned up at the appointed place for what proved to be a day and evening crammed with experiences I shall long remember. Every seat on the bus was taken. A few people crouched in the aisles. Although there were several men in the group, most were women, and many of them younger women in their twenties and early thirties. I began to talk to some of them sitting near me. Then once the bus was in motion, formal introductions began. It is the custom in Japan when groups take bus trips for any particular purpose, whether it be a company outing or a political demonstration, to have a microphone system set up so that each person can make a few remarks. When groups attend demonstrations together, these introductory remarks often include a statement of the individual's purpose in attending the demonstration and some remarks about how he or she became concerned about that particular cause. Statements of various women on the bus introduced me to a number of issues and causes in Japan that I had known little about. . . . The demonstration's attraction for women who were active in a wide array of political groups was a result of its focus on antimilitarism, a cause that in Japan unites the disparate groups in the progressive camp perhaps more than any other.

"When my own turn at the microphone came, I related, in a somewhat shaky voice, my own purpose for coming to Japan and my interest in the political goals of young Japanese women and their struggle to attain them. I was overwhelmed at the response.

---

[5]New York Times, "Japan Socialists Pick Woman as Chief," September 7, 1986.

Women from the Shufurengokai (Housewives' Association) march with rice paddle banners to protest the high price of rice.

Throughout the day, on the bus and later at the demonstration site, women young and old came up to me, expressed their interest in my work, and offered to help me meet young women to interview." [6]

One way in which Japanese women have been active in civic affairs is through involvement in the Parent Teachers Association. The P.T.A. has been a training ground and a network-building arena. Japanese mothers are expected to take an active part in the P.T.A. and young women who have served in the P.T.A. often have become involved in further social reform activities. One P.T.A. group, after trying unsuccessfully to raise funds for a school library, formed a library association and worked to improve the city library instead.[7] Another organization, The

Housewives' Association, which is particularly concerned about issues of inflation, toxic chemical use, and food prices, has also become involved in political campaigns.

One of the major environmental movements of the 1960's was the Anti-Minamata Disease campaign led by women, primarily Ishimure Michiko. The Chisso Corporation had been improperly dumping mercury wastes near the town of Minamata in southwest Japan. The people of the

---

[6]Susan J. Pharr, *Political Women in Japan* (Berkeley: University of California Press, 1981), p. 189.

[7]Higuchi Keiko, "The PTA — A Channel for Political Activism," Japan Interpreter, Vol. 10, No. 2 (Autumn 1975), p. 138.

village suffered from severe disabling diseases caused by the chemical pollution of the bay near their village and the fish they were eating. In the campaigns to end the dumping of the mercury, Minamata disease became an international symbol of the dangers of improperly disposed chemical wastes from manufacturing.[8]

Another issue women have been particularly interested in has been the campaign for "clean politics" waged by many women. This campaign aims to get rid of corruption in government and political campaigns by eliminating political slush funds and bribery of public officials.

Women in Japanese politics seem to involve themselves mostly with issues that relate to health, family consumer needs, and peace. Recently, however, there are some indications that women may be broadening their political interests. In 1975 almost 25 percent of all Japanese women over age 20 belonged to at least one women's organization, and the National Council of the Federation of Regional Women's Clubs had over six million members.[9] With increasing participation in service clubs outside their homes, may come increasing interest in political issues.[10]

Points to Consider

1. Women in Japan won full voting rights in 1945. Under the new constitution of 1947 they were granted full equality. Yet, Japanese women make up:

- 1.8 percent of the House of Representatives. (1983)

- 7.2 percent of the House of Councilors. (1983)

- about 1.3 percent of local government. (1979)

- one cabinet minister in 1986.

- 54.8 percent of the national advisory councils to the government had no women members. (1979)[11]

- no women among the 47 prefectural (state) governors.

- no women mayors of the 652 largest cities.

- only two women chief executives out of 2500 towns and villages.[12]

---

[8]Matsui Yayori, "Protest and the Japanese Woman" Japan Quarterly, Vol. 22, No. 1 (January/March 1975), p. 32-34.

[9]Morgan, *Sisterhood is Global*, p. 382.

[10]Pharr, *Political Women in Japan*, p. 184-185.

[11]Morgan, *Sisterhood is Global*, p. 376.

[12]New York Times, "Japan Socialists," September 7, 1986.

A Japanese woman and two women from Africa stand in front of the
Peace Tent at the United Nations Decade for Women conference at
Nairobi, Kenya, in July 1985. They hold paper cranes, ancient symbols
of peace. Members of the Thousand Crane Club, founded in Japan
after World War II, work for world peace.

Suggest some possible reasons to explain this low participation of women in Japan as elected and appointed government leaders while they have such a high rate of participation in voting.

2. Looking back at the election charts, what years had the highest numbers of women elected? How do you explain the larger numbers?

3. Using class or library sources, find out comparable statistics on women's participation in United States government as voters and elected and appointed leaders. Compare and contrast these to women in Japanese politics.

4. Women participate in all political parties but often come together over some particular issues. What issues do many Japanese women see as their common concern?

Why might women feel more comfortable demonstrating over issues they see as extensions of their role as wives and mothers? Why might it be more acceptable to Japanese society for women to march in public demonstrations over high rice prices than for other causes?

5. A prominent feature of Japanese culture is that people are group oriented. Many activities — from travel to political — are done in

well-defined and organized
groups. In Susan Pharr's
description of her participation in
a demonstration in Japan, what
evidence is there of this tendency
to form groups? How did this work
to her advantage as a scholar
carrying on research in Japan?

6. Thinking back over what you have
read about Japanese women in
contemporary times, list some
specific reasons why there might
be an increase in the level of
participation of women in
Japanese politics in the near
future.

F.   Issues for Women of Japan—A Summary

Takahashi Nobuko, director general of the Women's and Minors' Bureau of the Ministry of Labor of Japan in the 1970's, discussed the legal protection of Japanese women's rights. She said, "We have plenty of law. It's a matter of putting it into practice."[1] The constitution of Japan explicitly states that women are to have equal rights, and specific laws allow for maternity leaves and protection of women workers.[2] The 1947 Labor Standards Act says that it is against the law for employers to discriminate against women concerning wages, and the constitution gives women equal rights; yet many problems of discrimination remain for Japanese women workers.

Some forms of discrimination have been attempted openly; others less obviously. Until 1976, for example, it was common for companies to have two salary schedules — one for men,

one, with lower pay, for women. This violated the 1947 Labor Standards Act, and a Japanese court ruled this practice to be illegal. After the court ruled against the separate salary schedules, corporations downgraded the titles of women's jobs so they could still be paid less under the law. The tasks required, however, were not changed.[3] The dual track employment system continues to be discriminatory

---

[1]William H. Forbis, *Japan Today: People, Places, Power* (New York: Harper & Row, 1975), p. 36.

[2]Protection laws sometimes work against women as they are not allowed to work overtime and in certain jobs deemed dangerous.

[3]Robin Morgan, ed., *Sisterhood is Global* (Garden City, NY: Anchor Press/Doubleday, 1984), p. 376.

against women employees. A survey in 1978 showed the following:

- 91 percent of companies had jobs closed to women.

- 73 percent of companies had different (lower) starting salaries for women.

- 52 percent did not promote women.

- 77 percent had different retirement systems for women.

- 19.4 percent offered equal training to women.[4]

Although Takahashi Nobuko may be right that there is "plenty of law" to protect women, when the ministry of labor proposed an equal opportunity bill in 1984 it met with strong opposition from the business community.[5] Court challenges claiming discrimination which violates the Japanese constitution may be brought, but these are often hard to prove — and expensive.

Particularly for young women with four-year college degrees, the dual track employment system has meant a lack of opportunity to get meaningful jobs. This leads to a sense that women will not receive benefits from a four-year college degree and encourages women to settle for less education. It also means that women do not take business or technology courses in the same numbers as men. The following statistics bear this out:

Number of Female Students in 4-year Institutions by Department — 1982

(Persons)

Department	Total	Women		
		Number	Percent Distribution	As percent of total
Total	1,716,956	387,465	100.0	22.6
Literature	239,486	137,995	35.6	57.6
Law, Politics, Economics & Industrial management	681,045	56,034	14.5	8.2
Science	55,188	9,274	2.4	16.8
Engineering	333,387	6,698	1.7	2.0
Agriculture	59,072	7,685	2.0	13.0
Medicine, Dentistry, Pharmacy & Nursing	114,458	35,679	9.2	31.2
Mercantile marine	1,516	22	0.0	1.5
Home economics	31,453	31,197	8.1	99.2
Teachers training	133,724	68,593	17.7	51.3
Arts	44,183	27,788	7.2	62.9
Others	23,444	6,495	1.7	27.7

[4]*Ibid.*, p. 376.

[5]*Ibid.*, p. 376.

Enrollment of Women in Institutions of Higher Education—1982

(Persons)

Type of Institution	Total	Women		
		Number	Percent Distribution	As percent of total
Total	2,191,922	741,117	100.0%	33.8%
4-year institutions	1,817,649	405,125	54.7	22.3
Public	477,773	105,012	14.2	22.0
Private	1,339,876	300,113	40.5	22.4
2-year institutions	374,273	335,992	45.3	89.8
Public	36,151	22,438	3.0	62.1
Private	338,122	313,554	42.3	92.7

[6]

Many Japanese women work part time. As was seen in Chapter 11-C, this may mean working nearly full-time hours without the fringe benefits or eligiblity for pensions of a full-time job. Older married women have a difficult time finding full-time jobs. Women may also work in part-time jobs because of the lack of day care facilities and the social pressures to be a "good wife/ wise mother." Generally, women are still expected to take care of the home and children, even if they are employed elsewhere. According to 1976 statistics, women over 15 average 26.3 hours per week on work in the home while men average 1.5 hours.[7] Although these statistics include women who are full-time homemakers, it does suggest that women carry the overwhelming burden of home and child care. Therefore, women are attracted to part-time work, even if the pay, benefits, and opportunities for advancement are far less than full-time employment.

There is a lack of opportunity for meaningful work outside the home for Japanese women. The scope of volunteer work open to women in Japanese communities is also limited. The choices of outside activities for adult, married women tend to be narrow; therefore, mothers tend to live their lives through those of their children. Some mothers become overdemanding of their children's school performance and may feel useless when their children grow up and leave home. The high suicide rate for older women in Japan, compared to women in other world areas, may indicate these feelings of worthlessness after children are raised.[8]

Another issue for women in Japan

[6]Women's and Young Workers' Bureau, Ministry of Labour, Japan, *The Status of Women in Japan*, 1983, p. 8.

[7]Morgan, *Sisterhood is Global*, p. 378.

[8] For example, according to 1980 data, the United States' suicide rate for women 45-64 was 8.9 in 100,000 while Japan's was 16.3; for 65 and over, United States 6.1, Japan 44.4. Overall, Denmark, Austria, West Germany, and Switzerland had higher rates, as did men world-wide. See, *Information Please Almanac*, 1985. (Boston: Houghton Mifflin Company), p. 132.

discussed recently by some Japanese feminists is that there continues to be two, quite distinct, Japanese forms of speech — one masculine, one feminine. In social situations women are expected to use a female style of Japanese which involves speaking in softer tones, using few direct commands, and being less egocentric in their use of language. The prominent novelist, Enchi Fumiko, has said that this female Japanese should be discarded because it puts women at a psychological disadvantage.[9] The president of Nippo Marketing, an advertising company, described how she sometimes slipped into the wrong style of speech at inappropriate times:

"Whenever I attended a meeting of a women's organization where some of my mother's classmates were present, I used to talk as if I were still in the office. One of them came over and tugged at my skirt and whispered, 'Yuri, don't talk like a businessman!' I did not realize that I was talking in a very brusque businesslike manner, which was entirely inappropriate in a women's gathering in Japan. The words we use and the way we deliver them reflect our thinking and our attitude. I was very grateful that someone thought enough of me to bring this to my attention . . ." [10]

Other issues that have been discussed by women's groups include:

- The Japanese media's stress on youth has encouraged "30 and out" employment discrimination where women at 30 are forced to retire. Men, however, are not considered "old" at 30. The emphasis on a woman's youthful

beauty has meant that even women of 30 are considered inappropriate for jobs as "office flowers."

- Bar hostesses and geisha are an accepted part of Japanese businessmen's social lives, often to the exclusion of their wives or their family involvement.

- Professional women often have their abilities doubted. Female elementary teachers are sometimes seen as inadequate, and mothers ask, "How can [my] son possibly pass the college entrance exams if a woman teaches [him]?" [11] One critic of women teachers even said that Americans based decisions on "emotional consideration" because they have had too many female teachers.[12]

- Japan has been called a "man's country" because the judges, politicians, business leaders, and educational leaders are nearly all male.

Some signs of change in Japan may give women a greater voice in public affairs.

---

[9]Joy Paulson, "Women in Media" in, *Women in Changing Japan*, Joyce Lebra, Joy Paulson, and Elizabeth Powers, eds., (Stanford: Stanford University Press, 1978), p. 224.

[10]Yuriko Saisho, *Women Executives in Japan* (Tokyo: Yuri International, 1981), p. 82.

[11]Elizabeth Knipe Mouer, "Women in Teaching" in, *Women in Changing Japan*, Joyce Lebra, Joy Paulson, and Elizabeth Powers, eds. (Stanford: Stanford University Press, 1978), p. 185

[12]*Ibid.*, p. 168.

- Women are moving into the labor force in greater numbers — with more older women seeking and finding employment.

- Young couples are increasingly flexible about the wife working at outside jobs and the husband sharing family responsibilities.

- More women are receiving educations equal to those of men — and, armed with their degrees, are demanding equal job opportunities.

- Since 1978 the Group to Frame an Employment Equality Law, made up of women leaders, has lobbied for anti-discrimination in employment laws. In 1985, an equal opportunity law was finally passed, though many women were disappointed that it did not carry a stronger provision for legal enforcement.

- The first case against discrimination in promotion was brought to the courts in 1978.[13]

The Group to Frame an Employment Equality Law held a hunger strike in 1981. Women's Liberation Communication Networks have been formed in Osaka and Kyōto. A group of women workers refused to load rice into ships at Uotsu to protest high prices in 1981. This demonstration started national riots protesting food prices.[14] But these public demonstrations organized by women are somewhat exceptional. Generally, Japanese women have not openly confronted the male establishment.

Delegates from Japan to the United Nations Decade for Women meeting in Copenhagen, Denmark, in 1980 insisted that the Japanese government approve the mid-decade Program of Action and sign the Convention on the Elimination of All Forms of Discrimination Against Women. The Advisory Council to the prime minister on Women's Affairs developed a plan for the second half of the Decade for Women that included these priorities:

"(1) Reviews of laws and regulations with a view to improving the status of women.

(2) Acceleration of women's participation in policy-decision making.

(3) Promotion of education and planning.

(4) Promotion of equal opportunity and treatment between men and women in employment.

(5) Improvement of the [facilities] related to childcare.

(6) Respect for motherhood and promotion of maternal health.

(7) Stabililty of life in old age.

(8) Promotion of welfare and the improvement of the status of women in agricultural, mountainous, and fishing villages.

(9) Promotion of international cooperation.

In particular, as regards the

---

[13]Morgan, *Sisterhood is Global*, p. 382.

[14]*Ibid.*, P. 382.

305

Convention on the Elimination of All Forms of Discrimination against Women, in 1980 the Headquarters came to an agreement that it is considered a major priority task to take steps necessary for the ratification of the Convention, including revisions of relevant laws." [15]

The meeting marking the end of the United Nations Decade for Women was held in Nairobi, Kenya, in July 1985. One participant commented that in the non-government sponsored meetings the Japanese women, along with the militant anti-American Iranians, were the most visible. According to this observer, the Japanese women were well-organized — passing out colorful brochures and strongly supporting a number of causes for women. [16]

Whether or not the Japanese government will actively pursue these goals outlined during the Decade for Women remains to be seen. But in defining and listing these goals, in making women's issues a part of the national agenda, Japan illustrates a major change in government policy. In a relatively short period of time — from the early 1940's to 1985 — the Japanese government has gone from an assumption of second-class citizenship for women to a declaration of a goal supporting total elimination of sexual discrimination. The opportunities missed by the women of Japan in the 1930's may be part of the future of the women of Japan in the 1980's.

Points to Consider

1. Job discrimination against women in some forms in Japan has been openly practiced; in other forms have been more covert (less open). Looking back at the survey of businesses, which forms of discrimination seem very clear and openly practiced? Which forms of discrimination might be harder to prove? Other than those on the survey list, what barriers have prevented Japanese women from achieving employment equity with Japanese men? Which barriers might be the hardest for women to overcome?

2. People who worked for women's suffrage in the United States in the early 20th century felt that after women had the vote, they would soon achieve political power. This did not happen — no women have been president or vice-president of the United States, only a few have been senators or state governors. Japanese women have not achieved political power since achieving the right to vote.

   Why do you think having the right to vote may not give women much political power?

---

[15]Women's and Young Workers' Bureau, Ministry of Labour, Japan, *The Status of Women in Japan*, p. 40-41.

[16]Mary Hill Rojas, Associate Director of International Studies, Virginia Polytechnic Institute and State University, Blacksburg, Virginia.

Japanese woman collects signatures on a petition at the final
conference of the United Nations Decade for Women at Nairobi,
Kenya, July 1985.

Why might women in Japan and the United States make some progress toward more political power in the next 25 years or so? How might they?

3. Thinking over the issues and problems that seem to be the most important for Japanese women — and ones for which they wish to find solutions — decide which issues would be of the most importance to the following groups of women and explain your answers:

    - high school or junior college graduates entering the job market for the first time.

    - four-year college graduates entering the job market for the first time.

    - women between 30 and 40 years old that are returning to the job market after their children are in school or raised.

    - women over 40 who have been continuously employed and wish to complete a career.

4. Think back over this book and review this last selection; then write three summary paragraphs:

- First, describe what you see as the two or three major problems for Japanese women.

- Second, describe what you see as the major strengths of Japanese women.

- In summary, overall do you feel the history of Japanese women has been one of oppression, one of influence and equality, or some of both? Give specific examples to back up your views.

Glossary

Ainu: The original inhabitants of Japan, now refers to indigenous peoples of Hokkaido. They have non-Japanese physical appearance and have suffered from discrimination as members of a minority group.

Anthropology (anthropologist): The branch of social science that deals with cultural development and social customs of peoples. Often *anthropologists* study small groups of people to observe their social organizations.

Archaeology (archaeologist): Study of the ancient past, particularly through artifacts and other non-written remains.

Artifact: Any object made or shaped by humans.

Buddhism (Buddhist): A religion that originated in India, founded by the teacher/philosopher Buddha in the 5th century B.C. Buddhism later spread to China, Tibet, Burma, Japan, and other Asian countries.

Burakumin: A Japanese minority group who were considered "despised citizens" (senmin) or outcastes (eta) because they did tasks like slaughtering animals and burying the dead, which were considered ritually polluted according to the ideas of Buddhism.

Chronicles: Historical accounts usually written in order of events, as in a time sequence, but without discussion. Frequently ancient historical accounts.

Concubine (concubinage): A second wife with some of the rights and privileges of a wife, but less status than the regular wife.

Confucius: A Chinese scholar and teacher (c. 551-497 B.C.). Although his life is surrounded by legend, the sayings and writings attributed to Confucius form the basis of traditional Chinese philosophy. The philosophy based on these ideas, Confucianism, was introduced into Japan from China in the 6th century A.D.

Courtesan: A prostitute who associates with men of power or wealth. Courtesans traditionally were known for their beauty or intelligence.

Daimyō: Feudal lords who ranked below the shōgun but higher than the ordinary warriors or samurai. The daimyō controlled land and peasants but owed feudal obligations to the shōgun.

Diet (parliament): Bicameral (two house) legislative body of present day Japan. The more important lower house, the House of Representatives, has 511 members; the upper house, or

House of Councillors, has 252 members.

Empress-Dowager: The widow of an emperor who was often powerful in Japanese history as she acted as regent for her son or absent husband.

Feudal, feudalism: A social and economic system based on the holding of lands in fief (loaned in exchange for services) by lords (daimyō) who owed loyalty to the shōgun. For Japan, the time between 1185-1867 A.D. is known as the feudal period.

Filial piety: A Confucian idea that sons and daughters owed absolute obedience to their parents (or in the case of a daughter-in-law, to her parents-in-law).

Floating World (ukiyo): The world of sexual pleasures, theater, tea drinking, and music in geographical areas set aside in large cities for entertainment during the Tokugawa Period (1603-1867).

Fujiwara family: During the Heian Period this family held supreme power through political maneuvering, especially by marrying their daughters to imperial sons who were to become emperors.

Fundamental Code of Education (1872): A law in the Meiji period that declared that all Japanese had a right to an education and no one should be illiterate.

Geisha: Japanese female entertainers who, from the male view, complement wives who generally do not socialize with men.

Imperial Rescript on Education (1890): An order from the Meiji emperor that restricted the subjects to be taught to girls and emphasized Confucian values of filial piety.

Kabuki Theater: Japanese plays that include music, dancing, stylized costumes, and acting, with all parts being played, since 1629, by men.

Kami: Ancient deities, heavenly or higher spirits often associated with nature. Looked at as sources of power — both destructive and creative.

Kannon: Ancient Japanese female god of mercy, related to the Chinese deity Guan Yin.

Kimono: Traditional dress of Japanese women.

Kyōiku-mama (education mama): Japanese mothers who take a great personal interest in their children's education and strongly encourage them to study and excel.

Matriarchy (matriarchal): The mother is the head of the household, with descent lines traced through the mother.

Meiji Period: Period from 1868-1912 during which Japan was modernized.

Miko: Female assistants at Shintō shrines.

Moga (Modern Girl): This term was applied to girls during the Taishō Period in the 1920's who wanted to be thought of as up-to-date by adopting costumes and customs of Western countries.

Nakōdo: Go-between for a marriage. At times he or she plays a mainly ceremonial role but often actually arranges the meeting of the prospective couple.

Natal family: Family into which a person is born.

Neo-Confucian system: Social system based on Confucian ideas. It was revived in Japan during the Tokugawa Period (1603-1867 A.D.) and became the basis for the social order.

Neolocal marriage: A married couple who set up an independent household, not necessarily near to either the wife's or husband's parents.

Nō theater: A form of classical drama, often with masks, developed in 14th century Japan, using very formal patterns of dance, music, and verse with religions and mythical themes.

Obi: Wide, stiff, heavy sash that goes around the waist, when one is wearing a kimono.

Patriarchy: Where the father is head of the household, with lines of descent traced through the father.

Polyandry: The practice of having more than one husband at one time.

Polygamy: The practice of having more than one spouse at the same time.

Polygyny: The practice of having more than one wife at one time.

Prehistoric: History of people before recorded events and known mainly through archaeological discoveries.

Primogeniture and entail: The practice whereby the entire inheritance goes to the oldest son.

Protestants/Protestant Reformation: A number of European reform movements begun by people like Martin Luther and John Calvin who wished to change aspects of the Roman Catholic Church. These movements led to a number of different Christian churches in Europe by the mid-16th century.

Regent: One who rules for another; in historical Japan a Dowager-Empress often ruled for an absent husband or minor son.

Rokumeikan: Translated as the "Deer Cry Pavilion." A Victorian English-type building built in 1883 in Tokyo. Western-style entertainment took place at the Rokumeikan with both women and men in attendance.

Roman Catholic Church: The dominant Christian faith of medieval times in Western Europe. Francis Xavier and two other priests introduced Catholicism into Japan in 1549.

Samurai: A warrior class of noblemen who constituted about 5% of the population. Their unwritten code was called bushidō — "the way of the warrior" — which included the acceptance of physical hardships, loyalty to their leaders, and — as the most honorable fate — a heroic death on the battlefield.

Shaman: A person, female or male, acting through the supernatural as both priest and healer.

Shamisen (samisen): Three-stringed, fretless instrument associated with geisha.

Shintō, Shintōism (kami-no-michi, the way of the gods): The ancient native Japanese religion that sees higher spirits — kami — in all aspects of nature. Kami are appealed to in times of trouble or for rewards. The religious beliefs of most Japanese today combine Shintō and Buddhism.

Shōgunate (shōgun): Beginning in 1185 with Minamoto Yoritomo, a succession of military dictators or shōgun became the virtual (real) rulers of Japan, although the emperor remained as the nominal ruler. This system continued until 1867 when the shōgunate was abolished.

Shokuba-no-hana (office ladies or office flowers): Term used to refer to women in clerical jobs. Their duties include serving tea, cleaning desks, and brightening up the office.

Suffrage, Suffrage movement: The right to vote or — in this case — the movement for adult women to gain the vote.

Sushi: Japanese food made up of raw fish on vinegared rice.

Terakoya: Private schools open to commoners before the Meiji Reforms required universal education.

Virilocal marriage: The custom whereby a bride and groom live with the husband's parents, or nearby.

Yen: The major Japanese currency equivalent to the United States dollar.

Selected Bibliography

General

Bacon, Alice. *Japanese Girls and Women*. Boston: Houghton Mifflin, 1982.

Bernstein, Gail Lee. *Haruko's World: A Japanese Farm Woman and Her Community*. Stanford: Stanford University Press, 1981.

Condon, Jane. *A Half Step Behind: Japanese Women of the '80's*. New York: Dodd, Mead & Co., 1985.

Cook, Alice and Hiroko Hayashi. *Discrimination Against Women in Japan: Reform and Resistance*. New York: School of Industrial Relations, 1980.

_____. *Working Women in Japan*. Ithaca: Cornell University Press, 1980.

Dalby, Liza. *Geisha*. Berkeley: University of California Press, 1983.

Danly, Robert Lyons. *In the Shade of Spring Leaves*. New Haven, Connecticut: Yale University Press, 1981.

Lebra, Joyce, Joy Paulson, and Elizabeth Powers. *Women in Changing Japan*. Stanford: Stanford University Press, 1976.

Lebra, Takie Sugiyama. *Japanese Women: Constraint and Fulfillment*. Honolulu: University of Hawaii Press, 1984.

Pharr, Susan. *Political Women in Japan*. Berkeley: University of California Press, 1981.

Rexroth, Kenneth and Ikuko Atsumi, tr. *Burning Heart: Women Poets of Japan*. New York: Seabury Press, 1977.

Robins-Mowry, Dorothy. *The Hidden Sun: Women of Modern Japan*. Boulder, Colorado: Westview, 1983.

Saisho, Yuriko. *Women Executives in Japan*. Tokyo: Yori, 1981.

Sievers, Sharon. *Flowers in Salt: The Beginnings of Feminist Consciousness in Modern Japan*. Stanford: Stanford University Press, 1983.

Smith, Robert J. and Ella Lury Wiswell. *The Women of Suye Mura*. Chicago: University of Chicago Press, 1982.

Biography and Autobiography

Ishimoto, Shizue. *Facing Two Ways: The Story of My Life*. New York: Farrar & Rinehart, 1935.

McClellan, Edwin. *Woman in the Crested Kimono*. New Haven, Connecticut: Yale University Press, 1985.

Omori, Annie Shepley and Doi Kochi, tr. *Diaries of Court Ladies of Old Japan*. New York: AMS Press, 1970.

Sugimoto, Etsu Inayaki. *A Daughter of the Samurai*. Garden City: Doubleday, Doran & Co., 1934.

ABOUT THE AUTHORS

Marjorie Wall Bingham was born in St. Paul, Nebraska, received a B.A. degree from Grinnell College and M.A. and Ph.D. degrees from the University of Minnesota. She has taught high school history for the St. Louis Park school system since 1963. Dr. Bingham's experience also includes teaching in a junior high school in Davenport, Iowa, and at the University of Minnesota. She is presently co-director of WWAS (Women in World Area Studies) and has served as a member of the Minnesota Council for the Social Studies Executive Board and as president of WHOM (Women Historians of the Midwest). She currently serves on the Teaching Division of the American Historical Association, the Advisory Committee of the Organization of American Historians *Magazine of History*, and the Editorial Board of *The History Teacher.*

Susan Hill Gross was born in Minneapolis, Minnesota, and received her B.A. degree from the University of Minnesota and her M.A. degree in history from the College of William and Mary in Virginia. Ms. Gross taught secondary English and history in Denbigh, Virginia; Savannah, Georgia; and the Robbinsdale Schools in Minnesota before becoming a director of the curriculum project Women in World Area Studies. She has also taught at the University of Minnesota and has served as president of WHOM (Women Historians of the Midwest). She is currently director of the Upper Midwest Women's History Center for Teachers.

Dr. Bingham and Ms. Gross are frequently invited to lecture to various educational and community groups on issues concerning women's history, integrating women's studies into the curriculum, and on issues concerning Title IX.

The activity which is the subject of this book was supported in whole or in part by the Northwest Area Foundation, The Japan Foundation, The National Endowment for the Humanities, the Ise Cultural Foundation, and the St. Louis Park Schools. However, the opinions expressed herein do not necessarily reflect the position or policy of the Northwest Area Foundation, The Japan Foundation, the National Endowment for the Humanities, the Ise Cultural Foundation, or the St. Louis Park School system #283, and no official endorsement should be inferred.

Authors' Acknowledgments

The project *Women in World Area Studies* began with the support of two Minneapolis suburban school districts — St. Louis Park and Robbinsdale. The project was funded by the Elementary and Secondary Education Act, Title IV-C for three years. The Northwest Area Foundation, The National Endowment for the Humanities, and The Japan Foundation funded the research and writing of *Women in Japan.*

The Ise Cultural Foundation of Tokyo funded the printing of the *Women in Japan* student book and teacher's guide.

We would particularly like to thank the following administrators, teachers, editors, consultants, and friends who made possible this curriculum unit *Women in Japan.*

Carl Holmstrom, Superintendent, and Jim Gavenda of the St. Louis Park Schools.

Janet Donaldson who acted as editor for the text and as co-developer of the accompanying sound filmstrip.

Alyce Fuller, copy editor, who provided her secretarial skills, suggestions about readability of the text, and organized the permissions for photographs and quoted materials.

Eileen Soderberg who assisted as a final proof reader and acted as office manager for the project.

For *Women in Japan* we were fortunate to have the advice of four able academic consultants. Their suggestions and comments were invaluable to the project, helping us to avoid a variety of problems ranging from incorrect spellings to philosophical tangles. They are:

Gail Lee Bernstein, Department of Oriental Studies and Department of History, University of Arizona.

Susan J. Pharr, Holder of the Japanese Chair of Politics, Harvard University.

Tamie Kamiyama, Department of Chinese and Japanese Studies, Washington University.

Machiko Tomita, Consultant for the Global Studies Resource Center, St. Louis Park, Minnesota and a staff member of the Global Education Center at the University of Minnesota.

In addition we would like to thank Sally Sudo, teacher, Minneapolis Public Schools, who acted as pronunciation consultant for the sound filmstrip and Gretchen Heath, teacher and drama coach, Robbinsdale Schools, who narrated the filmstrip.

Gail Lee Bernstein, Russell Christianson, Susan Erickson, J. Edward Kidder, Jr., Merrill M. Kuller, Georgia Loutfallah, Kenneth McCullough, Mel and Renee Maisel, Betty Lee Nyhus, Julie Rasmussen, Saisho Yuriko, and the Japanese Housewives Association (Shufurengokai) donated excellent photographs used in both the book and sound filmstrip.

The University of Minnesota library staff made possible the research for the series of books of which *Women in Japan* is a part.

Finally, we would like to thank our husbands, Bert Gross and Thomas Egan, who assisted us throughout this project particularly by understanding the time involved in this curriculum project.